Yale Readings in Insurance

LIFE INSURANCE

Edited by
Lester W. Zartman, Ph.D.

William S. Hein & Co., Inc.
Buffalo, New York
2003

Library of Congress Cataloging-in-Publication Data

Life insurance / edited by Lester W. Zartman.
p. cm. -- (Yale readings in insurance)
Originally published: New Haven, Conn. : Yale University Press, 1909.
Includes index.
ISBN 1-57588-780-0 (cloth : alk. paper)
1. Insurance, Life. 2. Insurance, Industrial. I. Zartman, Lester W. (Lester William), 1878-1909. II. Series.
HG8771.L44 2003
368.32--dc21
2003047759

YALE READINGS IN INSURANCE

LIFE INSURANCE

EDITED BY

LESTER W. ZARTMAN, Ph.D.

ASSISTANT PROFESSOR OF POLITICAL ECONOMY, YALE UNIVERSITY

NEW HAVEN, CONNECTICUT

YALE UNIVERSITY PRESS

LONDON

HENRY FROWDE

OXFORD UNIVERSITY PRESS

1909

Printed in the United States

PREFACE

THE "Yale Lectures on Life Insurance" appeared five years ago. Although a considerable edition was printed, the unexpectedly large demand soon exhausted it, and as the plates were destroyed, for two years the lectures have been out of print.

It seems desirable that either a new edition of the lectures should be printed, or that something new should be published in their place. The latter alternative has been chosen, and instead of simply reprinting the old lectures, the plan has been adopted of selecting special readings, partly from the "Yale Lectures," partly from other sources. This plan was preferred for two reasons. In the first place, many changes have taken place in the insurance business since the old lectures were given, and much new and valuable material has appeared. In the second place, it has been thought that by not confining the readings to the old lectures a more comprehensive treatment could be secured. In this way it has been hoped to broaden the scope of the new readings, and thus to increase their usefulness. Only four of the lectures included in the old volume are reprinted, and three of these have been partly rewritten. Some of the matter now published has never appeared before, and much of the remainder has been revised.

In selecting these readings, the aim has been to avoid those authors who treat the subject in technical language, as well as to avoid those who make the subject more simple than it really is, and thus conceal its real problems. The broad selection of material would not have been possible without the coöperation of others. It is a pleasure to acknowledge the fine spirit of publishers in permitting reprints from copyrighted books, and the willingness of authors to revise articles where changed conditions made revision desirable.

LESTER W. ZARTMAN.

NEW HAVEN,
August, 1909.

CONTENTS

YALE READINGS IN INSURANCE

CHAPTER I

ELIMINATION OF RISK[1]

BUSINESS men try not only to estimate the risk which they must encounter and to adjust their accounts accordingly, but they also endeavor to avoid such risks altogether. This follows from the existence of the factor of caution. Where the coefficient of caution is abnormal, amounting to *in*caution, risks are not avoided, but are expressly sought, and the phenomena of gambling and indiscriminate speculation are the result. But in the great majority of men there exists a healthy fear of risks, and in consequence a tendency to avoid or reduce them.

There are five principal ways in which risks may be reduced, viz.: —

1. By increasing guaranties for the performance of contracts.
2. By increasing safeguards against incurring losses.
3. By increasing foresight and thereby diminishing the risks.
4. By insurance, that is, by consolidating risks.
5. By throwing risks into the hands of a special class of speculators.

These will be considered in order.

The ownership of capital wealth necessarily involves

[1] By Irving Fisher, Professor of Political Economy in Yale University. Reprinted from pages 288–300 of "The Nature of Capital and Income," by special arrangement with the publishers, Macmillan and Co., New York.

risk, since the income from it can only be estimated, — never precisely foreknown. But it is possible, by a division of the ownership of capital wealth, for one class of property holders to assume the burden of risks and to *guarantee* to another class a fixed income. This is the primary reason for the separation of securities into two great classes called stocks and bonds. In any large enterprise the stockholders take the risks, and by so doing guarantee to the bondholders a fixed income. As was remarked in a previous chapter, the capital stock acts as a buffer between the liabilities and the assets, which amounts to saying that it guarantees a fixed income to the holders of the liabilities. President Hadley has emphasized the fact that a bondholder "commutes" the precarious income of an enterprise into a fixed annuity, and that the system by which one class receives "interest" and another "profits" has its origin in the desire of one class to avoid and the willingness of another to assume risks.[1]

Nevertheless the general relation between creditor and debtor necessarily carries with it a certain amount of risk to the creditor. This risk may be reduced by the deposit of collateral security or indorsement[2] as in the case of bank loans and discounts; by mortgage on real estate, or occasionally on chattels; by legal regulations, as in the case of notes of national banks, and by other methods.

[1] But the "rate of commutation" is not a rate of interest, since any ratio of commutation is necessarily a ratio between two incomes, those respectively of the stockholders and the bondholders, whereas the rate of interest is a ratio of income to capital.

[2] The influence of indorsement in reducing risk is greater than would appear on the surface. Thus, if there is one chance in a hundred that the signer of a note will default, and a like chance for his indorser, both these risks being *independent*, the chance that the bank will lose is the product of these two, or only one chance in ten thousand. Hence, two-name commercial paper is ordinarily a safe security, provided, of course, the names are those of reliable business men, such as have a high "rating" in Bradstreet's or other standard commercial agency.

The method of guaranties is really a method of *shifting* risks rather than of avoiding them. The second method aims to reduce risk by special safeguards. Some articles of wealth exist, in fact, simply for the sake of meeting sudden unforeseen emergencies. This is true, for instance, of fire engines, fire extinguishers, safety appliances on railways, safety valves, and other devices connected with steam engines and machinery, burglar alarms, safety deposit vaults, etc. To a large extent this risk-meeting function applies to almost every stock of wealth. Food in a pantry usually exists beyond *certain* wants in order to provide for *un*certain wants, and when sources of supply are distant, such stores of food need to be large. Especially is this true in the case of armies. Again, a factory will usually have a large reserve stock, both of raw materials and finished products, in order to meet unexpected demands. In like manner, jobbers, wholesalers, and retailers maintain a sufficient stock of goods to meet not only the foreseen, but some of the unforeseen demands of their customers. The function of speculators in grain or other commodities consists largely in conserving the stock of a community as a safeguard against future scarcity. Almost all of what is called the reserve of a bank is used as a safety fund to meet the unforeseen demands of note-holders and depositors, and, in particular, to meet a special "run." These reserves often remain as idle as a fire extinguisher for years or even decades against the hour of need. It is said that there are bars of precious metals in the Bank of England which have lain there undisturbed for two centuries. A large part of the cash carried by an ordinary individual is quite analogous to a bank reserve, being held to meet special emergencies. Some individuals even keep in a separate pocket a special gold piece, lest some day they should become "stranded." It may be said that this risk-meeting function of pocket cash is the chief compensation for the so-called "loss of interest" on the money thus carried. The convenience and security obtained by having an adequate supply is a species of income replacing the income which might be earned were the sum invested. The same principles, from the standpoint of an individual, apply to bank deposits, and thus to the whole volume of the circulating medium.

The third method of reducing risks is by increasing knowledge. It has been seen that risk is nothing but an expression of ignorance, and decreases with the progress of science. It may be said that the chief progress now being made industrially consists in lifting the veil which hides the future. The countless trade journals now in use have their special reason for existence in enabling their readers better to forecast the future, by supplying them with data as to past and present conditions, as well as by instructing them in the relations of cause and effect. The government reports of crops, the technical schools and agricultural colleges, all tend in the same direction. Whereas formerly the mine prospector could only guess wildly at the ore "in sight" and the time and cost required to mine it, the graduate of mining schools is now able, through knowledge of geology and metallurgy, to bring these forecasts into some degree of scientific accuracy. And, whereas until recently farming was one of the most uncertain of occupations, it is to-day — thanks to modern scientific agriculture — almost if not quite as amenable to prediction as industry or commerce.

We come now to that important means of avoiding and shifting risks, called insurance. Insurance involves the offsetting of one risk by another; that is, the consolidation of a large number of chances whereby relative certainty is, as it were, manufactured out of uncertainty. To illustrate this, let us suppose that 10,000 houses of the same kind are too distant from each other to be destroyed by the same fire, and let us suppose that these houses in the average would be worth $10,000 each were it not for the risk of fire; in other words, that $10,000 is the capitalized value of the services to be rendered by each house, assuming that it lives out its natural life. The value of the total number of houses would then be $100,000,000. This is the "riskless value." It is the capitalized value of the income which the 10,000 houses would bring in, were there no loss by fire. If interest is at 5 per cent., the income which is thus capitalized is $5,000,000 a year. If now we suppose that the annual risk of fire is one chance in 200, there will be about 50 houses annually burned. Reckoning the value thus destroyed at an average of $10,000 for each house, there will be $500,000 annually lost by fire. We must now deduct this from the $5,000,000, which would be the income were it not for fires. We have left $4,500,000, the capitalization of which is only $90,000,000. In other words, the total property of 10,000 houses is worth in "mathematical value" $90,000,000 instead of $100,000,000, the reduction being because of the prospect of fires. If we suppose all of these houses to be owned by one corporation, this mathematical value of $90,000,000 might also be the actual value, for such a corporation could count on about 50 houses burning annually almost as a certainty. Each house would then be worth, on an average, $9000. But if such an individual house is owned by an individual person, this mathematical value would not be its "commercial value," on account of the element of caution. Let us say that the caution coefficient is $\frac{7}{9}$, in which case the house would be worth $7000. In other words, we have $10,000 as the "riskless" value of the house, $9000 as its "mathematical" value, and $7000 as its actual "commercial" value, assuming that there is not as yet insurance. Now if the owner of such a house could secure insurance on a purely mathematical basis of the risk, which, as we have seen, is one-half of one per cent., and, therefore, could pay only $50 per annum, in consideration of which the value of his house, if destroyed by fire, is restored to him, it is evident that he has made a good investment; for he is now assured of a house even should a fire occur, and he has, instead of the risk of fire, merely to pay his annual premium of $50 a year, the capitalized value of which is $1000. Consequently, his house is worth $10,000 — $1000, or $9000.

Such an insurance rate, however, being based on the mathematical or "pure" premiums, would not pay any profit to the companies conducting it. But even a higher insurance would leave a large margin of capital-value saved to the insured. If we suppose a "loading," so that the insurance premium is not $50 but $100, similar reasoning would show that the value of the house when insured would be to the owner $8000 instead of $7000. As long as the loading is not sufficient to absorb *all* the margin between the $7000 and $9000, it will be advantageous to insure.

Between the case of a man owning an individual house, when the element of caution would have a large influence, and that where 10,000 houses are owned by the same corporation, in which case the caution element is almost entirely absent, there are numberless intervening cases. The larger the number of houses owned by one individual or corporation, the less profitable becomes insurance. To express it in the language of the business man, the various risks insure each other. Thus, the North German Lloyd Company finds it profitable not to insure its vessels against shipwreck, because they have so large a fleet that their losses through a period of time can be counted on fairly well in advance.

One effect of insurance on the individual is to steady the income from his property. The owner of the house in question would receive, if it were not insured, a net annual income, after providing for depreciation, of 5 per cent. on $10,000, or $500 a year until the house was burned, after which he would receive nothing; whereas, if he insures, he receives this $500 income less his premium up to the date of the fire, and afterward the income from the indemnity paid him by the company.

The same principles apply to other forms of insurance,

as marine insurance, which, by consolidating in an insurance company the risk on a large number of vessels, reduces for the individual even the perils of the sea to relative certainty and regularity; or as steam boiler insurance, which in a similar manner treats the risk of explosion; or as plate-glass insurance, burglar insurance, live stock insurance, hail and cyclone insurance, fidelity insurance, accident insurance, employer's liability insurance, and, above all, life insurance. This form of insurance, like the other forms, tends to steady the income of the beneficiary. If a wife holds insurance on her husband's life, the consequence is that, although what he gives her during his life is somewhat diminished, her income will not suddenly cease at his death. The tendency of insurance here as elsewhere is to make regularity out of irregularity, relative certainty out of relative uncertainty; and where, under the form of insurance contracts, the opposite result follows, the case is not one of true insurance, but tends to become one of gambling. Thus, if a person insures the life of some one in whom he has no financial interest, he is merely gambling on that person's life. Some years ago in Michigan there was an abuse of this type called "graveyard insurance." Speculators went through the form of insuring the lives of certain old persons, in other words, of betting on their deaths, a procedure not only vicious as gambling, but calculated also to lead to crime. The same considerations apply to fire insurance, where a person insures a building in which he is not financially interested, or over-insures one in which he is.[1]

The range to which insurance can apply is always limited; but it is constantly being extended, as business men learn how to bring risks of any kind on to a statistical basis and to apply the theory of probability. At present the total assets of life insurance companies alone in the United States are nearly $3,000,000,000.

[1] For the moral effects of insurance, see "Insurance and Crime," by A. C. Campbell, Putnam's, 1902.

Where risks cannot be reduced to a statistical basis, and therefore cannot be insured against, recourse is often had to the shifting of the risk into the hands of those who are willing to take it. Such persons are speculators. A speculator is usually one in whom the caution factor is not so pronounced as in the ordinary individual. In extreme cases he tends to become a simple gambler. The distinction between a speculator and a gambler, however, is usually fairly well marked. A gambler seeks and makes risks which it is not necessary to assume, whereas the speculator is one who merely volunteers to assume those risks of business which must inevitably fall somewhere. A speculator is also usually fitted for his work by special knowledge, so that the risk *to him,* owing to superior foresight, is at the outset less than it would be to others. The indiscriminate prejudice against all speculation, which is so often met with, is beside the point; for, were there no speculators, the same risks would have to be borne by those less fitted to bear them. The chief evils of speculation flow from the participation of the general public, who lack the special knowledge, and enter the market in a purely gambling spirit. In addition to suffering the usual evil consequences of gambling, they produce evil consequences for the non-participating public by causing factitious fluctuations in the values of the products or property in which they speculate.

The evils of speculation are particularly acute when, as generally happens with the investing public, the forecasts are not made independently. Were it true that each individual speculator made up his mind independently of every other as to the future course of events, the errors of some would probably be offset by those of others. But, as a matter of fact, the mistakes of the common herd are usually in the same direction. Like sheep, they all follow a single leader. How easily they are led is shown by the effect on the stock market in the year 1904, when Thomas Lawson published scare-head advertisements in the newspapers advising the public to sell certain securities.

A chief cause of crises, panics, runs on banks, etc., is that risks are not independently reckoned, but are a mere matter of imitation. A crisis is a time of general and forced liquidation.[1] In other words, it differs from any other period in two particulars, viz., that the liquidations are more numerous, and that they are for the most part forced upon the debtors by the creditors because of threatened or actual bankruptcy. Neither of these conditions could exist unless there had been at a prior time a general miscalculation of the future. Both creditors and debtors must have made a wrong forecast when their ill-fated agreements were entered into. Hence a crisis is the penalty which must be paid when a previous *general error in prediction* is discovered. Such a general error *may* be due to the coincidence of a number of independent mistakes of individuals; but it almost always *is* due to lack of independence, — to the principle of imitation. The error, whatever it is, when committed by a person of influence, is like an infection; it is caught by hundreds of others and transmitted to thousands. A great mob of easily led investors, eagerly searching for "straight tips" which may bring instant wealth, make their mistake in common, and when the mistake is disastrous they try, *en masse*, to escape. A sudden rush of all the passengers on a ferry-boat to one side will produce a "list" in the boat's position, and sometimes cause it to capsize, though the independent movement of the individual passengers will seldom or never produce disaster. So also the sudden general realization of unforeseen danger on the part of the investing public may submerge the craft of credit and those whom it has hitherto borne along in safety. In short, a general crisis bears the relation to individual bankruptcies which a general conflagration bears to

[1] See Juglar, "Des Crises Commerciales," Paris, 2d edition, 1889, Chap. I.

individual fires. The key to the study of either crises or conflagrations is the existence, in place of independent hazards, of *interdependent* ones. So far as conflagrations are concerned, the principle of interdependence is distinctly recognized by students of fire insurance, and in consequence each company strives to keep its own fire risks independent of each other, by not having too many in the same locality; but so far as crises are concerned, the principle has not yet been sufficiently emphasized by students of economic history.

The same principle applies to the phenomenon of a run on a bank. The opinions of the bank's solvency are not formed independently but interdependently. A year or more ago the newspapers reported that, a policeman and a crowd of people being collected on the steps of one of the Wilkes-Barre savings banks to escape the rain, two Hungarian depositors who were passing jumped to the conclusion that the bank had been attacked by burglars, and circulated the disturbing news in the Hungarian colony, with the result that when the bank opened for business many depositors made a run upon it.

We see, then, that where speculation is imitative, it is dangerous alike to those who engage in it and to the public. Where, on the other hand, speculation is based on independent knowledge, its utility is usually enormous. It operates both to *reduce* risk by means of utilizing the special knowledge of speculators, and also to *shift* risk from those who lack this knowledge to those who possess it. The consequence is that normally speculative property will gravitate into the hands of those most able to forecast its true income.

Modern production has been called capitalistic-speculative production, owing to the fact that it is managed by "captains of industry," who are specially fitted at once to forecast and to mold the future within the special realms in which they operate. The industries of transportation and manufacturing particularly are under the lead of an educated and trained speculative class, whose function it is to assume for themselves the main risks, and leave the ordinary investor, who is not so equipped, to coöperate as a mere "lender" or silent partner. Yet it often happens that they betray the confidence placed in them, and continue to throw the burden of risk on those whom they pretend to shield.

In the special field more usually known as "speculative," — namely, that in which attempts are made to forecast prices in the great exchange markets, — we find a similar class who are specially trained. These speculators are either "bulls" or "bears"; that is, they speculate either for a rise or a fall. Those who believe that wheat or any other article is likely to rise in value and hence yield more than the "rate of interest," will hold it, or if they do not own it, will buy it or obtain an option on it. Such an option is known as a "call," and is put in force at a later time, at a price fixed in advance and considered low. On the other hand, those who believe that prices will fall will sell out their present holdings, or may sell "short," agreeing to supply such holdings at a later time at a fixed price which they consider high. Such a contract to sell is often made in the form of an option, in which case it is known as a "put."

To show how such contracts will shift risks, a few examples will suffice. A building contractor who had taken a large contract was asked if he were not taking large risks, since he could not foreknow the cost of building. He replied, "No, I am taking no risks at all except on 'labor'; I have made contracts to be supplied with all materials when needed, at fixed prices." Those who made these contracts thus assumed the risk of fluctuation in price in the special materials in which they dealt, relieving the contractor of the necessity of informing himself of the special market conditions for stone, brick, timber, etc., and enabling him to make a closer bid for the contract, inasmuch as there was less need of the element of caution.

The public, of course, get the benefit of such a shifting of risk in the form of reduced cost of building. Similar results follow from most other "short" sales. Again, a woolen manufacturer need not carry so large a stock of wool if he can make a contract by which some one will sell short, or agree to supply the wool at fixed prices and at certain dates. He can afford to use up his present stock fearlessly, with the certainty that when it is gone he can obtain a new supply.[1] Without such a contract, he would be under the necessity of carrying a large and idle stock.

An important method of shifting risks is "hedging," whereby a dealer, for instance in transporting wheat, may be relieved of the risk of a change in price. He buys wheat in the West intending to ship it to New York and sell it there at enough to cover cost of transportation and a small profit. In consequence of a sudden fall in price he might find all his profit wiped out; or he might, on the other hand, by a rise in price, make much more than normal profits. But, being of a cautious disposition, he prefers an intermediate course, — a small profit which is sure rather than the chances of both gain and loss. Comsequently he "hedges." He enters into some speculative market, knowing that it will move in sympathy with the New York market, and there he "speculates" for a fall, or sells "short." In case the price in New York falls, what he loses on the wheat which he has transported he gains through his speculative short selling. Contrariwise, if the price rises, what he gains on his wheat transported he loses in the speculative market. In other words, he is, as it were, betting on both sides of the market at once, and therefore eliminating all risk, so that he only obtains his normal profit, commission, or percentage on the actual wheat handled, having imposed the burden of risk of speculation on the speculative dealers to whom he sold short.[2]

[1] Cf. Hadley, "Economics," Putnam's, 1896, p. 106.

[2] See "Speculations on Stock and Produce Exchanges of the United

The effect of hedging on those who engage in it, such as the wheat dealers, is evidently to enable them to work on a smaller margin of profit. In consequence the public receives a benefit in lowered prices. The case is thus very similar to those respectively of the builder and of the woolen manufacturer. Short selling, binding the future to the past, enables the specialist to guarantee to the general public a definite foreseen series of events. The beneficial effect to the public, in saving useless stocks and reserves, in producing more intelligent direction of enterprises, and in encouraging accumulation through greater certainty of its future benefits, is both obvious and great. Risk is one of the direst economic evils, and all of the devices which aid in overcoming it — whether increased guaranties, safeguards, foresight, insurance, or legitimate speculation — represent a great boon to humanity.

States," by Henry C. Emery, *Publications of American Economic Association.* For the development of insurance speculation in England, see "The Put and Call," by L. R. Higgins, London, Effingham Wilson, 1902.

CHAPTER II

FUNCTION OF LIFE INSURANCE [1]

EACH family requires for its subsistence a certain sum of money, which varies, both as to its amount and the length of time during which it will be needed, according to the circumstances which surround each individual case. This income is, in some cases, derived from invested funds inherited or accumulated, but, in general, it represents the earnings of that one upon whom rests the responsibility of supporting the various individuals who have the right to look to him for maintenance.

The relations between life insurance and the family spring from this state of affairs, and depend upon the value which one human life has to another. To understand clearly how this may be ascertained, it will be useful to consider the rules which govern the worth of some varieties of property.

In the analysis of the question under consideration, it will be assumed that the security underlying the evidence of indebtedness is abundant and not regarded with doubt.

The simplest form of invested funds is, perhaps, a note or other form of obligation, the payment of which may be at any time demanded by the lender or made by the borrower. The value of this is always the amount it represents, for if the current rate of interest rises above the rate which has been agreed upon, the lender will demand his principal in order that he may put his money to

[1] By John M. Holcombe, President of the Phœnix Mutual Life Insurance Company, Hartford. Reprinted from pages 26–53 of the "Yale Insurance Lectures, Life."

more profitable use. If, on the other hand, the ruling rate falls below that stipulated for, the borrower will pay his obligation and secure his money on more favorable terms.

The present value of a bond running for a stated term of years, and bearing a fixed rate of interest, is a kind of property into which another element is introduced and which will serve to show the controlling force which interest exerts in all valuations. The price of such a bond will depend upon the rate of interest which it bears compared with the current rate which can be obtained by investors, and which, therefore, must be satisfactory to them.

If the rate provided for is greater than the market rate, the value of the bond will be greater than its face value, but will decrease as it approaches maturity, at which time only the face value will be payable. If, on the other hand, the stipulated rate is less than that current, the value will be less than the face, but will increase up to the time when the full obligation will be payable.

If the rate coincides with the market, the value will coincide with the amount of the bond.

If the current rate of interest changes, the value will change accordingly.

In valuing lands, still other elements must be introduced, although the interest question still exerts a force which, on the whole, is controlling.

Adam Smith in his "Wealth of Nations," published in 1776, remarks: "The ordinary market price of land, it is to be observed, depends everywhere upon the ordinary market rate of interest. The person who has a capital from which he wishes to derive a revenue, without taking the trouble to employ it himself, deliberates whether he should buy land with it or lend it out at interest. The superior security of land, together with some other advantages, which almost everywhere attend upon this species of property, will generally dispose him to content himself with a smaller revenue from land than what he might have by lending out his money at interest. These advantages are sufficient to compensate a certain difference of revenue; but they will compensate a certain difference only; and if the rent of land should fall short of the interest of money by a greater difference, nobody would buy land, which would soon reduce its ordinary price. On the contrary, if the advantages should much more than compensate the difference, everybody would buy land, which again would soon raise its ordinary price. When interest was at 10 per cent., land was commonly sold for ten and twelve years' purchase. As interest sunk to 6, 5, and 4 per cent., the price of land rose to twenty, five-and-twenty, and thirty years' purchase. The market rate of interest is higher in France than in England; and the common price of land is lower. In England it commonly sells at thirty, in France at twenty years' purchase."

In modern times this rule seems to hold good. In thirteen counties in the States of Iowa, Illinois, Missouri, Nebraska, and Kansas, there are now on record appraisals of farming lands made in 1876, showing an average of $20 per acre. At that time money was loaned on these lands at 10 per cent. In 1903 lands in these same counties were appraised at an average of $39.60 per acre, while loans were made at about 5 per cent.

In the varieties of property thus far considered, there will be found to be lacking certain elements which produce chances of change and deterioration, which must be combined with interest in valuing other classes of property. A lot in the center of a city has no value of its own, and can only be made income-producing by the erection upon it of a building for the use of which a rental will be paid. There are many circumstances which must now be considered in determining the worth of this property. If it is composed of or surrounded by inflammable materials, its value will be unfavorably affected. It is true that the owner can protect himself against loss by fire by a policy of insurance, but he must pay for this protection his full share of the risk, which will be accurately estimated, and the value which the building would have, were it not for this hazard, will be diminished by just the chance of that contingency. The present condition of the structure, viewed in the light of natural decay and its adaptability to the needs of the location and times, will demand intelligent discrimination. The amount, therefore, which an investor will pay for the block will be determined by his knowledge of what it now produces, and his estimate both of what it will yield in the future and the time when, either by gradual deterioration or by sudden accident, it will become unable to afford an income. If there can be obtained from it more than will suffice to meet necessary expenditures, then the property has an actual value which will vary according to the estimate that may be made of its future, always controlled by the current rate of interest which can be obtained on investments.

That neighborhood which to-day attracts business by the elegance of its buildings, or its nearness to lines of travel or transportation, may to-morrow be swept by fire or damaged by changes in modes of conveyance. No human foresight can provide with certainty for these contingencies, but the general future of a section is estimated by the careful student of the laws underlying commercial transactions, with an accuracy which, on the whole, enables him to reap the profits that legitimately belong to high intelligence. In the change of ownership, the purchaser thinks that he is receiving more than an equivalent for his money; else he would not buy. The seller differs as to the probable future, and believes that what he now receives will be of greater value; otherwise he would retain his possession. The result in almost any particular transaction will show that one or the other has erred in his estimate, but on the whole, real estate or any other property which is valued for its income will be found to conform to the general law which governs the value of money.

Repairs and alterations may be made which will check decay or even increase productiveness, but each change will call for a new expenditure which will not prevent the decline in the value of the original investment.

Having considered the elements which enter into the value of certain kinds of property, it can now be inquired whether a human life can have a definite worth which can be measured with any degree of accuracy. It would not be difficult to enumerate many lives which cannot be considered of any pecuniary value, because, for various reasons, they produce nothing. Such are those of the very old, the imbeciles, and the confirmed invalids. But the life of every man who earns more than suffices for his actual personal expenses is of pecuniary value to some one besides himself. This has been recognized from early times in the institution of slavery, which was based on the principle that the ownership of the services of a human being had a value in accordance with the excess of earnings obtainable above the necessary cost of subsistence. When a slave was purchased as an investment, he was examined in order that the state of his health and his muscular development might be known. These qualities, in connection with his age, his skill in any variety of labor, and his disposition, determined the price at which he seemed likely to be a profitable investment. A carpenter or blacksmith was worth 50 per cent. more, other things being equal, than an ordinary field hand, because, while the cost of his support was no greater, the quality of his service was much more valuable. In any case, however, certain important elements were either wholly lacking or but partially developed. "A person who can acquire no property can have no other interest but to eat as much and to labor as little as possible."

Family ties are needed to develop the highest value of a human life. But while this value thus reaches its greatest capacity, there devolves upon its possessor the responsibility of supporting those who have by his own choice and act the right to depend upon him for the necessities of life. The family, then, has a clear and indisputable interest in his earnings. This they have day by day, month by month, and year by year. If he dies possessed of property, this by right goes to them, in order that they may, so far as its income may enable them, continue to defray the cost of existence.

But what of the life itself? Has it a value beyond what it produces in a month or a year which can be measured with any degree of accuracy? Supposing its possessor to be of good constitution and free from hereditary taint, it has already been shown that he and others of his class will be governed, as to the length of their lives, by a law of mortality so certain that their average lifetime may be measured with as much precision as that which governs any series of future events. For example, a man is thirty years old, in good health, and his surplus earnings are $1500 a year, and money is worth 4 per cent. per annum; by a standard mortality table, the present value of the future surplus earnings of this life is $25,560. It is true that this value is based on averages, and that the assumption that he will, through his life, receive and spend just the amounts here set down will not probably be realized. It is well-nigh certain that his death will occur either before or after the date expected. Disease or accident may rob him permanently of his productive power. Circumstances which no skill guided by research can calculate, and no judgment foretell, may change the current of his life, and enhance or diminish the value of his efforts. And yet this value rests upon a foundation composed of elements no more uncertain than those which determine the worth of the business block. Both the building and the life are constantly exposed to the danger of destruction, but the chance can be measured even more accurately in the latter case than in the former.

The natural ability of one man is greater than that of another, and this advantage will be shown in the value of their respective services. These qualities as well as those of industry and perseverance are inborn traits, and will, considered in connection with education and training, determine the amount for which their possessor can lease his efforts to others or employ them for independent profit. What nature has done for the man may be said to correspond with the location of the building. What experience has taught him is like the quality of the structure. In each case there are certain necessary expenditures which must be met before any real value can exist, and in each case the worth rests upon estimates.

The family which depends upon this income has an interest in the life which produces it, which is not limited by a month or a year. It extends into the future as far as they need it. Without it they will suffer privation or be dependent upon charity, in either of which conditions their natural protector has no right to leave them. It is here that the institution of life insurance performs the service for which it was created. It renders immediately available the future earnings of a lifetime. It takes the place of him whose duty it is to care for his dependents until they can care for themselves.

The Federal Bureau of Labor has completed an extended investigation into the cost of living of workingmen's families, and the retail prices of the principal staple articles of food used by such families. The material for the detailed study of the cost of living consisted of the figures of income and expenditures furnished by some 2500 families in thirty-three states, although certain data not entering so much into detail were gathered from 25,000 families. The 2500 families furnishing the detailed material consisted on an average of 5.31 persons, a figure slightly (0.7) above the average of private families in the whole country as shown by the census of 1900. The average yearly expenditures for all purposes was $768.54 for the year 1901. Of this, 43 per cent. was for food, 13 per cent. for rent, 14 per cent. for clothing, and 5 per cent.

for fuel and lighting. Three-quarters of the expenditures was for the actual necessities of ordinary living, the remainder representing miscellaneous expenses, including the cost of education and sickness. If this average family is supported by one person, his death would diminish the total family expenditures by some amount. It is not unreasonable to assume that the cost of maintaining the remainder would be $500 per annum. Assuming that he is forty years of age, and in good health, and that money is worth 4 per cent. per annum, the present value which this family has in his life is $7546.50. Human and divine laws give them the right to the fruit of his labors. But does he perform his whole duty when he furnishes them with food, clothing, and the other necessities of life, or even with education suitable to their station? He may live to see his children self-supporting, and to provide for the old age of himself and his wife, but what if his life shall be cut off while they are still unable to earn their own subsistence?

Hadley says: "Although society insists as far as it can that each man shall be responsible for himself and his family, it cannot carry this principle out to its logical conclusion. We cannot kill off the weak merely because they have been unable to support themselves. Still less can we leave the unfortunate to die as a result of their incapacity. The ethical loss to the community which adopted such a course would indefinitely outweigh any material or physical gain. The independent and the unfortunate must under certain conditions be taken care of by society, even though the process of natural selection is thereby hampered."

Again, in discussing compulsory insurance and pensions, he says: "There are certain things which society must do in justice to itself, which it cannot safely allow individuals to demand in justice to themselves. If you give every man a right to a pension when he is incapable of self-support, you tacitly approve his failure to provide for himself and his children. That the necessary degree of production and of economy by the community as a whole would be maintained, if such a point of view were adopted, seems highly improbable. We need measures which shall increase individual responsibility rather than diminish it; measures which shall give us more self-reliance and less reliance on society as a whole. We cannot afford to countenance a system of morals or law which justifies the individual in looking to the community rather than to himself for support in age or infirmity."

It will not be denied that certain persons must and should be supported at the public expense, but the fewer there are of these, the better will be the morals as well as the finances of the community, and life insurance is continually reducing this dependent class. It is not the man who lives to old age, supports and educates his children and saves a competency, who contributes to the class who are applicants for public charity. But the one who is taken away while his children are infants and who has not had the time given him, no matter how affectionate and thrifty he may be, to provide for their needs, is a liberal contributor to the orphan asylum and the almshouse. He may avoid this danger by postponing marriage for such time as will enable him to accumulate a sufficient sum to insure the comfort of a family, but neither morality nor the public welfare will be best served by the establishment of such a principle. There is but one way by which he can follow the course which nature intended him to take, and that way is open to him through life insurance. By the payment of comparatively small sums at convenient intervals, he can relieve himself of the responsibility of the distress which would fall upon his dependents in case of his premature death, and he can, moreover, provide for his own future in case he should survive the time when, from physical weakness, he shall become incapacitated from earning his own subsistence.

In what directions and to what extent life insurance

promotes the best family life it is difficult to prove. That it tends to increase the sense of responsibility which leads to a thoughtful appreciation of affection and duty cannot be doubted. That man who enters upon his married life without consideration not alone of the probabilities, but also of the possibilities, will find himself weighted with a burden which he cannot transfer to another, and which will consist both of the necessity of self-denial and anxiety for the future. The first will develop and improve his character, will stimulate his ambition and increase his efficiency, but a combination of the two will dishearten and impede him and tend to cruelty, intemperance, and divorce, for he will seek to transfer to others that for which he alone is responsible.

Life insurance makes immediately available the future savings of a lifetime, and it is this element of its operations which is its most common and prominent characteristic. But its mission cannot be fully gauged without an understanding that it has another feature less used but not less useful. It has been shown that in a large number of human beings belonging to a known class, a law of mortality has been found to exist, and this has been used through life insurance to distribute among the many the unexpected disasters which must overtake the few, and which would otherwise bring distress, pauperism, and crime.

It is equally true that out of the many some will survive to old age, when they will have reared and educated their children and performed their whole duty toward them. If a man thus situated has been fortunate enough to accumulate property, the income of which is sufficient to maintain him independently of other aid, his natural desire and duty are to pass on his possessions to his descendants, who will thus eventually secure his surplus earnings. But in many cases he will in his old age find himself alone, his duty done, his children self-supporting and in the same condition in which he himself was in his youth, while the interest on his savings will not suffice to give him that comfort and independence to which he is fairly entitled.

Suppose such a man to be seventy-five years of age, and that he has saved $5000. If this is invested at 4 per cent. it will yield him an income of $200 a year. This will not provide for his needs, and he must depend upon others for a part of his support if he has lost his earning power, or he must, each year, spend a part of his principal, with a possibility of living long enough to exhaust it and finally to become wholly dependent. By the operation of the laws of mortality, life insurance can take this amount and give him an income of $800 a year so long as he may live.

This service also is a distinct and important element in the family life. While the responsibility which rests upon the man with a young and immature family is definite and unmistakable, and may extend to the end of an old age, involving the preservation and transmission of any property he may have, yet in some cases independence and happiness can only be secured by obtaining by means of life insurance the larger and sure income which involves the investment of the principal for the sole benefit of its owner.

The aged parent or relative who is no longer able to earn a living, and who has become a charge upon a family needing all its resources for its own members, is often an unwelcome guest, while this same one with an income sufficient for his maintenance will be an object of care and solicitude.

In these ways does life insurance serve the family in guarding against the losses of early death and in providing means to ameliorate the disadvantages of old age. But distributing the burden of the few among the many is not the only service which this institution performs for the family. The contracts which it offers to the public contain not only the element of protection, but of accumulation as well. The savings bank has its uses and has played an important part in the development of family thrift, but the payment which is called for at stated times will be more likely to be met than the deposit which is required only by an indefinite resolution. That the habit of saving, especially if it be for others, is uplifting and tends to strengthen family ties does not need demonstration.

Carroll D. Wright says that the family "must be considered as the crucial social unit — 'the very keystone of society' — for it results from happy association of the sexes by which the human species is perpetuated and extended, by which the affections are developed, and by which the interest which compels one unit to protect, preserve, and cherish another is fostered. It should be the purpose of society, as a whole, to protect the sacredness and integrity of that relation. Without the family unit no other social units would be possible; it brings the individual out of his seclusion into ethical relations, constitutes him a living evolutionary force, lifts him out of intensive selfishness to a more extensive selfishness, for in the family relation he must live for others, although in living for others he may live for his own higher enjoyment. The purpose of the individual unit in entering social relations and in inviting the force of association is to secure happiness. He may be well fed, warmed, and clothed, while in the disintegrated state of the individual, but in such state he can have no realization of the happiness which comes from appreciation of and service to others. Hence the family grows out of the psychic tendencies of men, and is perhaps the best demonstration of the highest aspirations of the individual. It is found in every condition of population, whether living in savagery, in barbarous or in civilized communities. It is the fundamental unit of civilized society."

If the family as thus described be thoughtfully considered, it will be apparent that life insurance is not only an important factor of this social unit, but that it is an absolutely essential part of an ideal condition of civilized life.

Although a policy of life insurance is a contract between an individual and a corporation and directly concerns only these two parties, yet the state which gives being to the corporation and undertakes to protect the individual can well be considered in its relations to this, the most far-reaching of all forms of business activity.

Woolsey defines a state as, "A community of persons living within certain limits of territory, under a permanent organization which aims to secure the prevalence of justice by self-imposed law."

It is clear that any agency which improves the mental or moral attributes, or the material circumstances of any one of its citizens, raises the condition of the community of which he is a member, and thus benefits the state. Savings banks encourage thrift and produce accumulations which would in many cases be otherwise wasted, and thus they constitute a distinct and tangible benefit to the state. Life insurance promotes a sense of responsibility, strengthens family ties, and thus elevates the general character of the nation. It lessens those family discords which end in divorce, it checks intemperance, and often by its requirements brings a realizing sense of the benefits of right living. The very restrictions which the companies transacting this business themselves place upon admission to membership bring a clear comprehension of the result which temperate living has upon the length of life. Careful observation has shown that the intemperate use of liquor weakens the human system, rendering it less liable to withstand disease, and thus shortens life. This is one of the risks which life insurance companies strive in every way to avoid. Not only are searching questions asked of the applicant as to his habits in this respect, but reports are often secured from independent sources as to his custom in the use of liquor. It is undoubtedly the case that many who have thoughtlessly fallen into habits of intemperate drinking, without realizing its ill effects, have, when brought face to face with the requirements of life insurance, changed their modes of life, and have become not only sounder physically, but improved in financial condition, and have thus become more valuable citizens and therefore increased the prosperity of the state.

The physical examinations which are required in all cases of life insurance also have their very marked effect upon the public, for until the true meaning of life insurance is brought home to an applicant, he seldom comes to an understanding of what the actual value of his life is, and how much this value is increased if the length of his life can be prolonged. Weaknesses and ailments not before known are often discovered, and remedies are applied which lengthen life, and thus add to the aggregate value of the state.

There can be no doubt, furthermore, that life insurance curtails the expense to the public treasury of almshouses and police, of criminal courts and prisons, and of the various other necessary branches of the public service which have to do with the prevention and punishment of crime, and the relief of the suffering and unfortunate.

Some years ago, a census was taken of the paupers in the Philadelphia almshouse, with the result that of the number observed — 1110 — only three were found who had been beneficiaries of life insurance, and these to the extent of $6,000, but through profligacy or improvidence they were reduced to a state of pauperism. In a census of the Montgomery County (Pa.) almshouse, 133 were examined and it was found that none of these people or their families ever had been the beneficiaries of life insurance.

In the year 1902 there was distributed to the holders of life insurance policies and their families in death claims, matured endowments, and annuities, by the life insurance companies of the United States, more than $140,000,000.

It is certain that in many cases the proceeds of a life

insurance policy are practically all that remain at the death of the one responsible for the support of helpless dependents, and in a vast number of these cases, were it not for this aid, many persons would be forced to accept public charity. There can be no doubt that an investigation of the records of the inmates of prisons, and of asylums, maintained at the public expense, for the care of those made helpless by disease and old age and unable to care for themselves, would show that with rare exceptions they do not belong to that class from which the membership of life insurance companies has been drawn.

The limits of this discourse do not permit an exhaustive analysis of the influence of life insurance upon the community, nor the benefits which it confers upon the living on the one hand and upon dependents on the other. Some other phases of the subject are of such importance as to make the study of them interesting and useful to all who are engaged in business, professional, or political life.

The state long ago recognized the part played in its affairs by this institution, and the peculiar nature of its service, by enacting laws to protect the family in the proceeds of life insurance policies as against the claims of creditors. As early as 1840 the State of New York passed an act in substance like the present law in that and other states. It clearly indicated that the government was justified in the position that the duty of a man not only to support his family during his lifetime, but also to provide for them after his death, should take precedence of all other obligations. This law as it now stands in the statute book of Connecticut is as follows: "Any policy of life insurance expressed to be for the benefit of a married woman, or assigned to her, or in trust for her, shall inure to her separate use; or in case of her decease before payment, to the use of her children, or of her husband's children, as may be provided in such policy. But if the annual premium on such policy shall exceed $300, the amount of such excess, with interest, shall inure to the benefit of the creditors of the person paying the premium."

The charters of some of these companies contain similar provisions. In order to make sure that the protection provided for by the insured shall in any event, notwithstanding his own pecuniary condition, reach those persons who properly look to him for support, and without whose protection might become charges upon the public, the law has been invoked both in the statute books and the articles of incorporation.

The business of life insurance is transacted exclusively by corporations deriving their powers from charters granted, in this country, by the governments of the various states. An ordinary contract of insurance is a promise to pay a given sum at some indefinite future time, in consideration of the present payment of a certain other sum. The peculiar character of this agreement makes possible the practice of deceptive and unsound methods, to an extent impracticable in those transactions where the purchaser can more readily examine and understand the real nature of the thing for which he pays. It was natural, therefore, that laws should be passed, intending to guard the public against the dishonesty and ignorance of the managers of these institutions by requiring reports of their affairs to be filed with public officials. The State of Massachusetts in 1807 adopted a resolution requiring insurance companies to render an account of their affairs to the next legislature. In 1828 an act was passed requiring these corporations to make annual statements to the comptroller, and in 1851 this official was given authority to make examinations of companies.

Massachusetts enacted a law in 1854 providing for the creation of an insurance department, which was organized in the following year by the appointment of three commissioners, whose duty it was to examine the reports and the conditions of all companies doing business in the commonwealth. Other states have followed the example set in the East, as the operations of these corporations have become extended and enlarged, until now there are fifty-two insurance departments, including Alaska, Porto Rico, and Hawaii.

It is likely that by reason of the statements made public through these reports, of vast sums collected from the people, a system of taxation has grown up which has become a serious burden upon members of these corporations, whose sole object it is to provide for future necessities. There was collected in the year 1902 from life insurance companies for taxes more than $8,300,000, by far the greater part of which was the tax upon premium receipts. It will not be claimed that these institutions should altogether escape some share of the cost of maintaining the governments, yet it is a question of very great public interest as to what burden of this kind should be imposed upon this particular class of institutions. If they are performing the public service which is claimed, the levying of these taxes tends to check the spread of insurance, by making it more costly than it otherwise would be. For several years the question of national supervision has been widely agitated, and while it is not at all probable that the various states will relinquish all supervision, it is certainly a fair question whether the public good will not be served, if some general supervision can be substituted for a considerable part of the present system, to the great saving of expense, without impairing the value of the present governmental inspection.

An examination of the items of investment is interesting and useful as indicating the influence which these accumulations undoubtedly have upon the growth and development of the country. The loans which these companies now hold upon real estate securities amount to not less than $600,000,000. These investments have enabled the owners of real estate in cities to improve their properties by building dwellings and business blocks, and to increase and extend every line of business. For more than thirty years some of the life insurance companies have made loans upon Western farming lands. These have enabled the farmers of the country to buy land and to cultivate it, to erect necessary buildings, to buy stock, and to continue their operations through unfavorable years. It is certain that these institutions have been largely instrumental in the growth of the farming interest. Lands in sections where these corporations have loaned money have very greatly increased in value, largely by reason of the reduction in the rate of interest which has come through the increase of these funds seeking investment. Vast sums of money gathered from the payments of policy-holders, and held and improved at interest, solely for the final payment of claims, have been used in the development of railroads and other corporations, and to improve cities and towns. Deposits in banks have served to aid commerce and have been largely instrumental in enabling those engaged in various lines of business to procure funds on reasonable terms.

Life insurance exists for the purpose of repairing the loss occasioned by the death of an individual who can produce more than the cost of subsistence. This has been shown in individual cases, and it has also been demonstrated how such value can be reached in any particular instance. In considering the relations which life insurance bears to the state, it is necessary to take such aggregate as can be ascertained, and to point to certain conclusions. The conditions which prevail in Connecticut may be used as a fair example. It is shown by the census of 1900 that there were 385,610 persons in Connecticut engaged in all occupations; of this number, 186,675, or somewhat less than one-half, were engaged in manufacturing, and the amount paid by these establishments in wages and salaries during the year 1900 was $95,053,775. Of this amount it is probably within the fact to assume that two-thirds, or say $60,000,000, was expended in the support of others than those earning this income. If it is assumed that the average age of these producers is thirty years, and that the present value of an annuity at that age is $17, and that on the whole the mortality among these persons will follow the table rate, it appears that this income represents a present value of future earnings of more than a thousand million dollars, any portion of which capital is liable to be cut off in any hour of any day. But these figures apply only to those engaged in one branch of labor, and this probably on the whole less remunerative than the sum total of other occupations. It is not claimed that these estimates even approach accuracy, but it seems reasonable to believe that they are within facts.

The grand list of Connecticut in the year 1900 amounted to $694,000,000. This represents the amount of property subject to direct taxation in the State, by far the greater part of it consisting of real estate and buildings. Theoretically these properties are placed in this list at somewhat less than their actual value, but it is doubtful if taking the whole State together, the value of real estate and buildings is materially greater than that placed upon them in the grand list.

From the estimates which have here been made, there can be no doubt whatever that the present value of the future earnings of those engaged in various occupations in this State is many times the amount of the grand list.

The material wealth of a state not only depends upon its citizens, but by far the greater part of real resources of the commonwealth is composed of the actual computable value of the lives of its inhabitants.

The report of the Insurance Commissioner of Connecticut for the year 1900 shows that there were at the close of that year life insurance policies outstanding on lives of citizens of the State representing $149,970,752 of insurance. Some of these have been in force for many years, and it is certain that the average age of these policy-holders is much higher than that of the general population. Assuming it to be fifty, it appears that this amount of insurance represents an income which it is intended to protect of about $12,000,000. It is evident that this protection is far less than the amount at risk, and that the community is therefore constantly sustaining losses by death, which are repaired only to a comparatively small degree. The life insurance agent is supposed to prosecute his business thoroughly, but he will not accomplish his full mission until the education of the public has proceeded to a point where the real purpose and the actual benefits of life insurance are far better understood than they are at this time.

The propriety of taxing the income or accumulations of life insurance companies has led to many discussions of the relations of these institutions to the state, and to an expression of opinion by many eminent men who have, by reason of such propositions, given much study to this question.

In a debate on an Income Duty Bill in the House of Commons in 1798, Pitt said: "Laying aside the proud idea of the vigor, permanence, and renewing energy which the measure secured, there is one case which, with a view to the class who are really willing to save for the benefit of those for whom they are bound to provide, makes some modification. It is in favor of those who have recourse to that easy, certain, and advantageous mode of providing for their families by insuring their lives."

In 1862, when this country was seeking means for meeting the extraordinary expenditures occasioned by the war, and the question of taxing insurance companies was before Congress, Charles Sumner said: "The business of insurance, it seems to me, is peculiar. It differs from other business. It is not strictly, if I may say so, a money-making business, but it is a money-saving business. I know that persons get up insurance companies in order to advance their own interests; but the primary object of the insurance office is to protect other people, and particularly the poor: it is to help the poor. I say, therefore, it is not primarily, as compared with many other businesses, a money-making business. On this account, it seems to me, it has a title to a certain consideration. Now, what is proposed? A tax on the premium. What are the premiums? The premiums are themselves a tax. The premiums constitute the tax which the person insured pays for his insurance; and now it is proposed to put a tax on a tax. This is the precise case. I state it in this way in order to simplify it; in order to reduce it, if I may say so, to its most naked form."

Francis A. Walker has said: "If a man's income belongs to him to spend, it belongs to him to save; and on the ground of equity, the state cannot lay its hands upon that which represents the double virtue of industry and frugality, while sparing that which represents the single virtue of industry. Economically considered, there cannot be a moment's question that the policy of laying the burden of the state upon that portion of the product of industry which has escaped the maw of appetite, which is presumably reserved for useful employment, which is in a sense consecrated by worthy social ambition and which represents the courage, prudence, and faith requisite to subordinate the present to the future, is thoroughly vicious."

Two-thirds of the adult men and women of this country are married. Some of the remainder are physically or mentally unfit for the marriage state, but it cannot be doubted that whatever agency increases marriages, among those who only postpone this act because of a natural and prudent apprehension of the results which death may bring, promotes the well-being and increases the happiness of the community. There is no way, except through life insurance, that many suitable and advantageous marriages can be entered into with a due regard for the happiness of the individuals directly interested, and for the protection and welfare of the state.

The public treasury must be supplied by those who are benefited by the expenditure of public money. Churches and schools lessen crime and pauperism, and thus diminish public expense. Their influence is rightly considered in distributing the burdens of taxation. In considering this question, which is of great and increasing importance, a knowledge not only of the theory of life insurance, but also of what it is accomplishing and of its possibilities, will be of advantage to every one who seeks to do his share for the uplifting of the state of which he is a part.

CHAPTER III

HISTORY OF LIFE INSURANCE; PERIOD OF EARLY BEGINNINGS[1]

It has been the endeavor of most writers to trace the practice, if not the principle, of assurance as far back as possible; but in doing this, trifles have been exaggerated into matters of importance. Some authors contend, on the authority of Livy, that it was in use during the Second Punic War; others, arguing from a passage in Suetonius, refer to the Emperor Claudius as the first insurer; because, in order to encourage the importation of corn, he took all the loss or damage it might sustain upon himself.

These cases are, however, entirely exceptional, and certainly indicate no settled plan, as the very fact that the Emperor guaranteed the contractor against damage is a proof that there was no other mode of doing so. Cicero is also quoted, because, in one of his epistles, he expresses a hope of finding at Laodicea security by which he could remit the money of the republic without being exposed to danger in its passage.

If, however, the assertion that marine assurance was known to the ancients is not demonstrable, there is no doubt that life assurance was unknown and unpractised, although the Romans had some wise regulations in connection with the economy of the people. From Servius Tullius downwards, they took a census every fifth year, and the right of citizenship was involved in any one failing to comply with the requirements of his age, name, resi-

[1] By John Francis. Reprinted from pages 25–40 of "Annals, Anecdotes, and Legends: a Chronicle of Life Assurance"; Longman, Brown, Green, and Longmans. London, 1853.

dence, the age of his wife, the number of his children, slaves, and cattle, together with the value of his property. They do not seem to have kept any exact mortuary register, as the chief object of their census was to levy men and money for the purpose of conquest. One of the commentators on the Justinian Code also gave a calculation of the worth of annuities, which, if it may be accepted as an expectation of life, gives far more correct views of its comparative value at various ages than was known in Europe until the time of De Witt.

Turning from these vague theories of an antique age to our own country, we find that associations founded on social principles, in which union for good or for ill, and in which provision was made for contingencies, were the prominent features, are to be found in our Saxon annals. The axiom, that "Union is Strength," the necessity of providing for casualties by mutual assistance, in other words, assurance on its broadest and most rational basis, was practised in the Saxon guild, the origin of which was very simple: Every freeman of fourteen being bound to find sureties to keep the peace, certain neighbors, composed of ten families, became bound for one another, either to produce any one of the number who should offend against the Norman law, or to make pecuniary satisfaction for the offense. To do this, they raised a fund by mutual payments, which they placed in one common stock. This was pure mutual assurance. From this arose other fraternities. The uncertain state of society, the fines which were arbitrarily levied, the liability to loss of life and property in a country divided against itself, rendered association a necessity. And if it was necessary before the Conquest, it became doubly so after it. The mailed hand of the Norman knight was ever ready to grasp the goods of the Saxon serf; and the Norman noble trod the ground he had aided to subdue, with the pride of a conqueror, at the same time that he exercised the rapacity of an Eastern vizier. To meet the pecuniary exigencies which were perpetually arising from fines and forfeitures, and to aid one another in burials, legal exactions, penal mulcts, payments, and compensation, — ancient friendly societies, somewhat similar to those of the present day, were established; and the rules of one which existed at Cambridge prove its approximation to the modern mutual friendly association. The following extracts will satisfy the reader of the truth of this assertion:

"1. It is ordained, that all the members shall swear by the holy reliques that they will be faithful to each of their fellow-members, as well in religious as in worldly matters; and that, in all disputes, they will always take part with him that has justice on his side.

"2. When any member shall die, he shall be carried by the whole Society to whatever place of interment he shall have chosen; and whoever shall not come to assist in bearing him shall forfeit a sextarium of honey: the Society making up the rest of the expense, and furnishing each his quota towards the funeral entertainments; and also, secondly, for charitable purposes, out of which as much as is meet and convenient is to be bestowed upon the church of St. Etheldred.

"3. When any member shall stand in need of assistance from his fellow-members, notice thereof shall be given to the Reeve or Warden who dwells nearest that member, unless that member be his immediate neighbor; and the Warden, if he neglect giving him relief, shall forfeit one pound.[1] In like manner, if the President of the Society shall neglect coming to his asssistance, he shall forfeit one pound, unless he be detained by the business of his lord or by sickness.

"4. If any one shall take away the life of a member, his reparatory fine shall not exceed eight pounds; but if he obstinately refuse to make reparation, then shall he be prosecuted by and at the expense of the whole Society; and if any individual undertake the prosecution, then

[1] About as much silver as is now coined into £3 1*s*. 11*d*.

each of the rest shall bear an equal share of the expenses. If, however, a member who is poor kill any one, and compensation must be made, then, if the deceased was worth 1200 shillings, each member shall contribute half a mark [1]; but if the deceased was a hind, each member shall contribute two oræ [2]; if a Welchman, only one.

"5. If any member shall take away the life of another member, he shall make reparation to the relations of the deceased, and besides make atonement for his fellow-member by a fine of eight pounds, or lose his right of fellowship to the Society. And if any member, except only in the presence of the king, or bishop, or an alderman, shall eat or drink with him who has taken away the life of a fellow-member, he shall forfeit one pound, unless he can prove, by the evidence of two witnesses on oath, that he did not know the person.

"6. If any member shall treat another member in an abusive manner, or call him names, he shall forfeit a quart of honey; and if he be abusive to any other person, who is not a member, he shall likewise forfeit a quart of honey.

"7. If any member, being at a distance from home, shall die or fall sick, his fellow-members shall send to fetch him, either alive or dead, to whatever place he may have wished, or be liable to the stated penalty; but if a member shall die at home, every member who shall not go to fetch his corpse, and every member who shall absent himself from his obsequies, shall forfeit a sextarium of honey."

These rules might have been certified by a Pratt, so simple and so excellent is their arrangement. But they must not be regarded as exceptional. The following form a portion of the regulations of another similar society at Exeter: —

"1. At each meeting every member shall contribute

[1] Equal in weight to about £2 1*s*. 3*d*. of our silver coinage.

[2] Equal in weight to 10*s*. 4*d*. of our present silver coinage.

two sextaria of barley meal, and every knight one, together with his quota of honey.

"2. When any member is about to go abroad, each of his fellow-members shall contribute five pence; and if any member's house is burnt, one penny.

"3. If any one should by chance neglect the stated time of meeting, his regular contribution to be doubled."

Well may Mr. Ansell say, "The guilds or social corporations of the Anglo-Saxons seem, on the whole, to have been friendly associations, made for mutual aid and contribution, to meet the pecuniary exigencies which were perpetually arising." Nor can the reader fail to be struck with the resemblance these rules bear to those of many of the modern societies; and, as they were framed 800 years ago, the similitude is somewhat remarkable. After the Conquest guilds were established for the express promotion of religion, charity, or trade, and from these fraternities the various companies and city corporations have arisen. The following, forming a portion of the rules of St. Catherine's Guild, seem like those of some modern fraternity:

"If a member suffer from fire, water, robbery, or other calamity, the guild is to lend him a sum of money without interest.

"If sick or infirm, through old age, he is to be supported by his guild according to his condition.

"If a member falls into bad courses, he is first to be admonished, and if found to be incorrigible he is to be expelled.

"Those who die poor, and cannot afford themselves burial, are to be buried at the charge of the guild."

Societies like these, established at a period when "the good old rule, the simple plan, that they should take who have the power, and they should keep who can," was almost the law of the land, cannot fail to surprise those who believe that the past was an age of barbarism, and the present the culminating point of civilization. It is certainly a curious truth, that that combination which has been esteemed a peculiar feature of modern times had its antetype in societies framed when commerce and law were yet in their infancy.

Of the rise of assurance generally in Europe the information is limited enough. Malynes and Anderson say it was known about the year 1200, and refer to the marine laws of the isle of Oleron; but a perusal of these has satisfied later writers that the theory was too hastily adopted, and that the earliest ordinance on the subject with which we are acquainted is that of the magistrates of Barcelona, in 1523, to which city must be attributed the honor, until some authentic evidence to the contrary has been produced.

The first English statute relating to marine assurance was passed in 1601. The earliest mention of it occurs in 1548, in a letter written by the Protector Somerset to his brother, the Lord Admiral, and that it was commonly known in 1558 may be gathered from a speech of the Lord Keeper Bacon. In the act alluded to above, "An Act concerning Matters of Assurances among Merchants," it is stated, that "it hath been time out of mind an usage among merchants, both of this realm and of foreign nations, when they make any great adventure, specially into remote parts, to give some consideration of money to other persons, to have from them assurance made of their goods, merchandises, ships, and things adventured, or some parts thereof, at such rates and in such sort as the parties assurers and the parties assured can agree; which course of dealing is commonly called a policy of assurance, by means of which policies of assurance it cometh to pass, upon the loss or perishing of any ship, there followeth not the loss or undoing of any man, but the loss lighteth rather easily upon many than heavily upon few, and rather upon them that adventure not than on those that do adventure."

If mercantile or marine assurance were so common, it is difficult to imagine that some approximation to life assurance, however imperfect or normal it might be, was entirely unpractised. It must necessarily have occurred to the captain of a trading vessel, that the storm or the whirlwind, which might send his merchandise to the bottom of the sea, might also send himself with it; and the thought that, if his goods were worth insuring for the benefit of the owners, his own life was worth insuring for the benefit of his family, arose naturally from the risks he ran. And in those days there was not merely a risk of storm or whirlwind. Man was more cruel than the tempest; and the galleys of the Turks were then as much feared, by the masters of trading vessels, as the corsairs of the Algerine were dreaded at a later period. They roved the seas as if they were its masters; they took the vessels, disposed of the cargo in the nearest market, and sold the navigators like cattle. The only way of mitigating this terrible calamity was by some mode of insurance, to procure their rescue if taken; and we find that to attain so desirable a result they paid a certain premium to their merchant freighters, who, in return, bound themselves to pay a sufficient sum to secure the navigator's freedom within fifteen days after the certificate of their captivity, the ordinary days of grace being lessened on such policies.

In those days, also, when crusades were common, and men undertook pilgrimages from impulse as much as from religion, it was desirable that the palmer should perform his vows with safety, if not with comfort. The chief danger of his journey was captivity. The ballads of the fifteenth century are full of stories which tell of pilgrims taken prisoners, and of emirs' daughters releasing them; but as the release by Saracen ladies was more in romance than in reality, and could not be calculated on with precision, a personal insurance was entered into, by which, in consideration of a certain payment, the assurer agreed to ransom the traveler, and thus the palmer performed his pilgrimage as secure from a long captivity as money could make him. It is true that this care for his personal safety may detract somewhat from a high religious feeling; but truth is sadly at variance with sentiment, and the pilgrims of the crusading period were but too glad to lessen the chances against them.

Another mode of assurance was commonly practised, by which any traveler departing on a long or dangerous voyage deposited a specific amount in the hands of a money broker, on condition that if he returned he should receive double or treble the amount he had paid; but, in the event of his not returning, the money broker was to keep the deposit, which was in truth a premium under another name.

In 1643 Captain John Bulmer published, "Propositions in the Office of Assurance, London, for the blowing up of a boat and a man over London Bridge." Nor was this an unusual mode of conducting an enterprise which was at once ingenious and costly, and which required a union of capital to support it. In the address above alluded to, Bulmer, an unsuccessful engineer, pledged himself to perform his promise within a month after intimating from the office that he was ready; "viz., so soon as the undertakers wagering against him, six for one, should have deposited enough to pay the expenses of boat and engine," he also subscribing his own proportion. The money was not to be paid until the Captain had performed his contract, when he was to receive it all. If, however, he should fail, it was to be repaid to the subscribers. "And all those that will bring their money into the office shall there be assured of their loss or gain, according to the conditions above named."

These facts are an evidence that the principle of assurance was making way, and that men endeavored to provide against the chances or mischances of life, to the best of their ability. Thus, any seafaring person proceeding on a voyage could insure his life for the benefit of his heirs; and if the information which has come down to us limits the practice to this particular class, it was because seamen were the chief visitors to foreign countries, and for them some such plan was essentially a necessity.

But there was a further and more remarkable fact in operation; as an annuitant enjoying a life-rent or pension could make an insurance on his life, by way of provision for his family. These, however, were only exceptional cases, for which the premiums were probably distressingly heavy, if we may judge from the fact that a century later the life of a healthy man, of any age, was estimated at only seven years' purchase. The great merchants of that day were chiefly responsible for such assurances, and many of the corporations engaged in these and similar adventures. The following will show that by 1569 the provident societies of the present day were anticipated. The writer is illustrating his opinion on usury.

"A merchant lendeth to a corporation or company £100, which corporation hath by statute a grant, 'that whosoever lendeth such a sum of money, and hath a child of one year, shall have for his child, if the same child do live till he be full 15 years of age, £500 of money; but if the child die before that time, the father to lose his principal for ever.' Whether is this merchant an usurer or not? The law says, if I lend purposely for gain, notwithstanding the peril or hazard, I am an usurer."

Again: "A corporation taketh £100 of a man, to give him £8 in the £100 during his life without restitution of the principal. It is no usury, for that here is no lending, but a sale forever of so much rent for so much money. Likewise, if a private man have £1000 lying by him, and demandeth for his life and his wife's life £100 by the year, and never to demand the principal, it is a bargain of sale and no usury."

But though these things are evidences of something closely akin to the principles of life assurance, it is certain that no system existed by which so happy a result could he habitually attained. The state of society was opposed to it. Life was then scarce "worth a pin's fee." The noble was at the mercy of his own fierce passions, and, if not engaged in some intestine warfare, was crossing and recrossing seas, was making or unmaking kings. The knight sought dangerous adventures with an avidity which would place his life on the trebly hazardous list of assurance offices, and pale the roses on the cheeks of directors. The citizen, again, was constantly embroiled in quarrels with which he had no business, and merchants would have looked doubtfully on any proposal to accept a life which was likely enough to end the day after its assurance.

In addition to these chances, there was the liability to "plague, pestilence, and famine." The black pest, the sweating sickness, the smallpox, are names to conjure up frightful images. Nothing is now certainly known of the numbers which these diseases swept away in our early history, but the rapidity with which whole families disappeared tended to exaggerate the feeling of insecurity. It seems, therefore, almost impossible to suppose that any plan of life assurance could have existed during these ages, when there were no documents to give the number of deaths, and no laws to determine the value of life. But if assurances were rare, we have constant evidence that annuities were familiar enough. The state employed them for its wants; scriveners enployed them for the necessities of their clients; Pole and Whittington, Canning and Gresham, invested their mercantile gains in them; the usurer made his money breed by granting them in many forms and on various securities; and although to arrive at a just system of annuities was as difficult as a just system of assurance, yet the usurer took as much care in the one case to secure his own interest, as he would in the other had it been an operation into which he chose to enter.

CHAPTER IV

ORIGIN OF THEORY OF LIFE INSURANCE[1]

In the early annals of this country there was no foundation whatever on which to form a theory of the value of life. The wars of succession, intestine strife, and civil discord, killed their thousands. Disease, arising from exposure to the air, from foul dwelling-places, and from an absence of the comforts of advanced civilization, slew its tens of thousands. They who were spared by the sword and escaped the pestilence perished too often by the fire of persecution. Death came in forms which were governed by no known laws; and, notwithstanding the insecurity of life, there was no possibility of making a provision for survivors. To this we owe that kind consideration for the widows and orphans of their members which is observable in many of the city corporate bodies.

Commerce was yet in its infancy, and all the capital which could be collected was necessary to its development. It was, indeed, on this that the wisdom of the executive was concentrated. Every half century brought rumors of some new land which was to enrich the adventurers who combined to explore it. The most gallant spirits of England sailed, and not always in the stoutest vessels, to explore a new passage, or to trade on the shores of some new country, alike indifferent where they went or how long they remained, provided they could bring home some attractive article of merchandise. Every

[1] By John Francis. Reprinted from pages 1–12, *et seq.*, of "Annals, Anecdotes, and Legends: A Chronicle of Life Assurance"; Longman, Brown, Green, and Longmans. London, 1853.

energy was, therefore, devoted to the extension of our mercantile interests; and although Lombards, goldsmiths, Jews, and usurers frequently granted annuities, there appears to have been no united attempt to grant assurances on lives.

This universal spirit of commerce produced, however, marine assurance very early, while the gradual progressive movements made in science and philosophy prepared the way for assurance on life. The rude notions of an uncultivated age were succeeded by broader and more statesmanlike views; the Roman Church, with its narrow notions and its denunciations of progress, ceased to exist; men feared no longer to give a free exposition of their principles; and the Provincial Letters of Pascal prove that a new era had arrived. The doctrine of probabilities, — originated at a gaming-table, — so curious, so interesting, and at the same time so necessary to the present subject, was first popularized by this great genius; but we are indebted to Holland for its earliest application to annuities; as when the States-General resolved to negotiate some life payments, the pensionary, John de Witt, added one more obligation to the many received from this distinguished man, by employing the theory which Pascal suggested, for the requirements of his government. His report and treatise on the terms of life annuities is the first document of the kind, and a most important paper it is. Step by step it explains the grounds on which the proposition of its author was based, and by which he arrived at the conclusion that the value of a life annuity, in proportion to one for a term of twenty-five years, was really "not below, but certainly above, sixteen years' purchase." It is probable that from political motives this paper was suppressed, but John de Witt was certainly the first who thought of applying mathematical calculations to political questions, and the first who attempted to fix the rate of annuities according to the probabilities of life. The essay of the pensionary was, however, but little known to the public, and had no sensible influence on the subsequent progress of the science.

Leibnitz, whose hobby was to investigate the theory of chances,[1] first drew attention to this production; but though often alluded to, its very title was not correctly given, and we are indebted to the researches of Mr. Hendriks for its rescue from an unmerited oblivion, and for the able translation of an essay which, had it been published at the time it was written, would have exercised an important influence on its subject.[2] Up to the end of the seventeenth century, therefore, as there were no laws to calculate the chances of mortality, life annuities were granted according to the caprice of the usurer, or the ignorance of the annuitant; and there is no occasion to remind the reader that the barbaric splendor of the Tudors witnesses customs which, rendering the conditions of life terribly uncertain, had a depressive effect on the science of assurance. The smallpox, a frequent and fearful visitor, was only met by an attempt to stare it out of countenance; for to effect a cure the patient was clothed in scarlet, the bed was covered with scarlet, and the walls were hung with scarlet; so simple and so ignorant were the leeches of the early ages. Dysentery, then known by its Saxon synonyms of the "flux," "scouring," and "griping," daily carried off the unwashed artificers of old London. Nor were dirty habits confined to the mere populace; the banqueting-halls of the palace were rarely or ever cleansed; the accumulations of months were left on the floors, which, to hide the dirt and preserve an appearance of decency, were periodically covered with rushes.[3] In such places disease was ever ready to spring

[1] When asked what benefit it would produce, he replied, "C'est pour perfectionner l'art des arts, l'art de penser!" This, at first regarded as a *mot*, became a proverb.

[2] The title of this essay is "Waardye van Lyf-Renten naer proportie van Losrenten"; or, "The Value of Life Annuities in Proportion to Redeemable Annuities."

[3] There was no just cause for surprise in these periodical visitations.

into vigorous life. Every few years, fevers which had been lurking in alleys and ravaging obscure places devastated the city under various names. At last, that awful sickness which, even at the present day, chills the blood but to think of it, seemed to be naturalized in this country, under the name of the plague; but to it we owe that the initiative step was taken in England, in founding the first principles which govern life assurance, for to it we owe our earliest bills of mortality.

Within a period of seventy years London had been visited by the plague five separate times; 145,000 having died from its collective attacks. As the visitation had been governed by no known system, as it came without any apparent cause and disappeared quite as capriciously, the Londoners never felt safe from its reappearance. It seemed always hovering over them; and as the intervals between its departure and return were sometimes only eleven years, and had never exceeded twenty-nine, its harassing impressions were constantly on the minds of the citizens. Its visits did not allow time even to soften or subdue the painful remembrances connected with it; and were it necessary,

The thinkers of the day understood the connection between cleanliness and health; and the following will show that such as these hit on the right source of pestilence: —

"I often wonder," says Erasmus in a letter to Dr. Francis, "and not without concern, whence it comes to pass, that England for so many years hath been continually afflicted with pestilence, and above all, with the sweating sickness, which seems in a manner peculiar to that country. . . . They glaze a great part of the sides with small panes, designed to admit the light, and exclude the wind; but these windows are full of chinks, through which enters a percolated air, which, stagnating in the room, is more noxious than the wind.

"As to the floors, they are usually made of clay, covered with rushes that grew in fens, which are so slightly removed now and then, that the lower part remains sometimes for twenty years together, and in it a collection of spittle, vomit, urine of dogs and men, beer, scraps of fish, and other filthiness not to be named. Hence, upon change of weather, a vapor is exhaled very pernicious, in my opinion, to the human body."

a reference to the letters, diaries, and chronicles of the day would show that the name of the plague turned men pale, and predisposed their constitutions for its reception; that the very thought made the merchant regardless of 'Change and of counting-house; and that the tradesman shuddered at the memory of a disease which slew his children, depopulated London, and destroyed his business.

The reports of the approach of the plague were, then, a positive and practical evil; and in 1592, when 30,561 died of the disease, the rumors of its horrors, appalling as these were in reality, were enormously exaggerated. An attempt to quiet public feeling by correctly indicating its progress was, therefore, made in the bills of mortality; and though they were not at first maintained consecutively, they were afterwards found so useful as to be continued from 29th December, 1603, to the present time.[1] The mode of their production was simple. When any one died it was indicated either by tolling or ringing a bell, or by bespeaking a grave of the sexton. The sexton informed the searchers, who hereupon "repair to the place where the dead corpse is, and by view of the same and by other inquiries they examine by what disease or casualty the corpse died. Hereupon they make their report to the parish-clerk; and he, every Tuesday night, carries in an account of all the burials and christenings happening that week, to the parish-clerks' hall. On Wednesday the general account is made up and printed; and on Thursday published and disposed of to the several families who will pay 4*s*. per annum for them." In 1629, two editions of the weekly bills were printed, one with

[1] The first parish registers were kept in England in 1538, in consequence of an injunction from Thomas Cromwell. They had been kept for a long time previous in Augsburg and Breslau, though it was not till the beginning of the seventeenth century that they were general in Europe. It is worth mentioning that, long ere this, the paternal government of Peru kept a register of all the births and deaths throughout the country; exact returns of the population being made every year by officers appointed by the state.

the casualties and diseases, and the other without. For a long time these papers were made but little use of by the public. A writer of the day says they were examined at the foot, to see whether the burials increased or decreased; they were glanced at for the casualties, as a matter of gossiping interest; and in the plague time, the progress of the pest was closely watched by the courtiers and the nobles, that they might escape its ravages; and by the citizens, with that morbid feeling which is as much attached to extraordinary calamities as to great crimes. But though this might be the case ordinarily, such was not the view with which a citizen of London, by name John Graunt, thought they should be regarded. This man was the author of the first English work on the subject, entitled "Natural and Political Observations on the Bills of Mortality." Little is known of his antecedents, save that he was the son of one Henry Graunt of Lancaster, that he was born in "Birching Lane," and that he had the ordinary education granted to the sons of tradesmen. He came early into business, passed through the chief offices of his ward with reputation, and became captain and major of the train-bands, when such an office involved danger as well as honor.

All that had hitherto been said of Graunt might be said of many. But Graunt's genius was far from being confined within these limits. It shone through all the disadvantages of mean birth and doubtful breeding. It broke down the barriers of rank and the limits of position, and gave him the first thought of a design, which was the earliest movement in economical arithmetic, and the closest approximation to the data on which life assurance is founded.

The exact time is not known when he began to collect and to consider the bills of mortality; but he says his thoughts had been turned that way for several years, before he had any design of recording certain notions he had formed. Until he published his volume, a more than

Egyptian darkness was on the eyes of the people, and he had to combat some very singular notions. Among others, that London was to be reckoned by millions, that the proportion of women to men was three to one, and that in twenty-six years the population had increased two millions. "Men of great experience in this city talk seldom under millions of people to be in London." To grapple with these and similar errors was Graunt's object; and it is easy to comprehend that his readers rebelled against assertions which lowered the pretensions of their favorite city. It is probable that he made some enemies by his book; as when the fire of London occurred, he was accused of having gone to the reservoir of the New River Company, and of cutting off the supply of water. As, however, he had changed, or was on the point of changing, his creed from puritanism to papistry, and the papists had the credit of originating the fire, the accusation was possibly a party one, and is of little importance now. It is with his work on the population we have to deal, and this, which contained "a new and accurate thesis of policy, built on a more certain reasoning than had yet been adopted," was first published in 1664; meeting with such an extraordinary reception that another edition was called for in the following year, the book being spoken of wherever books then made their way. It formed a taste for these studies among thinking men; and the fact is greatly to the author's credit, that he made a bold, if fruitless, attempt to deduce the law of life from bills of mortality which did not record the ages as well as the deaths of the people. In addition to the London bills, he gave one for a country parish in Hampshire; and in the later editions he added one for Tiverton, and another for Cranbrook. Charles II recommended the Royal Society to elect him one of their members, charging the Fellows "that if they found any more such tradesmen, they should admit them all"; and immediately after the appearance of the work, Louis XIV ordered the most exact register of births and deaths to be kept in France, that was then known in Europe. A few extracts from this rare and curious work will at once indicate its character, and show the simplicity of the existing information; but in their perusal the reader will do well to consider, that Graunt was the first who wrote on the subject; that he had but slight foundations for his calculations; and that, with all these difficulties, he was very successful in his conclusions.

. . . .

From an enumeration of his objects it may be seen that life assurance was not contemplated by the author when his important book was written; but as the earliest attempt to number the people, to classify their callings, and to ascertain the mortality among them, he assuredly laid the foundations of this science. His book gave new ideas. It first propounded the fact, that "the more sickly the years are, the less fruitful of children they be"; and though this was wonderfully ridiculed, time has proved that it was not less strange than true. It formed a taste for similar inquiries among thinking men. It was published at a period when, the city being less populous, there was additional facility in arriving at certain facts. From that time the subject was cultivated more and more. Increased attention was paid to the parish registers. The different diseases and casualties were gradually inserted; but it was not till 1728 that the ages of the dead were introduced. Graunt had forced people to think; and whatever merit may be ascribed to Sir William Petty, Daniel King, Dr. Davenant, and others, it may all be traced to the first observations of Graunt on the Bills of Mortality. To him we owe the care with which parish registers have since been kept, and the valuable material they have afforded to the science of political economy.

Contemporary with Graunt, and contributor to his attempts, was one of those strange, restless, speculative men whose love of money teaches them how to procure it, and whose desire to preserve it, by purchasing land, and leaving their heirs in possession, makes them the founders of noble English houses. This was Sir William Petty, who, in his "Essay on Political Arithmetick concerning the Growth of the City of London, with the Measures, Periods, Causes, and Consequences thereof," made a further onward movement. The earlier portion of his life was passed in battling with the world. He was as much a votary of mathematics as of money, and was eminently successful in both. Although only the son of a Romney clothier, he was the founder of a house which has exercised an important influence on English political life — the House of Lansdowne. He began his career with nothing, and he closed it possessed of £15,000 per annum. He lived at a time when social economy was but little regarded; and he published a volume which, however uncertain both in its data and its conclusions, was an attempt to apply arithmetic to economics of life.

He wrote "An Essay concerning the Growth of the City of London," "Observations on the Dublin Bills of Mortality," "Two Essays concerning the People of London and Paris," "Two Essays on Political Arithmetick"; and the name of Sir William Petty has come down to us more as the author of these works than as the successful speculator, as the founder of the Marquisate of Lansdowne, or as one who began life penniless, and left a princely inheritance.

. . . .

That the tables of Graunt and Petty had produced small practical effect, and that little or nothing was known as to the chances of life, may be gathered from a pamphlet printed in 1680, in which the whole doctrine of the value of the life as then understood and acted on is affirmed: the utmost value allotted to the best life was 7 years, at which the life of a "healthful man," at any age between 20 and 40, was estimated; while that of an aged or sickly person was from 5 to 6 years, the various limits between these two extremes constituting the whole range of difference in value.

Such was the limited nature of the statistics of life when the Astronomer Royal, Halley, compiled those calculations which make his name honored by directors and actuaries. To him we owe the germ of all subsequent developments of this science, in that general formula for calculating the value of annuities which is yet regarded with so much respect.

Up to the period in which he lived — the latter half of the seventeenth century — the town of Breslau, in Silesia, was the only place which recorded the ages of its dead; and from these Halley drew a table of the probabilities of the duration of human life at every age. This was in 1693, and was the first table of the sort ever published.[1] In it he taught, with great clearness and exactness, the conditions needful for the formation of rates of mortality; the manner of forming them with complete geometrical precision; of deducing a corresponding table of the present state and annual movement of the population; of reading in them the probability of survivorship of any person

[1] The following figures will give some idea of the chances of life as estimated by Dr. Halley: —

Out of	1000 born,	661	will be	living at	10	years	of age.
"	"	628	"	"	15	"	"
"	"	598	"	"	20	"	"
"	"	567	"	"	25	"	"
"	"	531	"	"	30	"	"
"	"	490	"	"	35	"	"
"	"	445	"	"	40	"	"
"	"	397	"	"	45	"	"
"	"	346	"	"	50	"	"
"	"	292	"	"	55	"	"
"	"	242	"	"	60	"	"
"	"	192	"	"	65	"	"
"	"	142	"	"	70	"	"
"	"	88	"	"	75	"	"
"	"	41	"	"	80	"	"
"	"	19	"	"	84	"	"

taken at random in a given society; of, in truth, concluding upon the probable duration of the coexistence of several individuals from the sole knowledge of their age. He also first developed the true method of calculating life annuities, taking for his guide the rate of mortality during five successive years in Breslau.

That the tables of Dr. Halley were very much wanted may be assumed, as in 1692 annuities were granted on single lives at 14 per cent., or only 7 years' purchase; and that the state took very little trouble to apply these tables is as true, for we read that, soon after they were published, annuities were estimated on 1 life at 9 years' purchase, on 2 lives at 11 years', and on 3 lives at 12 years' purchase. Some allowance must, of course, be made for the difficulty of raising money and the difference of interest; still the price paid was out of all proper proportion. But the most singular circumstance connected with government annuities at this period is, that, when life annuities were changed into annuities for 99 years, the owner of a life annuity might secure an annuity for 99 years, by paying only 4½ years' extra purchase. Thus, by the payment of 15½ years' purchase, a certain annuity of 99 years could be procured.

CHAPTER V

HISTORY OF LIFE INSURANCE IN GREAT BRITAIN [1]

LIFE assurance is the compound growth, first, of our commercial necessities, aided largely by a love of speculation, and later, of our progressive civilization. For the former, rough and ready means of estimation were resorted to; for the latter, a long and elaborate course of progressive investigation was needed.

The development of the business has extended over some three or four centuries, perhaps more. It has passed through three distinct phases, as (1) The experimental period; (2) The speculative or transitional period; (3) the period of scientific exactitude. These periods, of course, more or less overlap each other, but they each possess very marked distinctions.

It has to be remarked that during the constantly recurring epidemic visitations of the middle ages, anything depending upon the duration of human life could but be a lottery. There were no means even of approximate estimate other than tradition could supply. Life insurance, except as a bet or hazard between two or more individuals, was therefore impossible. And yet it was practised to an extent of which we can only judge by collateral circumstances — one of these being the existence of forms of contract exactly adapted to the nature of the business. These early contracts were indeed based, alike in form and expression, upon those adopted in marine insurance, which, it is generally admitted, had an earlier origin than that claimed for life insurance.

[1] By Cornelius Walford, F.I.A. Reprinted from Volume XXV, *Journal of the Institute of Actuaries.*

The class of life insurance chiefly in use during the experimental period was that of assuring mariners, *i.e.*, masters of ships, against death or captivity during the prosecution of their voyage; in insuring merchants against captivity by pirates — for in early times merchants accompanied their maritime ventures. The mode of undertaking these risks was by individual underwriters taking certain defined portions thereof at so much per cent. premium.

Again, there were also contracts for children's endowments, and various other contingent risks, specially devised in view of evading the usury laws, which latter were sought to be strictly enforced, by the Romish Church in the first instance, and afterwards by enactments in our own statute book; and there being no funded system of national finance in existence by which money could be steadily improved at a fixed rate of interest, until near the close of the seventeenth century (1690),[1] all manner of life annuity dealings were entered into as a means of gain and investment.

The speculative or transitional period is one of much interest. All subordinate offices in the service of the state were the subject of sale and purchase — sale by the patron, purchase by the incumbent. It was obvious that the value of a "place for life" depended upon the age of incumbents; but there were no scientific means of determining this proper value.

Church lands, and houses built thereon, were granted upon lives — "leases for lives" — usually three; on the death of the last of which the property reverted to the Church, and was only regranted, if at all, upon the payment of a considerable fine. Life insurance was much needed to render such transactions financially safe.

Mutual contribution societies were founded; and in default of the means of calculating the expected mortality

[1] In Venice a public funding system was brought into use as early as 1173. In Florence in 1340.

amongst the members, but little regard was paid to age on admission. The old were, indeed, frequently admitted on the same terms as the young, or where a distinction came to be made it was not based upon principles of computation, but was simply arbitrary; and various expedients had to be devised to meet the circumstance that nothing could be fixed in the way of accruing benefits.

Many annuity societies were formed in various parts of the kingdom; but in the absence of available scientific data on which to base their operations, they proved most delusive. Reversionary interests could not be accurately valued, and hence were the subject of speculation only. Even schemes of national finance were ventured upon in an equal absence of guiding principles: and extravagant advantages were offered, to say nothing of tontine projects. Friendly societies were founded without even an approximate idea of the pecuniary equivalents to be demanded for the benefits offered. Finally, there came the stage of scientific exactitude in the progress of life contingencies.

Life assurance associations could now undertake, in return for certain fixed contributions, to guarantee, on the expiration of the lives respectively insured, certain specific advantages. Such associations might therefore be founded and carried on either by trading companies, who entered into contracts in view of profit; and who, from the beginning, possessed funds which made the contract certain of performance in the absence of fraud. Under such conditions life insurance could be advantageously applied to many business purposes, wherein the element of certainty was the one thing needed; and the absence of speculation commended it to the judgment of prudent men, as a means of making provision for families.

In order to pass from the first of the preceding stages to the last, many steps had been necessary. First, in regard to the abatement of pestilence; steps were taken in most of the municipal towns, in the direction of cleansing the public streets, into which animal and vegetable refuse and other abominations had been heretofore indiscriminately thrown. As to the metropolis, which usually suffered more severely than the smaller towns from plague visitations, its burning in 1666 was the "baptism of fire" by which alone it became purified, and rendered even capable of its future development as the capital of the kingdom.

Bills of mortality came to be regarded as of importance in the light of being barometers of the public health. They were introduced into the principal towns by slow degrees; and their results were placed on permament record. From the bills so kept were afterwards deduced the true data for life measurement.

The laws of chance came to be developed, originally very much in the interest of the all-prevailing gaming which pervaded Europe during the seventeenth and most of the eighteenth entury. A yet higher class of mathematics soon afterwards elaborated the doctrine of mathematical probability. The application of these higher mathematical methods to the data supplied by the bills of mortality and other mortality observations led to the development of the science of life contingencies.

The first mortality table scientifically constructed, by means of which the probable duration of human life could be accurately computed, was prepared by Halley, the Astronomer Royal of England, and submitted to the Royal Society in 1622.

It seems necessary to state that Halley's table did not immediately lead to an adoption of the improved methods of computation which it made available. This was probably because its results were deduced from foreign observations, which it may have been thought did not apply to life in England.

Attempts were therefore made during the next century to construct other tables based upon English observations — especially upon those of London; and afterwards upon those of the central town of Northampton.

From the accomplishment of this last result by Dr. Price in 1769 dates what may be termed a general adoption of life assurance for its best and noblest purposes.

This preliminary survey of the stages through which life assurance has passed in its course to perfection is made with the view of preparing the mind for a more comprehensive review of the facts which are to follow. Stated generally, the progress has been a threefold one — juridical, as applied to the form of the contract and its construction; mathematical, as applied to the assumptions of the law of mortality, and the correct deduction of the financial elements; social, as securing the confidence necessary for its extended use as a branch of domestic economy.

. . . .

In 1622, Gerard de Malynes, merchant in London, published his famous work, *Vel Lex. Mercatoria, or the Antient Law Merchant, &c.*, which contains a chapter "of the Office of Assurances, and the antient custom of the same"; and the nature of the assurances there made is described in much detail. *Inter alia:*

"Other assurances are made upon the lives of men for divers respects; some because their estate is merely for term of life, and if they should have children or friends to leave some part of their estate unto, they value their life at so many hundredth pounds; and if he do depart this life within that time the assurers pay the money: as it happened of late that one being engaged for, Sir Richard Martin, Knight, Master of the Mint, caused £300 to be assured upon the life of the said Sir Richard, being some 90 years of age, and therefore gave twenty-and-five *per centum* to the assurers. The antient knight died within the year, and the said assurers did pay the money."

Here is the earliest mention of life assurance being employed as a provision for families. The first portion of the paragraph is rather involved, and probably describes two modes of insurance practised at that period and long before: 1. A man going into foreign parts, say on a religious pilgrimage, having more money than was required for his purpose, lent sums to his friends upon the condition that they paid, say, twofold on his return. They underwrote his life, to secure such a sum of money as would be required. 2. A merchant going on a trading expedition borrowed money of his friends upon the condition of repaying twofold the amount on his coming back. He might be required to insure a sum in case of his failure to return; or he might offer to do this himself, so as to secure the advance upon easier terms.

In 1693 that ingenious computer Leybourne, in his *Panarithmologia* — "a sure guide for purchasers, sellers or mortgagers of land, leases, annuities, rents, pensions, etc., in present possession or reversion" — describing the branches of insurance which then prevailed, said: "Other assurances are made upon the lives of men and women, at a rate that is moderate. For by this means, if you buy any place or office that is worth £1000 or more, or less, and you have not money enough to purchase it, you borrow £400 or £500. Now if you die, and are not in a condition to pay this money, it is lost: but if you insure your life, then your friend that you did borrow of will have his money honestly paid him."

Thus far all had been speculation and darkness. A new period takes its rise with the first efforts towards true light.

It is one of the most remarkable features in the history of life assurance, that at the very moment when the business could, for the first time, have emerged from the reign of experiment into the more satisfactory path of something like mathematical certainty — at that moment the course of events led it into a channel almost purely speculative. This was probably due to the temper of the times rather than to any other single cause. It is certain that the first step towards associated operation was intended to be respectable, although its basis was not very substantial;

it is equally clear that the movement of 1706 was intended to be in the direction of permanence; but it will be made too apparent, as we proceed, that the very attractiveness of the features of the business seemed to render it the prey then, as it has done since, to a band of most unscrupulous adventurers. It seems of the utmost consequence that the events of this period should be carefully surveyed; without this, no deductions can be drawn which will be permanently reliable.

The earliest project of associated life assurance was made in 1699. It was called "The Society of Assurance for Widows and Orphans." Its founder was Mr. Stansfield, "at St. Austin's Gate, near the east end of St. Paul's, London." The association was to consist, "when full," of 2000 members, who were to contribute five shillings each towards every death that occurred among the members, this contribution being designed to raise £500 on the death of each member, contingent upon all members paying up. I will give a brief outline of the main provisions of its "Articles of Settlement."

The scheme was to commence as from 6th April, 1699, to be kept in some public place in the city of London; two register books were to be provided and kept in the said office — one for entering the name and age of every subscriber, and the names and ages of his wife and children, or of any other person or persons to be provided for; and the other for entering the claim of every widow, or of every orphan or orphans, person or persons, made upon the society, and the sum or sums of money paid upon every claim. These books to be open to the examination of subscribers. All claims and matters relating to the "Society" were to be heard and determined by thirteen persons, who were named, and who were all persons of good social position, as clergymen, etc. They were to be trustees for the year. Any three of them might hold a "court" for admission of subscribers, and any five of them for determination of other matters, being lawfully summoned by the "Master of the said Office." Vacancies might be filled. Trustees to be appointed every year by the votes of the subscribers.

Every subscriber, on registering his name and the names of those for whose benefit the assurance was to be made, was to pay 5*s*. for entrance, and 5*s*. more to meet the next claim; and should these have a policy under the seal of this office, nominees might be named, and from time to time changed, for all benefits under the policy. Policies might be changed on paying the cost of stamp. In case of death, *timely notice to be sent to this office, that its "Visitor" might see the person deceased.* An affidavit of death to be made by parties interested in the policy, supported by a certificate of death under the hands of the minister and churchwardens of the parish, or of three substantial housekeepers.

Persons on entering were to sign the deed, and within six months were to appear at the office before three or more trustees, and have their policies approved and signed by the secretary in their presence; at which court every subscriber should, if required by the trustees, or by the master of the office, produce *certificate of his age,* and also an affivadit *that he had not any known distemper upon him, and that he was in a very good state of health,* and the trustees should have power to refuse the person *if it appeared he was sickly and infirm,* or did not produce the certificate, or that in any other respect he was not qualified for membership. Any person of the clergy or laity, "excepting such as live in the marshy and unhealthy parts of England," might be admitted by proxy, if known to some of the trustees, or to the master of the office, or to some two subscribers or substantial housekeepers living within the bills of mortality, as a person of good report; also not above 50 years of age, as also a certificate signed by the ministers of three neighboring parishes, testifying that they did believe him to be in health, and of such an age as he declared himself to be. All members being outside the bills of mortality to have a proxy to pay contributions and quarterages.

There was a stringent provision against *personation,* and in the case of persons who had become members becoming *soldiers and dying in warfare, or dying at sea, or in foreign parts,* all interest in the society and its funds was to be forfeited.

There were well-considered provisions for giving notice of and getting in contributions. On the death of any person after six months' membership, the master to be ordered to pay £500, abating a proportionate amount if there were not the full 2000 members; also deducting 3 per cent. towards defraying charge of office. The master of the office to settle the value of £1000 in ground rents as guarantee of fidelity. The remuneration of the master of the office was to be 1*s*. quarterly from each subscriber, the 5*s*. entrance fee, and the 3 per cent. deduction from the death claim.

Any subscriber not paying contributions within seven days after notice to lose all benefit in his previous payments, and his policy to be canceled. But members might by a deposit of money provide for future contributions and have account rendered. Subscribers dying by hands of justice to forfeit all contributions made.

Mr. Stansfield, the master of the office, was to have full power to control the office and regulate the staff; also to alter the regulations, subject to the approval of the trustees.

The number of subscribers did not get completed very rapidly. In 1704 there were 600 members; in 1705 there were 908; in 1707 the number had increased to 1,104; and early in the working of the scheme the age of entry was reduced from 50 to 45. Notice of the change was given, with this further condition: "When the Society shall consist of 1200, it is designed to be reduced to 40; when of 1600, to 35; when it is full, to 30 years of age."

. . . .

This was the first of the mutual contribution life offices. It seems desirable to call attention to the fact that all the essential conditions of life assurance were here provided for. The lives were to consist of persons in good health, and not over a specified age; persons whose social position enabled them to be identified. Military, naval, and seafaring risks were excluded, and also deaths by the hands of justice. There was to be a probationary period (six months) within which if death took place there should be no claim. This last regulation was to compensate for the absence of medical examination — a practice introduced at a later date.

In the following year (1700) the same Mr. Stansfield founded another and similar association, which became designated *The Second Society of Assurance for Widows and Orphans*. This was to consist of 1000 members only, hence the sum to be raised on each death could not exceed £250. The entrance and other fees were to be less than in the other society. No claims were to be paid until "there be actually £250 in the joint stock." Operations were not to commence formally until there were 600 subscribers. The general regulations were much the same as in the former case; but the nominee feature was expanded, by adding powers for changing them, etc. The master of the office was to give security in ground rents to the value of £500, to secure a sum sufficient to have always £250 in hand to pay claims. The reasons for starting this second society are very obscurely stated — for instance, it was started to be a means to help to fill up the first! Strong inducements were held out to join early, as afterwards the younger ages would be selected in preference to the higher ones. It was thought some would join both. "The first society, which has already made a considerable progress, has supply'd several widows, and is ready to answer all claims that may happen." Among the twelve promoters there were three doctors of divinity. The two societies worked on side by side for some years, and then suddenly disappeared from the scene — eclipsed, probably, by a later creation.

We now arrive at the period of the formation of the fourth mutual contribution life office established in London. This was designated the *Amicable Society for a Perpetual Assurance;* and it was destined, if not to be perpetual, to live long enough to become famous. It differed in some material respects from its predecessors, the chief distinction being that the contribution to its funds was fixed at £6 4*s*. per annum. The first 2000 members to pay, in addition, 5*s*. to the registrar and 5*s*. to the joint stock of the office; and all subsequent members were to pay 10*s*. to the joint stock. The founder and the registrar of the society was John Hartley; and he was to receive, permanently, 1*s*. per quarter out of each contribution.

The plan of working was this; the number of members was to be 2000. Amongst those who died in the first year *one-sixth* of the total contributions was to be divided; in the second year, if the full number of members were enrolled, £4000 was to be divided; in the third year, £6000; in the fourth, £8000; in the fifth, £10,000; and so on forever afterwards — with a proportionate reduction if the full number of members were not enrolled. The full contribution from the complete roll of members would be £12,000 per annum; the undivided surplus was to accumulate together with the proceeds from the sale of annuities — a new feature in life assurance. The uncertain element was the amount that would be realized for the fixed contribution. This depended entirely upon the number of deaths during the year, the sum appropriated for annual division being equally divided by the number of deaths. Each person had an interest, therefore, in recommending none but healthy lives. There was no limitation of age for membership in the first instance; but the court had the power of rejection. Candidates for admission attended before the committee, and were put through a species of cross-examination as to health, habits, etc. There was no medical examination. There were powers to change nominees. The original subscribers were men of good social position, and by their influence obtained in the following year a charter of incorporation from Queen Anne. This charter authorized the commencement of business as from March 25, 1706. The association had been formed in the preceding year.

The number of subscribers during the first year was 875, of whom 29 died — a very heavy mortality; only £875 was divided, the proportion of each being therefore £30 3*s.* 8*d.* only. In the second year the full 2000 subscribers were enrolled, 96 died, and the share of each was £41 13*s.* 4*d.* Third year, full number being made up by new entrants; 122 members died, and the £6000 divided gave £50 3*s.* 6¼*d.* per share. In the fourth year only 87 deaths; share of funds, £91 19*s.* 0¾*d.* At that time the accumulated stock had reached £25,000, and the stipulated £10,000 was henceforth annually divided amongst the nominees of deceased members.

This mode of working, which was financially safe, converted the society into a species of mortuary tontine, except that the smaller the number of subscribers dying in each year the better for their nominees. The heavy mortality of the first three years — the result of an undue anxiety to fill up the regulation number — combined with the absence of limit of age and medical selection, caused the speculation to be a very poor one for the representatives of those who died. The established tariff for life assurance amongst the underwriters at Lloyd's and elsewhere, who undertook life risks, was, and long had been, £5 per £100 for one year; here they had paid more and received much less! At a later period, the age of membership was limited to between 12 and 55 years of age.

The *Amicable* had no sooner become established than it was in conflict with the *Society of Assurance for Widows and Orphans.* It was one of those open, old-fashioned fights, wherein each said the worst it could of its opponents, without resorting to actual abuse. The idea of being "perpetual" was greatly ridiculed by the earlier society. "Perpetual is too great for any human undertaking, and especially for one of this nature. This must be granted if we consider the frailties and vices of men, the hazard that lies in employing a great stock in order to improve it; the tricks, the fraudulent combinations and practices which companies and societies are liable to when the temptation is great." Some of these predictions were in part realized a few years later when, in 1713, Mr. Hartley, the principal officer of the society, absented himself with some £6500 of its funds. This event caused great inconvenience and loss of repute to the society, and was not its only early misfortune. It turned out that some portions of the funds of the society were invested in lottery tickets in (I assume) the state lotteries of 1710 and 1712. Before these events, in 1711, several of the policies of the society were offered for sale. This was probably the first instance of the sale, or attempted sale, of a life policy. There is no record of the price realized. Later still, insurance brokers advertised that they desired to buy policies in the society.

It is not my purpose to follow the detailed history of this association through the entire 160 years during which it carried on business, until in 1866 it was merged into the *Norwich Union* Life Office, under the authority of Parliament. The idea is rather to trace the growth of the successive institutions founded for carrying on the business of life assurance, and indicate their progressive and fundamental differences. In that manner the growth and development of the business may be sufficiently seen.

. . . .

In 1707 there was projected by Mr. Charles Povey (a name that will always be remembered in insurance annals as the founder of the *Sun Fire Office*, and the advocate of numerous other projects), a scheme of life assurance, under the title of *The Proprietors of the Traders' Exchange House.*

In 1708 elaborate "proposals" were put forth in view of establishing a "*Perpetual Assurance Office,* by a voluntary subscription of two thousand persons who, for certain annual payments into a joint stock during their lives, may and will secure to themselves, or to any person or persons they shall name (at or before their respective deaths), such advantageous sum or sums of money as are hereafter expressed."

All through the years 1708–20 the newspapers teemed with advertisements of projected schemes of insurance, of which but comparatively few addressed themselves to life assurance alone.

The year 1720 is a memorable one in English history. It is hardly less so in life assurance history. An atmosphere of speculation had pervaded the metropolis from the commencement of the century. In the crude life assurance project of 1699 a new mode of aggregating wealth had been propounded. The notion, having taken hold of the public mind, was skilfully but unscrupulously worked by projectors of new schemes. Each year more attractive projects were put forward. The very unsoundness of the schemes enabled unscrupulous persons to realize promptly by putting forward for assurance unhealthy lives. In a mutual contribution society, the managers have no special reason (apart from motives of honor) to object to the introduction of lives of the worst class. They receive the entrance fees and the percentage deduction from the claims; the more that enter, the more the managers make personally, as the subscribers themselves pay the claims; the more claims that are paid, the more rapidly contributors come in. Time alone can dispel the illusion.

The movement, now inaugurated, of founding joint-stock insurance companies, shows that the earlier system was becoming exploded. The merits of life assurance were growing increasingly apparent. The people now said, — give us solid institutions to insure in. Hence the two projects of 1719; hence also several other attempts in the early months of this year: for instance,

1. A Copartnership for Insuring and Increasing Children's Fortunes, held at the Fountain Tavern.

2. Symond's Assurance on Lives.

3. Baker's Second Edition of Assurance on Lives. (The first was a scheme of annuities.)

4. Le Brun's Marriage and Widows' Assurance Company.

Simultaneously with the life assurance projects here already enumerated, there had been projected hundreds of other insurance schemes and of joint stock enterprises, altogether apart from assurance, almost from the commencement of the century. One of these outside projects — outside insurance, I mean — was the *South Sea Company*, founded in 1710, for the assumed purposes of trade and emigration. The stock in this company became a favorite one with speculators, and had gradually risen to an enormous degree of inflation from par (£100) to over £800. Many circumstances seem to point to the fact that money made in insurance projects passed into South Sea stocks, certainly some of the young assurance offices invested their members' money in these stocks, and advertised that they had done so. I am disposed to think that the promises of some of the later assurance societies enumerated were founded upon the results of past operations, and a belief that such opportunities would be continued. To what precise extent the various projects of this eventful period were interlaced, it is now impossible fully to unravel. Certain it is that with the bursting of the South Sea bubble every one of the life assurance projects of which I have already given a record, with the single exception of the Amicable (1706), passed into thin air and were heard of no more.

By way of adding to the confusion of the period (although not so intended) there came the passing of the

"Bubble Act" — 6 George I, Chapter 18 — "An Act for the Suppression of Bubble Companies," which recited (Section 18), "Whereas it is notorious that several undertakings or projects of different kinds have at some time or times since 24 June, 1718, been publicly contrived and practiced, or attempted to be practiced within the City of London and other parts of the kingdom and also in Ireland, and other His Majesty's Dominions, which manifestly lend to the common grievance, prejudice, and inconvenience of great Nos. of your Majesty's Subjects, in their trade or commerce and other their affairs; and the persons who contrive or attempt such dangerous and mischievous undertakings or projects under pretence of the public good, do presume according to their own devices to open books for public subscriptions, and draw in many unwary persons to subscribe therein, towards raising great sums of money; . . . and whereas in many cases the said undertakers or subscribers have since the said 24 June, 1718 presumed to act *as if they were corporate* bodies, and have pretended to make their shares or stocks transferable *or assignable, without any legal authority either by Act of Parliament*, or by any Charter from the Crown for so doing. . . ." It was therefore enacted that all such undertakings and all subscriptions thereto should, from and after 24 June, 1720, be deemed illegal and void. The effect of this measure was to kill the more solid of the later insurance associations — those that had a capital at their back — in favor of other weaker associations which had no legal status to support them, and which would almost necessarily succumb in the panic which prevailed.

I have tried to estimate the extent of the dealings of the many mutual contribution life assurance offices which passed out of sight in the year 1720. It is not possible to define the amount of assurances they had in force. That in the nature of the case was always an unknown quantity. We can only estimate the aggregate of the contributions, as against the aggregate returns made by the offices to their subscribers; the balance constitutes the loss to the public. There had probably been some fifty life assurance schemes set on foot between 1699 and 1720. Of about forty of these I have already given a more or less detailed account. Some "entered lives" by thousands, and others by hundreds only. Some lived for many years, others for very few. If we estimate the average duration to have been five years, and the average receipts in the way of entrance payments, contributions towards claims and to the management, at £5000 each (a very small estimate in view of scattered facts learned during my investigations), we have a total of £250,000 — which, at the current rate of £5 per £100, would have insured *five millions* sterling. Probably two-fifths, £100,000, of the contributions had been returned in the way of claims, etc., leaving the loss to the public at £150,000.

We commence our third epoch with the year 1721, and with the fact that there was at that period but one life assurance office in existence in Great Britain — the *Amicable*, founded 1706. That too, so far as we have the means of knowing, was the only life assurance association in the world. It was very defective in its mode of working, at the best; but it stood alone. The society had at this date an accumulated fund of about £50,000; it had distributed in death claims £118,000. Thus it had obtained a solid hold upon public confidence, but I suspect its business suffered considerably from the general shock to public credit. The days of mutual contribution life assurance associations, as such, were gone forever in England. This society had to take steps to mitigate the element of uncertainty, or it would most probably have died out. Solidity was now the one thing sought for.

The solitary survivor was not long to remain in undisturbed possession of the field. In the June of the preceding year there had been founded, under very special circumstances,[1] two powerful corporations for the transaction of marine insurance business — the *London Assurance Corporation,* and the *Royal Exchange Assurance Corporation.* On the 29th April, this year (1721), they each obtained additional legal powers, whereby they were enabled to accept life assurance risks, on the ground that it had been found advantageous for persons having offices and employments to effect assurances on their own lives and those of others.

Each of these corporations, under the powers of their additional charters, commenced to issue life policies.

Life assurance as a domestic institution, if not actually killed by the events of 1720, was thrown back at least one full generation. By what processes it became revived it will be our next purpose to trace.

In 1725 De Moivre published his work, *Annuities upon Lives: or The Valuation of Annuities upon any number of Lives, as also of Reversions: To which is added an Appendix concerning the Expectation of Life, and Probabilities of Survivorship.* In this work he propounded a method of calculating annuity values on a much simpler process than that which Halley had adopted. This proposal afterwards became developed into what is known to actuaries as "De Moivre's Hypothesis": consisting of the assumption that any specified number of persons born would be subsequently decreased from age to age, by some uniform number of deaths. From this it was evident that as the number of deaths was supposed to be invariable, so such number would annually be in greater proportion to the diminishing number of survivors, and thus consistently represent, at successive ages, a yearly decrease in the probabilities of life.

In 1726 John Smart published the large edition of his well-known *Interest Tables,* to which he appended a few remarks on annuities upon lives.

A small edition of Smart's tables had been published

[1] I do not recount the circumstances here; they are so widely known.

as early as 1707. Herein he gave what may be termed a hypothetical table of mortality for London — the first of its kind.

In 1727 Richard Hayes published *A New Method of Valuing Annuities on Lives*. It has been previously noted, that to him appears to be due the origination of the "whole-term" assurance principle. He puts for solution the case "To provide for a family: A clergyman or layman, aged 47 years, holding a benefice or place during life, and having a family, would willingly make some certain provision for them; but finding that his income will let him lay up about £46 a year, and that upon no better security than his own uncertain life, therefore chooses to sell the surplusage of his income — what is it worth?"

In 1730 there was published: *The Gentleman's Steward and Tenants of Manors Instructed*, &c. *The Tables for Valuing Estates on Lives being founded on Dr. Halley's Hypothesis, and calculated by the method laid down by Mr. Abr. De Moivre to* 4, 5, 6, 7 *and* 8 *per-cent., &c.*, by John Richards. This author, although no mathematician, had the acuteness to perceive that the true method of valuing leases for lives was really dependent upon specific calculation, and that the imaginary estimates currently adopted frequently proved entirely fallacious. He accordingly gave, in popular form, a series of tables, calculated upon the principles laid down by Halley and De Moivre, and which were of great practical utility.

Mr. Lawrence, Mr. Gael Morris, and Mr. Weyman Lee, all published works upon leases and annuities about the same period; and each (except the latter, who fell into a misapprehension of an untenable character) conferred benefit in promulgating correct views upon these questions.

In 1740 Mr. Thomas Simpson published *The Nature and Laws of Chance, &c., &c.*, a work which was, to a very considerable extent, an abridgment of De Moivre's; and which, being published at a much smaller cost, obtained a considerable circulation. And being thus known, he published in 1742, *The Doctrine of Annuities and Reversions deduced from general and evident principles, with useful Tables, shewing the values of Single and Joint Lives, &c.* He seems to have foreseen that the doctrine of life contingencies was destined to be extensively employed at a future time, and that consequently more real utility would result from endeavoring to discover general demonstrations applicable to *all* tables of observations that might be produced from time to time, than from inventing particular hypotheses, which, however interpretative of contemporary data, might cease to be useful if new data should arise. He expressed a view which, no doubt, had been generally felt and acted upon, namely, that Breslau, "a place where the generality of the people live to a greater age than at London (as appears by comparing the bills of mortality here with those observations) can be no just measure of the probability of life in this place" (London). He accordingly prepared a mortality table for London, showing what he believed to be the true rate of mortality for this city, which differed from that produced by Smart in 1726.

Other works followed of a similar character, such as Hodgson's *Calculation of Annuities on Lives deduced from the London Bills of Mortality, &c.*, and Corbyn Morris's *Essay towards Illustrating the Science of Assurance* (1747), and Short's *New Observations, &c.* (1750), and other editions of the works already noted; but the main result desired had been accomplished. Mortality tables had been constructed on English data, and the essential principles of life measurement were now generally understood in England.

CHAPTER VI

HISTORY OF LIFE INSURANCE IN THE UNITED STATES [1]

THE colonists who settled America were doubtless somewhat familiar with the practice of insurance as it was then carried on in Europe. But at the time when America was first settled, of the different kinds of insurance, even in Europe, marine insurance was the only kind which had been carried on to such an extent as to be really called a business, and even with this it was a full century after the landing of the Pilgrims that the first corporations were chartered in England whose purpose was to insure against the perils of the sea. Fire insurance as a business was just taking form in Europe at the beginning of the seventeenth century, and life insurance did not develop on a sound basis until the American colonies had been settled for a century and a half.

If such were the situation in Europe in regard to insurance, we should expect to find during most of the colonial period of American history insurance playing but a small part. As shipping increased, marine insurance developed somewhat, mostly carried on by a method of inter-insurance between merchants, and all of it by means of individual underwriters, that is, instead of a policy being written by a corporation, it would be written by one or more individuals. This was commonly done in England even upon exports from this country, but that there was some underwriting of marine risks in America is evidenced by the fact that a public insurance office, which in the

[1] By Lester W. Zartman, Assistant Professor of Political Economy in Yale University.

language of the time meant an office where insurance might be effected through the medium of a broker whose function was to obtain individual underwriters, was opened in Philadelphia in 1721. Though most of the underwriting continued to be done in Europe, yet all during the eighteenth century these public insurance offices could be found in the larger coast cities.

There was some life insurance business done in the first century and a half of our colonial existence, but it was of the nature of marine insurance rather than of an independent growth. All such policies on lives as were in existence were written by the public insurance offices which existed primarily to write marine policies. People had not yet realized that life insurance could be developed as a regular business, covering all the contingencies to which life is subject. Therefore so far as any trace can be found of life insurance during the colonial period of our history, it is found in connection with what were then considered extraordinary risks. If a merchant contemplated a voyage to Europe, or to the West Indies, or a journey to the frontier regions of the West, he was likely to secure a policy of life insurance. There were no companies from which a policy could be secured and the common method was to have a number of men in the community agree to share the risk. The policies were written usually for not longer than one year. Since the risk of death from a sea voyage corresponded closely to the hazards of the ship in which the merchant sailed, the rate charged corresponded to the rate then usually charged for marine insurance, 5 per cent. of the amount insured.

As an example of one of these policies, we have recorded the following written upon the life of one Benjamin Lincoln, of Boston: "Insurance is hereby made by Benjamin Lincoln, Esq., on his Natural life, aged about fifty-six years, for and during the space of twelve Kalender months, to Commence from the date hereof. . . . and we the Assurers do agree that the life of the said Benjamin Lincoln shall be rated at the sum of one Thousand pounds lawfull money. . . . For which we have received the premium due us of five pounds per cent. . . . In case he shall during the said Term happen to die, then we will well and Truly pay unto his heirs, the Sums we have hereunto Subscribed."

The first definite step in America toward the establishment of insurance as a business was the organization of a fire insurance company in Philadelphia in 1752. In 1748 a fire had occurred in London destroying some 200 houses. This fire seems to have directed the attention of one of the Philadelphia marine underwriters towards London fire insurance. Just who worked out the plan of organization of the new company is not known. Before any public mention of the company had been made, the project had received the approval of the Lieutenant-Governor of the Colony, and that most distinguished citizen of Philadelphia, Benjamin Franklin. The first manifest incident was the appearance of an advertisement in the Philadelphia *Gazette* of February 18, 1752, asking all persons inclined to subscribe to the articles of insurance on houses from fire to appear at the Court House.

A charter was obtained from the Pennsylvania government. The new company was called the "Philadelphia Contributionship for the Insurance of Houses from Loss by Fire." This first American insurance company was organized on the mutual basis. Organized by public-spirited men to protect the citizens of Philadelphia, it never changed its original purposes and still survives, thanks to the fact that Philadelphia has never suffered from a disastrous conflagration, the oldest fire insurance company in America.

It was seven years after the first fire insurance company came into existence in America that the first life insurance company had its origin. In 1759 the Presbyterian synods of New York and Philadelphia procured a charter from the proprietary government of Pennsylvania for a corporation whose purposes were fully expressed in its title, "A Corporation for the Relief of Poor and Distressed Presbyterian Ministers and of the Poor and Distressed Widows and Children of Presbyterian Ministers." This institution, which has become a life insurance company, the oldest now existing, was a growth, not a creation of one year. A fund had previously existed in aid of the poorly supported clergy, and the ministers had expressed a wish that, by some fund, like payment could be granted to their surviving wives and children. Donations had been received from Great Britain as well as from America for this purpose. The intention in organizing the corporation was to provide for systematic relief of unfortunate clergymen by more systematic contributions. It was not expected that the clergy would contribute the full amount of funds necessary to provide for the benefits promised, but that outside contributors would still aid. Under such circumstances it was not likely that much, if any, attention was given to the principles of scientific life insurance. That attention could not have been given to these principles seems evident, since it was not until three years later that the first life insurance company in England was organized along sound lines. Although the organizers of this Presbyterian corporation knew little of the science of life insurance, the company survived its early mistakes, changed its plans when the principles of life insurance did become known, and still prospers in a humble way.

Since so much of historic importance centers around this old company, it is interesting to note some of the provisions of its first plan of agreement. It was provided that:

"1. The yearly amount of the contributions shall be two pounds, three pounds, four pounds, five pounds, six pounds, or seven pounds, current money of Pennsylvania; and that the respective amounts to be paid to the widows and children of the contributors, be ten pounds, fifteen pounds, twenty pounds, etc., respectively: and that no alteration be ever made in the rates but that every contributor abide by the rate he first chooses.

. . . .

"3. That no annuity be transferable or liable to be sold; inasmuch as that practice would frustrate the very end of the charter, and of the pious contributions for this purpose.

. . . .

"5. That every contributor at his marriage and as often as that happens shall pay one year's rate extraordinary as he thereby makes the chance worse, by bringing, in general, a younger widow upon the fund.

. . . .

"8. That the contributor's widow, if there be no children, shall be entitled to her whole annuity during her widowhood, but to no more than half the annuity after her marriage, during her natural life.

"9. That if there be a child, or children, and no widow, it, or they, shall be entitled to the whole annuity for thirteen years after the father's decease and no longer."

Ten years later, the clergymen in the Communion of the Church of England in America, of New York, New Jersey, and Pennsylvania, organized companies in each colony, similar to the one already existing among the Presbyterian ministers. There were to be contributions by the ministers and the churches, as well as by charitably disposed persons. During the American Revolution the preservation of the funds held by the Episcopal corporation, as well as those held by the Presbyterians, was an object of solicitude. This anxiety was justified by the outcome, for the New Jersey fund was lost — the New Jersey treasurer, a royalist, left the country, taking the funds with him. After the war the Episcopal companies fell largely into inactivity. In 1797 the State of Pennsylvania passed an act authorizing a complete separation of the Pennsylvania members from the New York and New Jersey companies, and the reorganized Pennsylvania company entered upon a long career, confining its activities to insuring only ministers of the Episcopal denomination in the State of Pennsylvania.

These two denominational corporations, half insurance, half charitable institutions, form the transition stage in American life insurance from insurance by individual underwriters to insurance by corporations on a business basis solely. A beginning in life insurance had been made, but progress was slow for almost another century. Apart from annuity contracts, it is probable that there were not a hundred policies in force in the United States on the risk of life at the beginning of the nineteenth century.

The Insurance Company of North America was chartered by Pennsylvania in 1794 to do a general insurance business, including the insuring of lives. But by 1799 it had not written over half a dozen policies of life insurance and in less than a decade had given up this branch of the business entirely.

That life insurance did not prosper in the United States during the eighteenth century, and for some time during the succeeding century, is not strange. Life insurance cannot be successfully prosecuted in any country which is subject to serious fluctuations in the death rate. In Europe life insurance developed slowly because of the terrible plagues which swept over the country. It developed slowly in the United States for much the same reason. The cities in the United States during their early history suffered seriously from epidemics. Philadelphia and New York had many visitations of different diseases. Small-pox was a recurring epidemic. In 1741 an unknown disease carried off 5 per cent. of the population of Philadelphia, in 1746 diphtheria caused wide-spread terror, in 1756 small-pox was prevalent again, and in 1776 small-pox took 8 per cent. of the population of that city. So late as 1805 the deaths from yellow fever added 50 per cent. to the normal death rate in Philadelphia. Much as is now known about life insurance, it is doubtful if life insurance could flourish under such conditions. In fact there are considerable areas in the United States to-day in which the best companies refuse to write any policies.

Soon after 1800, however, there began to be some active interest shown in life insurance covering the whole of life. Level premium life insurance had now been in operation in England for more than a generation. Some correspondence had taken place between people in the States and the English life insurance companies. Early in 1807 the Pelican Life Insurance Company of London established an office in Philadelphia. In various sections of the country the idea of insurance was penetrating from England. Already an association called the "Pennsylvania Company for the Insurance on Lives" was projected, and while the project matured slowly, it was in readiness for formal organization late in 1809. The organization of this company marks the beginning of life insurance in the United States upon a business basis. This company was capitalized at $500,000. The policy forms were copied from those in use in England and the rates charged were those charged by the London companies, raised in some localities to offset what was considered a heavier mortality rate.

In 1818 the Massachusetts legislature chartered the Massachusetts Hospital Life Insurance Company. This was a stock company capitalized at $500,000 and empowered to do a life insurance and trust business. One feature of the charter provisions should be carefully noted. The corporation was required to pay the Massachusetts Hospital one-third of the net profits on its life business after deducting legal interest on its paid-up capital, and the same requirement was to be imposed upon any other life company that should be chartered. The reason back of the provision was evidently the belief, a belief all too prevalent yet, that life insurance is an especially profitable business, and that for the privilege of doing business the company ought to pay liberally to the state. The result of this charter provision was twofold — the company did very little life insurance business, and no other life insurance companies were organized in Massachusetts for twenty years.

The next company organized to do a life insurance business was the New York Life Insurance and Trust Company. Chartered in 1830, it issued during the first nine years of its existence nearly two thousand policies. It, too, was a stock company with a capital of a million dollars.

Several characteristics are common to all three of these first corporations organized in America to furnish life insurance. All were stock companies with large capitalization; all were chartered to do two kinds of business, life insurance and trust business; all have given up the issue of life insurance policies and all survive as prominent trust and banking companies in the cities where they were first chartered.

With the chartering of the New England Mutual Life Insurance Company by Massachusetts in 1835, and the Girard Life and Trust Company by Pennsylvania in the following year, a new era in life insurance history in the United States began. So far, outside of the half charitable plans of the Presbyterian and Episcopal corporations already noticed, all life insurance was being conducted on the stock plan. News of the great success of the Equitable of England began to be known in America. Even the stock companies were advertising this success as a means of inducing people to take out life insurance. Thus in 1830, in the so-called "proposals" which the Massachusetts Hospital Life sent out, it is stated: "Life insurance has increased very much in England during the last forty or fifty years. . . . The Equitable Society in London, in the course of twenty years from the year 1800, made insurance on 151,754 lives, being more than 7500 policies executed annually by that single office."

The Equitable was a mutual company, that is, a corporation without capital stock. Every policy-holder was a member and shared in the profits which were made. With the constant attention which was now being directed to the Equitable, it would have been strange if a company had not been organized in America on a similar plan. The New England Mutual Life Insurance Company of Boston was chartered by Massachusetts in 1835 to emulate the Equitable of London. But the Massachusetts legislature was afraid of a mutual company without capital, and so provided that the organizers of this company should furnish $100,000 of guarantee capital which later was to be refunded. This made it difficult to complete the organization of the company, and it was not until 1843 that the company commenced to write insurance. In the meantime, it happened that a stock company took the first real step towards the adoption of the mutual principle. The Girard Life and Trust Company of Philadelphia, organized in 1836, while holding to joint stock management, made provision whereby the profits of the business might be shared with the policy-holders. In 1844, in accordance with its promise, it declared its first dividend. The plan proved so popular and the Girard prospered so much that its competitor, the Pennsylvania Company, announced that thereafter all premiums for one or more years of insurance would entitle the policy-holder to a credit of one-half the profits.

Once started, the mutual plan of life insurance spread rapidly. The time was opportune. The conflagration of 1835 in New York had ruined many of the stock fire insurance companies, and a large number of mutual companies had been organized to furnish fire insurance. Until the next conflagration in 1845 they had a very successful existence. In marine insurance, the mutual plan was proving equally successful. If the mutual plan was successful in furnishing fire and marine insurance, why should it not also be successful in the field of life insurance? Furthermore there was the known success of the mutual companies in England. The American stock companies had recognized this success and were granting one-half the profits to the policy-holders. If a mutual company were organized, the policy-holders could get all the profits. The time was ripe for the spread of the mutual system.

In 1842 the Mutual Life of New York was organized. In 1843 the New England Mutual completed its organization. In 1845 the Mutual Benefit of New Jersey was chartered. In the same year the New York Life Insurance Company succeeded in fulfilling the requirements which the legislature had laid down as prerequisite for organization.

With the formation of these companies begins the great development of life insurance in the United States, a development which has resulted in a larger per capita amount of insurance in force in the United States than is found in any other country in the world. Interesting it is to trace the spread of insurance at that time over the country. With the formation of more companies, competition for business began. The three early stock companies had been content with such business as had come unsolicited to the office. Under competitive conditions, the companies began to appoint men in different cities to solicit life insurance as a side issue to their other work. Ministers, teachers, and lawyers were appointed agents and given a small commission. With agents soliciting business, more people began to be interested in life insurance. As they became interested they wondered why a local company could not be organized. Thus it was that life insurance was spread over the country. Take, for instance, the manner in which life insurance started in Connecticut. The Mutual Benefit appointed an agent in Hartford in 1846. An active campaign for policy-holders was inaugurated. The idea of life insurance was so new that wide attention was given to it in a way little understood at present. Public meetings were held to discuss the question. All at once the novelty of life insurance became the talk of the town. The Mutual Benefit agent did a large business. The thought struck some Hartford business men that they could as well organize a home company. In February, 1846, the agent had been appointed for the Mutual Benefit; three months later the Connecticut legislature chartered the Connecticut Mutual Life Insurance Company.

The stock companies had opposed the chartering of mutual companies on the ground that the mutual system was insecure, and that already sufficient facilities were available for furnishing life insurance. Once the mutual companies were organized, they soon drove the stock companies out of the life insurance field. In 1847 one more mutual company was organized. In 1848 three more, in 1849 two, in 1850 four mutual life insurance companies came into being. In 1851 three more mutuals were organized, in 1852 two mutuals, in 1853 three mutuals, in 1854 two mutuals, and so on until, by 1860, thirty-four companies had been organized to do a life insurance business on either the strictly mutual plan or on a plan whereby all but a limited amount of profits were to go to the policy-holders.

In 1843 the ten life companies then in existence did not have over six and one-half million dollars of insurance in force. By the end of 1860 this amount had increased to one hundred and sixty million dollars.

Rapid as was this growth in the insurance business from the successful organization of mutual companies in 1843 to 1860, it was but the beginning of one of the most interesting periods in any life insurance history. With the outbreak of the Civil War there were grave doubts among the managers of the companies as to its effect upon their business. A large territory was cut off from communication and thousands of men were going into a hazardous occupation. The result was not what was expected. Life insurance business prospered as it had never prospered before. During 1862, as well as during each of the two succeeding years, three new life insurance companies were organized. In the closing year of the war nine new companies were organized, and in the following year thirteen more were brought into the field, thus almost doubling in two years the number of life insurance corporations. Still greater growth came. In 1867 nineteen more companies were organized, in 1868 nineteen again, and in 1869, which saw the end of the movement, eleven more.

Thirty years earlier life insurance had been represented by a few stock companies, writing a small amount of insurance each year. At the close of 1869 there were one hundred and ten life insurance corporations in the United States actively competing for business. The amount of insurance in force had increased to nearly a billion and a half dollars.

The tremendous development which took place so suddenly in American life insurance has never been satisfactorily explained. Men who witnessed it were puzzled at the rapidity with which the growth took place. Undoubtedly there were a number of contributing causes. Chief among these causes was the newness of the idea, and the almost universal ignorance even among those who were in control of the companies as to the basic principles of the business. False assumptions were made in conducting the business and deceitful results followed. In the first place, actuarial science had so little developed in America that few people knew that when a company insures a number of people for life, charging the same premium for each year of life, that the company must save something out of the first year's premiums in order to pay the heavier losses that are sure to come as the group becomes older. It was generally understood by this time that the risk of death increased somewhat with increased age, but how much it increased, and what provision should be made for the greater hazard, was not known except by a very few.

The early American companies were simple imitations of the London Equitable. That company had prospered for nearly a century, therefore its plans must be sound. Its plans were good, and if the American companies had followed the Equitable in all things, many of their mistakes would not have been made, and part of the speculative, feverish growth in life insurance might have been prevented. But the imitation of the London Equitable was only partial. The Equitable was charging excessively high rates for insurance. American managers understood that the rate of interest entered into the computation of the premium; the higher the rate of interest that could be realized, the lower the premium might be. As the interest rate was much higher in the United States than in England, so premiums for insurance might be less. Thus while the London Equitable was charging $40 per $1000 of insurance at age 30, the highest premium charged by any American mutual office was $23.60.

These rates charged by the American companies were adequate if other mistakes had not been made. But with rates scarcely half those of the London Equitable, the American companies set forth the great dividends which had accrued to policy-holders in the London company as illustrative of what might be expected from American companies. Furthermore even greater dividends were paid. At the end of the first few years' transactions the managers of the companies found that they had considerable amounts of money on hand, and not knowing that most of these sums should be kept as a reserve to make up for future losses, they were given back to the policy-holders as dividends. Thus some companies were able even with low premiums to declare 80 per cent. dividends on the premium paid.

Even later in the period, when knowledge of life insurance began to be known more widely, a deceitful way of declaring dividends was adopted by some companies. Instead of paying back cash to the policy-holders, scrip dividends in the shape of non-interest-bearing notes were given by the companies, payable at some future date, sometimes at death. In this way large dividends could be and were declared. All this had its effect upon the growth of the business. The desire for family protection is strong among all Anglo-Saxons; it has proved to be particularly strong in this country, and if insurance can be obtained cheaply it is desired by nearly every one. With the companies ignorantly transacting business on false assumptions, the masses of people were led to believe that a new device had been discovered whereby men could obtain protection for almost nothing. In fact the impression spread that life insurance was a good investment, and it was little wonder that the business prospered.

Delusive dividends and faulty reserve plans were the first causes of the rapid growth of the business. Another cause of popularity was the method adopted by many companies of receiving premiums. With the advent of the mutual companies, a number of them adopted the plan of accepting interest-bearing notes instead of cash for the premium. In many cases, from half to four-fifths of the premium would be accepted in the shape of a note. The agents promised that the dividends made by the companies would be so high as to repay the notes, and hence insurance could not only be secured cheaply, but with scarcely any outlay of cash.

So it was that with the novelty of the business, with a delusive way of declaring dividends, and with the adoption of the system of paying premiums with notes, life insurance in the United States from 1850 to 1870 had a development unparalleled for its rapidity and extent.

A change soon took place. The prosperity of the life insurance business had brought men to it who ought not to have been attracted. Even if the country as a whole had not soon suffered one of the most severe financial and industrial depressions it has ever experienced, there would probably have been trouble in the life insurance business. The growth in the number of companies had been too rapid. Many of the companies had been organized for the sole purpose of furnishing lucrative positions to the men who organized them. Even in the many cases where honest management was desired, the business as we have seen was conducted unwisely. In some instances, honesty was never intended, and such companies quickly brought trouble.

In 1868, even while new companies were still being organized, three companies went into the hands of receivers, one insured in another company which subsequently failed, and one was closed at the suit of stockholders. In 1870 seven companies went out of existence. In 1871 two went into the hands of receivers, and the disaster was but started. In 1872 thirteen companies failed, or reinsured in companies which failed. Thus before the financial depression which affected all lines of business had begun, thirty life insurance companies had been forced to discontinue. When the general hard times did set in, and failures in other lines of business became frequent, the rate of insurance failures was accelerated. In 1873 fourteen companies were closed up, in 1874 four, in 1875 nine, and in 1876 nine. Six companies went to the wall in 1877, making a total of seventy-one life insurance corporations which had been forced out of business in ten years. The weaker companies had been weeded out and failures became less frequent. Between 1878 and 1888 a few more companies failed, but mostly as a result of conditions arising in the previous decade.

Along with the actual failures of many companies had come a decline in the business of all. There was nearly two billion dollars of insurance in force in 1870; by 1880 it had decreased to less than a billion and a half.

The causes of this disastrous period in life insurance history have been indicated. The delusive methods of the companies in the preceding period had caused an unwise stimulus to the business. Companies had been organized more rapidly than capable men could be developed to manage them. The premium note system had resulted in many dissatisfied policy-holders. It had been shown what yet has not been learned by many, that life insurance cannot be secured at a small cost. This had made it difficult to secure new business, just at a time when there was much competition for new business. Severe competition resulted in the acceptance of inferior lives; inferior lives resulted in heavy death losses; to recoup these losses speculative investments were made; and then came the financial panic at the crucial time. The cumulative result of all these causes was wide-spread disaster among the companies.

By 1880 began the revival in business. The companies which had survived had been subjected to a hard test. Gradually they recovered their ground as financial conditions improved and as memories of life insurance in the seventies became less vivid. No new companies were organized for twenty years, but from 1880 to 1905 the business done by the old companies increased apace. In 1885 the total insurance in force passed the two billion mark, five years later it had doubled, by 1900 nine billion dollars of insurance was in force, and by 1905 five million level premium life insurance policies were in force in the United States, insuring for a total amount of twelve billion dollars.

Space will not permit more than a passing mention of the striking characteristics of this later period from 1880 to 1905. There was the extensive development of the agency system, the increase in the expense ratio, the liberalizing of the policy contract, the wide use of the deferred dividend system, and the invasion by some of the New York companies of foreign countries. All these have had a prominent part in the great development of the business and have been the subject of much discussion.

During the summer of 1905, starting with a personal quarrel for control of one of the largest companies, revelations were made of bad management which led New York and other states to make an investigation into the management of a number of companies. Exposures were made in some cases of betrayal of trust which shocked the public. These disclosures, coming at a time when the public mind was already inflamed by exposures made in other lines of business, resulted in a demand by the public that remedial legislation should be enacted, and during the following two winters, many legislatures busied themselves in revising the insurance laws. Nothing has been said in this sketch of life insurance in the United States about legal regulation of the business, but it has played a conspicuous part. From 1860 on, nowhere else in the world have so many laws, attempting to regulate the business to such a great extent, been enacted as in the United States. But what was attempted before 1905 has been surpassed by the laws placed upon the statute books since that year. Laws have been passed regulating salaries, expenses, and premiums. Standard policies have been provided. The amount of insurance that could be written has been prescribed. Surplus is limited in amount. Methods of allotting dividends have been defined. Systems of control by the policy-holders have been enacted into law. More publicity is demanded. In short in many cases the climax of state regulation has been reached. Any further attempt at control would practically result in the states taking over the active management of the business.

As a result of the disclosures and of the restrictive laws which followed, the year 1905 marks something of a halt in life insurance progress. Whether the laws will ultimately have good results remains yet to be seen.

In any history of life insurance in the United States, however brief, some attention should be given to assessment plans of life insurance. Level premium or old line life insurance, the history of which has been traced, involves the idea of charging a policy-holder a relatively high premium during the earlier ages, and accumulating a reserve in order that the premiums may not go higher at the later ages as the risk of death increases. Assessment insurance has followed so many plans that it is difficult to define, but in general it involves the idea of assessing members just enough to pay current expenses, and current death losses, leaving a higher death rate in the future to be provided for by higher or more frequent assessments.

Normally, in the evolution of life insurance, assessment insurance should precede level premium life insurance. It is a sort of half-way development from the primitive plan of taking up a collection for the family left in need, and modern level premium life insurance. But life insurance did not develop normally in this country as it did in England. With no system of life insurance in this country, the fully developed, level premium system was imported from England. An abnormal beginning in the United States resulted in an abnormal development. After level premium life insurance had become firmly established, there arose the assessment associations. What brought them into existence, or where their originators got their ideas, is not known. Assessment societies had flourished in England in the early part of the eighteenth century, but had long passed away. It is probable that the first assessment societies in the United States were suggested by the English friendly societies, and took the form which they did in the United States because of the life insurance condition in America at the time, namely, the prevalence of the premium note system.

The first assessment society was organized in New York in 1867. In 1868 there was organized the famous secret association, the "Ancient Order of United Workmen." These two early associations represent the two types which assessmentism has taken in this country. One type has been the associations organized for the sole object of furnishing life insurance on a business basis. The other type has been the fraternal association combining life insurance with more or less of social objects.

Both methods of furnishing life insurance on the assessment plan flourished during the seventies and eighties. It was cheap insurance again, and proved popular. In 1880 no less than 236 of the business assessment organizations had been chartered by Pennsylvania alone. By 1885 fifty-six had been chartered by Massachusetts. By 1889, the country over, the business assessment associations had a billion dollars more insurance in force than did the old line companies. Their life, however, was to be short. Conducted on unscientific plans, these companies soon commenced to fail. In the early nineties, they failed in large numbers. Some state legislatures, finally realizing the weaknesses of the plan, passed prohibitory laws, and at the present time the assessment companies conducted merely as a business venture are of little importance in the life insurance world.

Assessmentism as developed by the fraternal society had a slower development. The fraternals, while growing more slowly, have had sources of power which the business assessment does not possess. The fraternal ties keep men in the order long after they would have stopped paying assessments to a business company. Again, they have been almost untrammeled by state law. Having close organizations, the political party in power has not dared to enact legislation inimical to the desires of the fraternalists, so that even yet in most of the states the fraternal orders are not subjected to any supervision whatever. To-day fully seven million people are insured in the fraternal orders in the United States, two million more than are insured in the level premium companies.

In concluding this sketch of American life insurance, let us consider the more important problems connected with the business to-day. In the old line field there is the important one of the influx of new companies. As a result of the exposures in 1905 there developed almost a mania for new companies in the West and South. At least two hundred new companies have been organized. This seems too many. Competition between them and with the old companies will be so keen that many companies will not be able to continue. There will be probably a period of failures and receiverships somewhat akin to that of the seventies, but without the disastrous effects upon the business which the failures in the seventies caused.

A second important problem is what to do with the fraternals. Something should be done. The assessment plan of collecting premiums cannot but result in failure and disappointment. These associations educate some men to take out level premium policies, but in too many cases failures of the fraternals give men an excuse for not insuring at all. Some of the fraternal societies are voluntarily adopting the level premium system, and if it proves successful, the movement may solve one of the greatest problems in American life insurance, the problem of heavy expenses. The state should encourage these transformed societies and provide that no more on the old assessment plans shall now be organized.

Lastly, of many important problems which may be mentioned is the problem of securing good management of the level premium companies. There are companies which to-day have five hundred millions of invested funds, and the power which control of such sums involves is enormous. Can big enough men be found to entrust with such power, and will they be found? What can the states do to help? If proper management can be secured, life insurance in the United States has just begun its development.

CHAPTER VII

THE THEORY OF RISK [1]

To live and labor in uncertainty is the common lot of all men. Life and health, property and income, are all exposed to countless dangers. The precariousness of the results of human effort has been a favorite theme of poets and philosophers of all ages. "The best laid schemes o' mice an' men gang aft agley," and the possibility of such a mischance profoundly modifies the conduct of rational beings. In their economic activity in particular the influence of uncertainty can be clearly discerned. While exact mathematical measurements are in the nature of the case impossible, the direction of this influence, and to an approximate extent its degree, may be ascertained. It has long been considered a commonplace of economic theory that the reward of capital, and to a less extent the reward of labor, varies directly as the degree of risk to which they are exposed as a result of their economic activity. But until recently, no attempt has been made to isolate the phenomena of risk and risk-taking, and to determine the laws which govern them. The new interest in the subject has sprung for the most part from discussions as to the exact nature of the function and reward of the entrepreneur. Professor Mangoldt in Germany, and Mr. Hawley in the United States, have made independent attempts to elaborate a theory of distribution in which the assumption of certain risks shall be the special

[1] By Allan H. Willett, Instructor in Economics, Carnegie Technical Schools. Reprinted from pages 25–34 of the "Economic Theory of Risk and Insurance"; Columbia University Press. New York, 1901.

function of the entrepreneur, and his income the reward for risk-taking; and though few writers have adopted their general doctrine, the notion that in some way the function of the entrepreneur has a peculiar connection with risk is by no means uncommon. In all the previous discussions, however, one will search in vain for a thorough treatment of the nature of economic risk and the way in which its influence makes itself felt.

We are told by the philosophers that all the activities of the universe are obedient to law. Nowhere have they left any opportunity for the intrusion of chance. Events which appear to take place in a purely accidental way are just as much determined as those whose occurrence can be accurately foretold. The appearance of accident is due entirely to human limitations. It is because we do not know all the previous conditions or all the laws governing them that a particular phenomenon appears to us to occur by chance. In this sense, then, chance is purely subjective; it is merely an appearance, resulting from the imperfection of man's knowledge, and not a part of the course of external nature. But the term may be used also in an objective sense. By chance in that sense is meant the degree of probability that a particular event will occur, as it is estimated with the aid of all the attainable knowledge of the preceding conditions. If the only fact known about the condition of a number of balls in a bottle is that there is an equal number of white ones and of black ones, there is an even chance that the first ball to come out will be white, and this chance is independent of any personal peculiarities of the person who estimates it. It is in this objective sense that the term is commonly used, and, to avoid any possibility of ambiguity, it is in this sense alone that it will be used in the following pages. By chance will be meant the degree of probability of the occurrence of any future event.[1] It may vary all the way

[1] This term may also be used to denote the probability that an event has occurred in the past, when it is impossible to obtain any

from absolute certainty that an event will not occur, through the different degrees of probability, to absolute certainty that it will occur.

Chance affects economic activity through the psychological influence of uncertainty. Man's conduct is modified in one way by coming events which he can definitely foresee and provide for, though he can do nothing to prevent their occurrence; it is affected in a different way by events which are only possible, and which may never occur, or may occur at an unexpected time. In the latter case he will not act just as he would if he knew that they would occur, and occur at a definite time, and he will not act just as he would if he knew they would not occur at all. His conduct will be modified by the very uncertainty as to the occurrençe of the future event, that is, by what appears to him as chance.

A distinction must be made and kept clearly in mind between the chance, or the degree of probability, and the degree of uncertainty. Manifestly the greatest degree of uncertainty does not accompany the greatest degree of probability. When the chance is zero, the uncertainty is also zero. A slight degree of probability brings with it a slight degree of uncertainty. But the two cannot go on indefinitely increasing at the same rate, as at the end of the series we should have the absurd combination of the highest degree of probability, which is certainty, with the highest degree of uncertainty. The uncertainty is the greatest when the chances are even, that is, when the degree of probability is represented by the fraction $\frac{1}{2}$. In such a case we say that there is nothing to show what the outcome will be. As we go from an even chance either towards greater probability or towards less probability, the uncertainty diminishes, and at either end of the series it entirely disappears. For example, there is an

certain information about it. Premiums for the insurance of overdue ships are determined partly by the chance of loss as estimated from past experience.

even chance that the first card drawn from a perfect pack will be red or black, and there is absolute uncertainty as to which it will be. If, however, one of the red suits is replaced by a third black suit, the degree of probability is altered. The chance of drawing a red card is now one in four, and the chance of drawing a black one is three in four. The chance has been increased or decreased, according to the color whose appearance is made the basis of comparison. But the degree of uncertainty has been reduced, and this is equally true of the uncertainty about the appearance of either color. And after a black suit has been substituted for the remaining red suit, the chance of drawing a red card has been reduced to zero, and the chance of drawing a black card has been increased to a hundred per cent., while all uncertainty as to which color will be drawn has disappeared.

I have dwelt at such length upon this simple distinction because of its fundamental importance for the determination of the nature of risk. The word risk, as it is employed in common speech, is by no means free from ambiguity. It is sometimes used in a subjective sense to denote the act of taking a chance, but more commonly and preferably in an objective sense to denote some condition of the external world. To avoid ambiguity its use in the following pages will be confined to this latter sense. The act of incurring a risk will be called risk-taking or the assumption of risk.

But even when used in this objective sense its significance is not always the same. It is possible to think of risk either in relation to probability or in relation to uncertainty. As the degree of probability of loss increases from zero to one hundred per cent., the degree of risk may be said to increase *pari passu.* This is undoubtedly the way in which the term is ordinarily used. A person who should enter upon an undertaking in which the chances were ninety in a hundred that it would result in failure would undoubtedly be said to run a tremendous risk.

But if the term is used in this sense, it will not be true, as I shall attempt to show later on that the special net reward for assuming risk invariably increases as the degree of risk increases. This net premium increases as the uncertainty increases; but after the point of even chances is passed, the uncertainty diminishes as the probability increases. Beyond that point, therefore, the net premium for risk-taking will also diminish as the probability of the occurrence of the loss increases. When the loss is certain to occur the premium entirely disappears, as in the case of the ordinary replacement of capital used up in productive operations. As, however, the risks assumed in industrial life are usually well below the point of even chances, so that the uncertainty as to the outcome increases as the probability of loss increases, it will be more convenient to continue the discussion as though such risks only were to be considered. Whatever statements are intended to apply to greater chances will be put in a form that will make their application clear.

This is not the place to undertake to establish the law laid down above. My only reason for mentioning it here is to show why it seems necessary to define risk with reference to the degree of uncertainty about the occurrence of a loss, and not with reference to the degree of probability that it will occur. Risk in this sense is the objective correlative of the subjective uncertainty. It is the uncertainty considered as embodied in the course of events in the external world, of which the subjective uncertainty is a more or less faithful interpretation.[1]

Considering risk in this sense, we find that the method

[1] This definition involves considerable departure from ordinary usage. The word *uncertainty* might be used in this objective sense, or a new term might be coined to designate its objective aspect. But it has seemed better to keep to the term ordinarily used by economists in this connection. It is important not only to develop more clearly than has yet been done the effect of risk on economic activity, but also to note that many of the statements commonly made about it are true only when the term is defined in this way.

by which the degree of risk may be ascertained depends upon the relative perfection of the knowledge of preceding conditions. In some cases it may be known directly from the circumstances attending it. The uncertainty about the color of a card drawn at random from a perfect pack is of this kind. No one would consider that the chance at the tenth trial was altered by the fact that at every one of the preceding nine trials a red card had been drawn. But when no such definite knowledge of preceding conditions is attainable, the degree of risk is estimated in a different way. It is ascertained by applying the laws of probability to the accumulated results of past experience. The chance that a particular loss will occur is denoted by the fraction expressing the ratio between the actual number of such losses and the possible number in a given period of time. If during each year for a series of years the loss has been one in one hundred in the case of buildings of a certain kind, the chance that a similar building will be destroyed during the following year is expressed by the fraction $\frac{1}{100}$ — on condition that there is no appreciable change in the methods adopted for preventing loss. If for the moment we assume that it is known that the actual number of losses every year will correspond with the average number, the only uncertainty for the group as a whole will be as to which of the buildings will be the one to suffer the loss. The chance that any particular building will be destroyed will be one in a hundred, but the number of losses for the group as a whole will be fixed.

But as a matter of fact the loss for the group as a whole is not likely to correspond exactly with the average loss as determined by past experience. The actual number of losses in any year will vary more or less from the average. This variation is not absolutely indefinite. By the laws of chance a figure can be obtained which will indicate the probable variation of the actual number of losses from the average. This figure will vary in different cases according to the nature of the series from which the average has been obtained. The probable variation will be much less in the case of a series in which the losses from year to year have varied little from the average, than it will be in the case of a series which shows great fluctuations. Thus, to take a simple illustration, if the losses for four years have been 1, 11, 30, and 18 per hundred, the average is 15 per hundred, but it is evident that the actual number may vary greatly from the average. If on the other hand the series had been 13, 14, 16, and 17, while the average would have been the same as before, the actual number for the following year would be much more likely to be near the average. The probable variation of the actual number of losses from the average may be ascertained by calculating the average of the actual variations during the series of years under observation. Thus in the first illustration given above, the variations were respectively 14, 4, 15, and 3, giving an average variation of 9. In the second series the variations were 2, 1, 1, and 2, and the average was 1½. It is evident, therefore, that the greater the fluctuations are from year to year in the number of losses, the greater is the uncertainty as to the number which will occur in a particular year. It must be borne in mind that risk is connected with the uncertainty. If the number of losses may vary from 1 to 30, the area of uncertainty includes the entire number of possible losses; but if the number may vary only from 13 to 17, that whatever may be the uncertainty about the fate of any particular building, for the group as a whole 13 losses can be counted upon, and the area of uncertainty includes only the 5 losses from the 13th to the 17th.

This distinction between the certain and the uncertain losses is of the utmost importance. If, as I shall attempt to show, uncertainty imposes a cost upon society, the removal of the uncertainty will in itself be a source of gain. Not that the replacement of the possibility of a small amount of loss by the certainty of a large amount would result in a net gain. The effect of the occurrence of disaster is in itself the same, whether it was foreseen or not. It is the destruction of a certain amount of capital. But the net result of the occurrence of a certain amount of loss which was definitely foreseen is different from the net result of the occurrence of the same amount of loss plus previous uncertainty whether it would be greater or smaller. And the influence of the latter element is greater when the anticipation of future loss is based on an average obtained from a fluctuating series of past losses. The greater the probable variation of the actual loss from the average, the greater the degree of uncertainty.

Finally it must be noted that the probable variation varies with the number of cases included in a group. According to the well-known statistical law, the figure denoting the probable variation increases only as the square root of the number of cases. Increasing the number of similar risks a hundred-fold increases the probable variation by only tenfold. If, for example, we assume that past experience, based on the observation of 10,000 cases for a number of years, has shown that on the average one house in every thousand is destroyed by fire each year, the average loss has been 10 houses a year. But the actual loss has varied from year to year. The probable variation of the actual loss from the average can be determined only by a calculation based on the actual losses during the years under observation. But we will assume that for 10,000 cases this variation is 5. Then if there is no change in the chance of destruction to which the houses are exposed, the loss next year will probably be between 5 and 15. It is probable that as many as 5 and no more than 15 of the houses will burn. The area of uncertainty, then, is 10, or $\frac{1}{10}$ of 1 per cent. of the number of cases. If we now increase the number of houses exposed to the same danger a hundred-fold, from 10,000 to 1,000,000, the average loss will be 1000, but the probable variation of the actual loss from the average will not increase a hundred-fold, from 5 to 500, but only tenfold, from 5 to 50. The actual loss next year will probably be between 950 and 1050. The area of uncertainty is now 100, or $\frac{1}{100}$ of 1 per cent. of the number of cases. We have used the term *area of uncertainty* to denote the number of cases lying between the largest probable number of losses, or the average plus the probable variation, and the smallest probable number, or the average minus the probable variation.[1] We may say, then, that the area of uncertainty increases as the square root of the number of cases, and that its ratio to the entire number of cases becomes correspondingly less.

Risk, in the sense in which we are to use the term, is, so to speak, the objectified uncertainty as to the occurrence of an undesired event. It varies with the uncertainty and not with the degree of probability. In that sense the degree of risk in any individual case is a definite quantity. It may be ascertained in some cases by direct observation of the conditions on which the possibility of the occurrence of the event depends. When such knowledge can not be obtained directly, it is sought indirectly by a statistical study of the results of past experience. The chance of the occurrence of a loss is denoted by the fraction expressing the ratio between the actual number of losses and the possible number in a given period of time. The value of this figure varies with the regularity of the series from which it has been obtained. There is greater uncertainty about the number of losses that will occur in a given year when the average

[1] I need not point out that the average variation itself denotes only a probability and not a certainty. There is additional uncertainty as to the extent to which the actual variation in any year will vary from the probable. I have not thought it necessary to consider the various devices of the mathematicians for obtaining more significant figures than averages. My only purpose is to show that with the increase in the number of cases the actual degree of uncertainty for the entire group diminishes, and that fact is sufficiently well brought out by the use of crude averages.

has been obtained from a fluctuating series than when it has been obtained from one which was comparatively uniform. The figure expressing the average variation of the actual losses from the average loss for a number of years is called the probable variation. The greater the ratio between the probable variation and the whole number of cases, the greater is the uncertainty. The probable variation increases only as the square root of the number of cases, therefore its ratio to the whole number becomes less as the number is increased. Consequently the more individual cases there are included in a group, the less is the uncertainty as to the amount of loss which the group as a whole will suffer.

CHAPTER VIII

MORTALITY TABLES [1]

TABLES of mortality, although they form the scientific basis, were very little used for life assurance purposes until towards the end of the eighteenth century, after the Northampton tables had been published. Other tables were in existence nearly one hundred years before, one of the first being that compiled from the statistics of the population of the town of Breslau in Silesia by the British Astronomer-Royal, Halley, and published in 1692. Halley at the same time advocated correct principles for annuities and assurances, which were not adopted until nearly seventy years later.

There are two principal sources for obtaining such information as is necessary for compiling a good mortality table, namely:

(1) Population statistics, including registers of births and deaths; and

(2) Life assurance statistics.

Other sources are occasionally used, such as particulars of peerage families which have been carefully recorded and published for many generations; widows' and pension funds; employees in large corporations; army and navy statistics, etc., etc.; but the two above mentioned are sufficient for our present consideration, as they bring under review all the salient features of mortality.

In order to form tables correctly from population records, it is necessary to have an enumeration of the

[1] By Henry Moir, Associate Actuary of the Home Life Insurance Company of New York. Reprinted from pages 32–45 of the "Life Assurance Primer"; C. C. Hine's Sons Company. New York, 1904.

people with their ages, together with a record of the deaths which take place and the ages at death. Even with such statistics, the results are influenced by movements in population in the nature of emigration or immigration during the period over which the observations extend. Frequently, also, when an enumeration of population is taken, the ages are misstated or given approximately. Discriminating judgment is essential in dealing with mortality statistics — otherwise erroneous conclusions may be reached.

The Northampton table may be taken as an interesting example of erroneous construction, because Dr. Price, who published the table in 1783, ignored several important factors affecting the mortality. The statistics on which he based his results consisted of a record of the deaths in two parishes in the town of Northampton. No enumeration of the population was taken, but the tables were formed from the deaths, with ages at death. Dr. Price had also a record of the baptisms which had taken place in the community, and he found that the number of deaths exceeded the baptisms in the period under observation (1735–1780). He therefore *assumed* that the additional deaths were caused by immigration into Northampton at the age of 20. As a matter of fact, however, the additional deaths were largely the result of baptisms being less numerous than the births. There were many Baptists in the town, and the names of their children did not appear on the records of christenings. The baptismal records were on an entirely different basis from the death records, and they should not have been used together. The assumption above mentioned was therefore inaccurate, and moreover the mortality of the two parishes from which the figures were taken was higher than the average of other towns; so that the Northampton table was in several respects unreliable. It was, however, extensively used for many years; and, as it showed excessive mortality, large profits were earned by life assurance companies which adopted its figures. On the contrary, annuity companies suffered severely because their annuitants lived longer than the table indicated. It is a strange and unaccountable fact that this Northampton table is still used in the United States for certain legal purposes, and in some courts appears to be the only recognized table of mortality.

On the other hand, the Carlisle table may be quoted as one which was prepared on scientific principles and from satisfactory statistics. This table was published in 1815 by Joshua Milne. It was constructed from a census of the population of two parishes in Carlisle in 1780, and the deaths in the same parishes from 1779 to 1787 inclusive. It is usually supposed that a second census was taken in 1787; but the figures themselves indicate that this is doubtful. Anyhow, it was found that an increase (treated as being exactly 1000) in the population had taken place, and allowance had to be made for this increase as affecting the deaths also, so that the ratio of the deaths to the numbers living could be satisfactorily obtained. There was a larger proportion of female than of male lives included in the statistics, and the result was to show light mortality at the older ages. The table has been very extensively used, and even to the present day is considered of great value, especially in the calculation of survivorship benefits. For general life assurance purposes, however, it has been superseded by tables formed from mortality amongst assured lives.

Mortality tables from the general population of England have been formed on five occasions, the latest having been published in 1897, dealing with the period from 1881 to 1890. The mortality of the entire population was given and compared with that in various occupations. A most useful series of tables was submitted, with details of mortality in one hundred different occupations, showing not only the mortality rates in those occupations, but giving also the causes of death.

One of the population tables has received more prominence than others, namely; the healthy English table. It was formed by Dr. Farr from the census returns of 1851, and the records of the births and deaths, from 1848 to 1853 inclusive, in 63 of the healthiest registration districts of England and Wales. In all of these districts the mortality of the general population did not exceed the rate of 17 annual deaths to 1000 living; and at the census of 1851 the total population in these selected districts was nearly one million persons, of whom about 493,000 were males and 503,000 females. The mortality of the sexes was investigated separately. This table (male section) was selected by a committee of the Actuarial Society of America for comparison with the specialized mortality afterwards referred to, with slight modifications at ages under 21 and at ages from 51 to 60, and with a special adjustment for the reduced mortality arising from medical selection during the first five years of assurance.

The records of life assurance companies are almost free from the errors and misstatements to which population statistics are subject. The ages of those who take out policies are correctly taken, and a complete record is kept from which can be obtained the number under observation at any age, and the number of deaths which take place amongst them. The first table formed from the experience of a life assurance company was prepared by Mr. Arthur Morgan, Actuary of the old Equitable Society, and published in 1834. The records of any individual company are not, however, so valuable as records formed from a group, because individual companies have frequently peculiar conditions affecting their mortality, while a group is more likely to represent a fair average, such as may be equaled by any well-managed corporation.

Accordingly, in 1843, there was published the experience of 17 life assurance companies, now known in America as the "Actuaries" or the "Combined Experience" table.

The statistics from which that experience was compiled embraced nearly 84,000 policies running from 1762 to 1833, of which nearly 14,000 terminated by death. The average duration of all the policies was less than eight and one-half years. The mortality amongst females was taken out separately and it was found that between ages 20 and 50 the mortality was considerably *heavier* than amongst males, but the reverse was the case above age 50.

This condition as regards male and female mortality has been confirmed from many other sources. Amongst annuitants, however, even at the younger ages the mortality of females is less than that of males; and a careful distinction must therefore be drawn regarding the nature of the contract entered into. The reason for the different condition at younger ages probably is that annuities are generally purchased on the lives of spinsters and widows in good circumstances; while in life assurance transactions the same conditions do not so frequently apply.

The American experience table of mortality, now recognized as the standard table in the United States, was formed by Sheppard Homans and was first published in a schedule attached to an act passed by the legislature of the State of New York on May 6, 1868. The author never gave full particulars of the data employed. It is generally supposed that he used the mortality statistics deduced from the experience of the Mutual Life Insurance Company of New York as his basis, but these figures were inadequate at the older ages and accordingly he must have arbitrarily adjusted the table. It has been very much used, and has grown in popularity because it is found to represent faithfully the American mortality amongst assured lives after the first effects of selection have disappeared. It is now generally prescribed in the state laws as the standard for valuation purposes. Moreover, the table has been successfully graduated by Makeham's law of mortality, so that the calculation of complex benefits is thereby made comparatively simple.

Many other important tables of mortality have been formed, but there is no need to enter into minute details of these, as such details do not involve particular principles. Three different tables have been constructed from the experience of annuitants, more or less directly connected with the British government schemes. The first two of these tables, published in 1829 and 1863 respectively, included some special lives carefully selected by speculators who purchased annuities and drew the proceeds for their own advantage, a practice which was afterwards discontinued by law in Great Britain. They also included certain old tontine funds formed in the seventeenth and eighteenth centuries. But the last of such tables, published in 1883, gave statistics of government annuitants only. The rates of mortality shown by the three sets of tables do not differ to any material extent, and they all prove that female annuitants are much healthier than male. The same feature is still more marked in the latest publication relating to the mortality amongst annuitants, namely: the British Offices Life Annuity Experience, published in 1903. *For example,* the expectation of life at age 50 of a male annuitant is 20.7 years, while the corresponding expectation of a female annuitant is almost 23 years. This experience embraced a period from 1863 to 1893, and included particulars of about 10,000 male lives and 25,000 female lives.

The most important investigations of recent years are those conducted by the British actuaries covering the period from 1863 to 1893. There are three particular features of that experience which had never before received so much attention and care, namely: — the tracing of the mortality (1) according to the duration of the policy, and (2) according to the kind of policy taken; and (3) the publication of full tables of withdrawals. All of these are important influences, and as regards the mortality in policy classes, it was clearly proved that endowment policies, and those which call for heavy premiums in proportion to the risk, were subject to lighter mortality rates than whole life policies and other forms where the premium rate is light as compared with the risk incurred. The reason for this is that those who take limited payment and endowment assurance policies are generally well-to-do people in their own sphere, thrifty and prudent, who look to the future and prefer a little self-sacrifice now if it will provide greater comfort hereafter. The prudence they show in their life assurance is an index to their whole mode of life, and the discretion they exercise is rewarded by length of days. The most important tables are those based upon ordinary whole life policies with profits, and in that class more than 550,000 lives were included. The effects of selection in that class of policy were also carefully analyzed for each year during the first ten years of duration, and full monetary tables have been published.

The following table shows the classes of policies which were separately investigated, and gives also the number of lives included in the aggregate observations:

Male Lives:	No. of Lives.	Years of Risk.
(1) Whole Life Assurances, With Profits	551,838	7,056,863
(2) Whole Life Assurance, Without Profits	56,807	602,591
(3) Endowment Assurances, With and Without Profits	132,043	897,673
(4) Whole Life, Limited Premiums	36,839	410,251
(5) Whole Life, Ascending Scale	23,280	207,709
(6) Joint Life Assurances	9,195	90,171
(7) Contingent Survivorship Assurances	3,482	Over 15,500
(8) Temporary Assurances	11,603	Over 36,000
Female Lives:		
(1) Whole Life Assurances, With Profits	42,293	507,042
(2) Whole Life Assurances, Without Profits	11,050	112,010
(3) Joint Life Assurances	7,222	77,078

The Female Lives in the other classes are so few as to be of no value statistically.

The mortality amongst lives assured who take policies with the right to participate in surplus is noticeably lighter in Great Britain than that amongst those who take non-participating policies. The reason probably is that non-participating policies are generally effected on the lives of borrowers and for financial reasons; and, as already stated, debtors and borrowers are not on the average so healthy as thrifty people. There is reason to believe, however, that the same condition does not hold in America. It is thought rather that the opposite effect is experienced, viz.; that non-participating policy-holders are subject to lighter mortality rates than those who take policies with the right to participation. The reason is that non-participating policies in America are taken with a purpose in view entirely different from that above outlined; in many cases this form is taken as the result of extreme conservatism.

One very important investigation recently completed was that made by the Actuarial Society of America into special classes of assured lives. In all there were 98 separate classes of risks, covering a wide range of material, and the particulars of about two and one-half millions of lives were furnished by the American life assurance companies. The classes of risks may be generally described as follows:

(1) *Policies for large amounts:* one class over $20,000.

(2) *Policies granted on terms other than applied for* (2 classes).

(3) *Nationality:* divided into 4 classes.

(4) *Occupation:* divided into 35 classes and covering army, navy, and marine service; the more important hazardous trades; liquor dealing; and railway service.

(5) *Personal disability:* covering 32 classes, including past history of diseases such as gout, blood-spitting, etc., unusual weights and unusual heights.

(6) *Family history unsatisfactory:* covering 2 classes dealing respectively with cancer and insanity.

(7) *Place of residence:* 22 classes, each relating to a different county in the United States.

The mortality experience in these different classes was compared with a table which was adopted as representing standard mortality amongst healthy lives, with allowance for the effects of medical selection during the first five years from the date of issue. Great care must be exercised in making use of the results of this investigation, and discriminating judgment is necessary because of two important considerations which an inexperienced reference to the published tables might not at first reveal. The first and most important is that the lives assured in these special classes were all *accepted* by assurance companies; and presumably, therefore, they represented the very best material from these special classes. One prominent example may be given by way of illustration, namely, the class relating to personal history where the applicant "has had blood-spitting." The rate of mortality shown in that class is only 108 per cent. of the tabular rate adopted as representing normal mortality. This cannot be considered as the true mortality amongst people generally who have suffered from blood-spitting; but it does represent the mortality which was experienced by assurance companies *on lives accepted* who had disclosed this feature in their past history. It may be taken as certainty, however, that any person giving a history of blood-spitting within a period very shortly before the date of taking a policy would be absolutely rejected; and moreover, even in the case of a history of blood-spitting some years before the date of application, the case would be declined unless the physique of the applicant in other respects were almost perfect. If any applicant showed an under-average physique, and gave at the same time a history of blood-spitting, he would almost to a certainty be declined by any assurance company. The statistics do not always indicate the *average* mortality amongst persons coming within any one of the specialized classes; but only the mortality experienced by companies on lives accepted by them — ignoring entirely rejected lives of the same class. Analogous remarks apply to many other cases; and, as already stated, the results must be used with great care and discrimination.

The second consideration is not of so much importance — it is the question as to whether the standard table has been accurately chosen as representing the average mortality amongst assured lives in America. If the standard show high mortality, then all the results appear more favorable than they ought; while if the standard be low, then the opposite effect is obtained.

One important question in connection with the mortality of life assurance companies is the effect of what is called selection. Before a policy is issued on the life of any person he has to undergo a medical examination and other restrictive tests designed to set aside all who are below a certain standard of vitality. The result is that persons who obtain policies of assurance are subject to lower mortality rates than the general population at the same age, and particularly is this noticeable in the period immediately after the policies are taken. At that time there are none but healthy lives; of course even those are subject to accident and to what might be called accidental diseases, such as fevers, pneumonia, etc. By the recent O(M) experience the death rate per thousand amongst selected lives at age 40 is less than 5. In the course of a year or two, however, illnesses of a more permanent nature make their appearance amongst policy-holders: heart, lung, and brain diseases affect the lives to a greater or less degree, and indeed the mortality gradually approximates to the same rates as affect the classes of persons from amongst whom the selection had been made. At the same age of 40, amongst persons who have been insured for five or more years (*i.e.*, who effected policies at 35 or a younger age and were 40 at date of investigation) the death rate is about 10 per thousand, or more than double the rate applicable to selected lives of the same age.

Another feature which has received a great deal of attention as affecting the rate of mortality is the right always enjoyed by policy-holders of withdrawing and lapsing their policies, either by taking a surrender value in cash or otherwise. The opinion was formerly held quite generally that the healthier policy-holders discontinued their contracts, while those who were unhealthy and could not obtain assurance protection elsewhere continued their policies year after year. It was therefore thought that the effect of lapses would be to increase the average mortality amongst those retaining their policies, as the tendency would be to lower the average vitality by the withdrawal of an undue proportion of healthy lives. Of recent years it has been pointed out that policy-holders who discontinued their contracts do so more frequently because of financial embarrassment than because they are healthy and do not require the protection. The protection offered by life assurance is more thoroughly appreciated after it is possessed than before; and healthy, prosperous people value the benefits more than the improvident. It follows, therefore, that a great many lapses take place because the policy-holder has fallen into irregular habits, and it is well known that the rate of mortality affecting such people is much heavier than that which applies in the case of thrifty and prosperous men. Lapses of this nature tend to improve the mortality amongst those remaining, because they reduce the proportion which the unhealthy bear to the total number.

As is indicated above, there is an element of discrimination on the part of policy-holders themselves according to the class of policy they may take. Those who take policies which provide large assurance protection at small rates are subject to heavier mortality than those who take policies of investment forms which require larger premiums, although each class is subjected to the same initial tests by the assurance companies. The circumstances and the basis of argument are exactly the same as those referred to in the preceding paragraph. Prosperous and thrifty people, who are looking to the future, prefer investment forms of policies which provide not only immediate protection, but at the same time build up a capital for themselves in later life. The man who is struggling along from year to year and living close up to his income may feel the necessity for assurance protection for the benefit of his family or of his business, but he strives to obtain this protection at the cheapest possible rate; and, as already indicated, men of this temperament are subject to heavier mortality rates.

It is sometimes said that if a company were to issue policies for $1000 each, on the life of every person passing along a certain street on a given day, without medical examination or any other test, and at the ordinary premiums for the respective ages, and if the policies were duly maintained, the result would be a most profitable one for the company. This remark is probably quite correct; but it is not correct to pass from this statement as is frequently done and say that the companies could afford to take all who apply without selection. If any company were to do this, the unhealthy would apply for large amounts, because it is easy to convince an unhealthy man that life assurance is desirable; while on the other hand the healthiest would refuse to be classed amongst them, and would rather take the risk upon themselves. In like manner, it would not be correct to accept every person passing along a certain street *for such amounts as they might themselves choose*, because in that case the healthy would take small amounts and the unhealthy large. The average, therefore, would not be maintained because there would be a greater preponderance of business on unhealthy persons.

No single company can ever afford to dispense with careful selection, although it is possible that at some time in the dim future, when social science has developed much more fully than at present, the companies may unanimously agree (or legislation may require) that all who apply should be assured for an amount determined according to the assessed value of the life. Something in this direction might take place if it were possible to assess the monetary value of a person's life in a manner similar to the assessing of the value of property for fire insurance; and it is the only direction in which it would seem to be possible to conduct life assurance without medical examination in its complete sense.

Various plans of life assurance without medical examination have been adopted and are more or less popular in Great Britain, but restrictive measures other than examinations are in vogue to secure that the experience under such policies will be of an average character. Mention may be made of the compulsory assurance of employees in the service of large corporations where every person must be assured, the premium being often payable wholly or in part by the employer. In such case, the average is maintained because the assurance is obligatory on all. Or again, as the effects of medical selection are supposed to be of little consequence five years after policies have been taken out (not that this supposition applies to individual cases in any way, but only *on the average*), one or two companies offer policies, subject to participation in the surplus of their own class, and with the proviso that, during the first three or five years, only a portion of the face value would be payable in event of death. Another plan which has been found very successful is to issue only what is known as a double endowment policy. Under such a contract, if the life assured were to survive a fixed period, then the amount payable at that time as an endowment would be double the amount which would have been paid in event of death during the period. In this case, also, such policy-holders participate in the surplus of their own classes, and the premiums are sufficiently large to ensure that there will be a good surplus for distribution.

These plans are all said to be successful, but they could not under existing laws be practised throughout the United States, because in several states life assurance companies are expressly forbidden from issuing policies unless a medical examination of the life shall have been made by a duly qualified examiner.

When the rates of mortality have been ascertained from the data of assurance companies or from population statistics, it is usually found that they fluctuate from year to year and do not run smoothly. For example, in an individual case the rate of mortality at age 30 might be found lower than at age 29, although other experiences would indicate that the contrary *should* be the case, while at age 31 again the rate might be abnormally high. Such accidental irregularities are to be expected, more particularly if the numbers under observation are small; and it is therefore necessary, in order to obtain a mortality table of practical utility, to submit these statistics to a process known as "graduation." Graduation aims at removing irregularities which may be accidental, without disturbing what may be peculiar features of the statistics investigated. The adjusted results should be compared with the ungraduated figures. The tests of a good adjustment are stated to be:

(1) General regularity in the mortality rates;

(2) Close agreement in the total number of deaths in graduated and ungraduated tables; and

(3) The frequency in change from positive to negative deviations, which indicate that the original figures have been closely followed.

The simplest methods of graduation consist merely in smoothing over the irregularities by averaging the results at two or three ages; and the process has been amplified from this, through the graphic method, by which the mortality is represented by a diagram, to the assumption of a law of mortality which has been found to adhere very closely to the facts in several large investigations, and which provides great facility for the solution of complex problems. It is, however, outside the scope of an elementary work to enter with any minuteness into this subject, which is one of considerable intricacy.

CHAPTER IX

ASSESSMENT LIFE INSURANCE [1]

THE subject of assessment life insurance represents the pathological side, if I may so express it, of life insurance. Instead of dwelling upon the physiology of life insurance, upon the normal phases of it, I am invited to discuss those phases which are abnormal and which we hope are now passing away. In order to do so, I find it necessary to make some explanation of how it happened that the disease of assessmentism set in.

It is worth while for the young men of the new generation, who scarcely know assessmentism at all, except as connected with another form of insurance, to be made acquainted with that which was well known to their fathers, and but scarcely known to their grandfathers. When I say it was scarcely known to their grandfathers, I mean that there was a time when the pathological side of life insurance, that is insurance of a pathological nature of this particular type at least, did not exist, and when, whatever other diseases life insurance might have been inflicted with, this particular disease known as assessmentism was not to be found. I shall point out to you why assessmentism in this country became prevalent; because diseases or disorders in life insurance, quite as physical disease, do not originate independently, but grow out of other pathological symptoms.

Now, the particular situation which gave rise to assess-

[1] By Miles M. Dawson, Consulting Actuary, New York City. Reprinted from pages 120–127, Volume XXVI, of the "Annals of the American Academy of Political and Social Science."

ment life insurance and its great growth in this country was the following: In their early history the regular life insurance companies of the United States addressed themselves to furnishing protection. To-day one will often hear representatives of the fraternal societies distinguishing between insurance and protection, and claiming that their organizations are for the express purpose of furnishing protection, as distinguished from investment; and I think it is a matter of common knowledge that regular companies doing a life insurance business in the United States at this time give a very large part of their attention to investment insurance, and their agents scarcely talk protection, separate from investment, at all. This was not the case in the early days. On the contrary, *the* insurance policy was the whole life policy, a policy with level premiums payable so long as the insured lived, the amount being payable when the insured died, and with no other benefits. These policies had no surrender values originally, although there was every reason why some surrender value might have been allowed; but while they had no surrender values, the rates, being computed upon certain conservative bases, were what we may call redundant, and the expected mortality was much greater than experienced. In consequence, there was a large margin on these premiums and, as most of the companies were mutual, or, if not mutual, sold participating mutual policies which promised the insured a share in the surplus, it necessarily followed that there were large dividends, so called, to be paid to the insured.

Now, when men are seeking for protection, there are two questions for them to consider, quality of protection and the price; and these companies, or some of them at least, at the start expected to earn dividends and to pay them annually, equal to fully 50 per cent. of the premiums they were charging. In order to convince the public that they would earn these dividends, and believing that it was a perfectly safe and prudent thing to do, they offered to permit a portion of the premium, usually 40 per cent. or 50 per cent., to stand against the policies as a charge, bearing interest; and the expectation held out to the insured was that the charge would be wiped out by dividends. Now consider what this would mean. Take it on a 50 per cent. basis. It meant that when a man was actually paying $16 for $1000 of insurance, the insured was led to believe that his insurance was worth only $8; and that was all he paid in cash at the time. In point of fact, largely because men conducting companies did not understand what they were doing, the annual dividend expectations, in connection with which these charges against the policies had been made, were disappointed; and the insured found himself with an increasing charge against his policy which amounts to a diminution of the amount insured, and with an increasing rate to pay, including the interest upon the increasing charge; in other words, with more to pay and less to get. This was unsatisfactory, and the plan became unpopular; but it left one psychological result in the minds of unthinking people, and that was that insurance at that age was worth only $8. Moreover, it chanced that the death losses in some companies were only 8, 9, or 10 per thousand for a time. So the policy-holders declared they were robbed, mistreated.

Men also learned at this time that there was a reserve in life insurance, and that the state required the company to hold a reserve; but they had no idea concerning its function, and they believed it to be unnecessary. They said, these losses are only 8 or 9 out of every thousand; there are some variations from year to year, but it is evident there is no natural increase. So a company can pay its losses out of current premiums, can pay liberal expenses, and have a large surplus left. There is, consequently, no use for a reserve. That was their reasoning. The want of surrender values, giving back to the insured a portion of the reserve in case he was compelled or desired to stop his insurance, was one reason why that psychological result was to be found in the minds of the policy-holders. So we have two things, the issue of the fallacious, misleading, annual dividend, loan note policy, and the refusal to give surrender values, representing some part of the reserve. These two things, working together, produced in the minds of the people two ideas, one being that there was no reason for holding the reserve, which was only a means of robbing the policy-holders, and the other that the insured need pay only about one-half the premiums they had been charged by the old-line companies, which was all that was required to pay the losses.

In the year 1868, after all these conditions which I have described had long been present and were growing worse, there was launched in the State of Pennsylvania, in the little city of Meadville, an assessment plan. That was the beginning practically of assessment life insurance in the United States. It was not really the intention to make this association an insurance society, but something akin to a labor union. It was given the name of the Ancient Order of United Workmen. Incidentally, as one will find to be the case now in a good many thriving unions, it was proposed to give a small protection to the members of the union out of a common fund to be contributed by the payment of $1 by each member whenever another died. Subsequently, however, the organization dispensed with the idea of assessing the members until the funds on hand were wiped out by death losses. The labor union part of the proposition was an utter failure from the start; but owing to the conditions I have just mentioned, the assessment life insurance feature became, after two or three years, extremely popular. Similar institutions multiplied throughout Pennsylvania, and in a short time throughout the entire country, the ground having been well prepared for assessmentism, as has been mentioned.

I want to call attention to the fact that about the time that it became popular there also arose an extremely favorable condition for it, viz., the panic of 1873. For when the panic came it caused the downfall of a large number of the regular life insurance companies. During the years 1872 to 1880 the amount of insurance in force in the regular companies diminished about 50 per cent. by the failure of companies and on account of hard times. It was necessary for men to find some sort of life insurance from month to month as it were and at level cost, and according to what an extremely happy phrasemaker recently named it, the most "comfortable" method of payment, namely, by monthly payments. About the same time the tontine, or deferred dividend, plan became a feature of life insurance. It provided that all money paid in by the insured should be pooled for ten, fifteen, or twenty years. We have practically an abandonment of the pure insurance field by the regular companies at this time, or at least by the most enterprising and progressive of the regular companies. They began to address themselves to those persons who, observing the enormous number of lapses and discontinuances which took place during the panic times, and the hard times that followed, were convinced that they could make a good speculation out of what agents called their "financial strength," *i.e.*, their ability to keep their policies in force; and as the hard times caused people to want cheap insurance, protection policies as distinguished from investment policies, conditions became extremely favorable for the introduction of assessment insurance in the United States.

It may be well to say a little more, by way of introduction, as to what assessmentism was, what it did, and how it came to be; and to state that if such a plan had not been introduced at just this time by the Ancient Order of United Workmen, it might never have been known in the United States. The idea was conceived by Father Upchurch, who had learned of the friendly societies of Great Britain and knew that insurance on the assessment plan had been furnished by these societies. Another thing that he would have known, had he been a deeper student, was that the plan had been an utter failure in Great Britain, and that the friendly societies were reforming their methods and abandoning systems such as he introduced, adopting more scientific modes of doing business. Traces of something like assessment life insurance societies are to be found far back in history, in the ancient guilds of Rome and Greece, of Germany and Great Britain, but the sums to be paid were usually small funeral benefits or benefits for the last illness. Now suppose the members were charged 10 cents a month to furnish a benefit of $50 upon the death of one of them, it would be a high price, but it is evident that the members would not be likely to try to ascertain whether they should have paid 12 or 8 cents, for the simple reason that the contributions were small and the benefits were small. We find, however, that when a large portion of the membership found that there was discrimination and the amounts were larger a totally different case presented itself.

Somewhere about the close of the seventeenth century, the year 1706, I think, there was chartered by a special act of the British parliament a society known as the Amicable Corporation, for the purpose of furnishing insurance upon the lives of its members. Its system was as follows: Every member made a contribution, without regard to age, each year. At the end of the year the funds that were on hand were divided equally among the claimants of the persons who had died during the year, and also without regard to age. About a quarter of a century later there was organized a regular life insurance company, which furnished policies for only one year, or five or seven years, and at a high price; so that the Amicable Society for a half century or more had a monopoly of what we now call whole-life insurance. Notwithstanding this monopoly, it became necessary for the society to make different provisions concerning the distribution of its funds and also concerning the collection of funds.

In 1762, as a result of lectures in London by a former professor of mathematics in Cambridge, Mr. Dodson, and by a man whom the Encyclopedia Britannica calls the ablest non-academic mathematician Great Britain ever produced, Mr. Thomas Simpson, a society called the Equitable Society was founded. It was refused a charter by the British Parliament on the ground that the plan it proposed to give its members was a new idea, untried, dangerous, and difficult to understand, and that if such a thing was attempted at all the company should be compelled to raise a very large capital, all of which seems amusing at this time, for the system proposed was the level premium plan. This society, the Equitable of London, was the first regular life insurance company in the world to do a whole life, level premium business. It is in existence to-day with more than twenty-five millions of assets and about forty millions of insurance in force.

After the organization of the Equitable, there continued to be assessment plans in Great Britain, and some societies of the "$1 a month" or "$1 every time a member died" sort, grew to great size, and then failed or changed their plans. All this was before the time of Father Upchurch and might have been known by him.

As a result of the introduction of the plan in this country, and the favorable conditions for its spread, there came to be numerous societies on the assessment basis. Please bear in mind that the plan introduced by Father Upchurch was to collect just enough money to pay the claim by levying a certain sum on all members without regard to age. There sprang up numerous small associations, some of which grew to large proportions. The Ancient Order of United Workmen now has more than 400,000 members and over $700,000,000 of insurance.

In addition to the above-named societies, there are others known as business assessment associations, where the management is vested in persons who have the power of perpetuating their control by means of proxies from the members. These societies claimed to be superior to fraternal societies, because of the business men's services that they were able to secure and utilize, and their superior attention to the details in the conduct of the business. Some of these became large institutions, and ten or fifteen years after their first appearance a very large portion of the life insurance of the country was in "business assessment" societies.

They did not, however, proceed very far on the equal levy, or flat assessment, system. They felt it was not only unfair to put a man of 60 and a youth of 20 in the same class and to charge the same rate of premium for both, but that it also resulted in the young man aged 20 or 30 not going in or not remaining in, on account of the excessive cost, while the old man persisted. In the State of Pennsylvania at this time, for example, there were myriads of these societies. No other part of the country was so pestered with them as Pennsylvania. Many were called "graveyard" associations because they allowed speculation on the lives of old men in feeble health by persons who had no interest in their lives whatever. These concerns were short lived, of course.

They did not, however, proceed very far on the equal levy, or flat assessment plan of life insurance, which was so unfair and dangerous on account of no regard being paid to the ages of the members upon entering. Most of the business societies were organized on the basis of charging a different levy or assessment according to the age of the member at his introduction into the society. That is to say, for instance, charging a member introduced at the age of 20, 40 cents, one introduced at the age of 40, 60 cents, one introduced at the age of 50, $1, or whatever the case may be. Frequently these rates were based on a misapprehension of the mortality table. At the age of 20, men die at an average say of 7 per 1000; at the age of 40, 10 per 1000; at the age of 50, 15 per 1000, and at the age of 60, 30 per 1000. Therefore, said they, the monthly rate for the man at 20 will be one-twelfth of $7, or 60 cents; at 40 it will be 90 cents, and at 50 it will be $1.25, and at 60, $2.50. This they called equitable distribution of cost and thought it met all requirements, forgetting that it was good for but one year. Almost all of these so-called business assessment life insurance societies were organized on that plan.

Later in the development of the business there were two modifications of the plan, one consisting of the creation of a reserve by adding a percentage to the assessment, which reserve was to be called upon to help out the excess cost over what the net assessment would provide. A second method of making reserves was invented by one of the most ingenious minds that has been engaged in life insurance. According to this method it was proposed to utilize the gains from lapses, that is to say, over-payments by members who did not keep up their policies, to reduce the premiums for all members. It was designed that under this system both the premiums and reserves of the persistent members would be lower than under the usual plan which does not count the gains from lapses. Investigations since that time have shown that if these gains are discounted and applied to reduce the premiums the reserves will not be reduced; while only in case the premiums are not reduced will the reserve be reduced. Only one company made extended use of this plan. That company was able later to reorganize as a regular life company, and is now conducting a prosperous business as such.

For the most part, the business assessment societies have passed out of existence. In any event, they occupy relatively a much less important place than hitherto. The proportion of the total life insurance in the country, held in the business assessment associations, has steadily decreased, and for many years the amount in force has diminished. A considerable number of smaller societies are still held together by special influences, and in a few cases great economy and skill in management, resulting in low expenses and low mortality, has enabled the companies to thrive even to this day, notwithstanding the defects of their plans. Many of those which have gone out of business have failed, but a respectable number were reorganized as regular companies, dealing with their assessment business in various ways, which I shall not here attempt to discuss.

CHAPTER X

FRATERNAL LIFE INSURANCE[1]

MORE than seven millions of American citizens are today looking to fraternal societies like the Knights of Honor, the Ancient Order of United Workmen, the Independent Order of Foresters, and others whose name is legion, for protection to their families in case of death. The distinguishing feature of these societies is that they are associations whose members are banded together through a spirit of charity or fraternity for mutual assistance and protection. They are wholly outside the line of our ordinary life insurance companies, which deal in insurance for the general public on a business basis. Their membership is chiefly made up from those of limited means who are seeking insurance at the smallest outlay. Over one-fourth of the population of this country may be said to be directly or indirectly interested in these societies. A knowledge of their principles and of the character of the insurance which they offer is a matter which concerns every American citizen regardless of his interest in insurance as a profession.

Nearly all our existing fraternal societies have started within the past thirty or forty years, but they have a long line of predecessors extending back through centuries. Their proper understanding requires a glance at their historic relations. To the student of sociology as well as of economics a peculiar interest attaches both to their origin and history. As a race we are communal as well as

[1] By Walter S. Nichols, Editor of the *Insurance Monitor*, New York. Reprinted with additions from pages 162–183 of the "Yale Insurance Lectures, Life."

social in our very instincts, and in those instincts are the fundamental impulses that have developed all our political and social organizations. To the evolutionist they are the inherited traits of a remote ancestry which man shares with lower forms of life. We find the social organism in its simplest type in the ruminants, which herd together for mere association or protection. We find its fuller developments in the more strictly communal animals and insects. The beaver lodges join their forces to build the common dam for the benefit of all, but when the dam is built each separate lodge confines its attention to its own affairs. In the ants and bees we find this communal instinct in its extreme development. The female bee surrenders her maternal functions to a single queen and becomes a mere worker, to build and provision the common hive and care for the offspring. The ant marshals its warriors to guard the common nest or to enslave its neighbors. Thus do we find the germs of those social and political organizations which characterize our twentieth century civilization implanted in the lower orders of creation.

It may seem a far-away thought from the habits of the insect and mammalian world to the subject of the present lecture. But there is a deep significance in the fact that the fundamental principles which underlie fraternal insurance are thus operative in the lower orders of life. The fraternal society must be studied not as the mere artificial product of an advanced civilization, but as an organization whose roots and tendrils are implanted deep down in our common humanity. Civilized communities have no monopoly in this spirit of fraternalism. It was the active force at work in primitive days when the family relationship grew into the patriarchal form of government and this in turn expanded into the tribal state. As tribes solidified into nations this social evolution moved along lines so familiar in the physical world. The homogeneous pursuits of the tribesman became the heterogeneous occupations of the civilized state. Each occupation had its separate corps of workers, who banded together in a society for their common interest and protection in the economic struggle which followed the barter and trade between the groups. Thus was evolved the early benevolent or fraternal societies that are met with in so many of the nations of antiquity.

We find them in the ancient Roman empire as numerous and influential as now. Rome had her trade unions, and her religious confraternities devoted to the service of her gods, and her social clubs, and was compelled to legislate for their regulation. Contribution to a common fund for the assistance or burial of their needy members was then as now a familiar feature. The downfall of Rome scarcely interrupts the story. Phenix-like, they arose out of the ashes of her empire when her distant provinces developed into the industrial states of modern Europe. In Great Britain, to which our own fraternal societies directly trace their origin, they were known as guilds, and during medieval times when agricultural serfdom was being broken up and when centers of trade and manufacture were developing, these trade societies wielded a strong political influence. Along with them too were religious fraternities, which were the foundation of some of England's most important schools of learning. Aid to their needy members in ways more or less crude was a common feature of these associations.

As the power and influence of the guilds declined they were succeeded by the modern British friendly societies, from which our own have been so largely patterned. Members chiefly from the working classes united for mutual aid in sickness and for funeral benefits, through contributions to a common fund. They recognized the distinctly insurance character of their work and sought to frame scales of moneyed contributions which would be adequate. But they knew little of the principles of insurance, and their frequent and disastrous failures at last attracted the attention of the British Parliament. Investigations by that body, aided by leading British actuaries, disclosed the total inadequacy of their rates and the mismanagement which characterized their affairs. Attempted legal reforms were strongly resisted for a while by the members, and it has required nearly a century of legislation to place the friendly society system of Great Britain on the comparatively sound basis where it now rests. Under the existing laws in that country, such societies are induced to register and to accumulate reserve funds and charge rates which, like those of ordinary life companies, will be adequate to meet their future obligations. When registered they are required to have expert valuations periodically made of their resources and liabilities and proper balance sheets published of their affairs. The knowledge of their condition thus furnished to their members and to the public is relied on to check mismanagement. The law makes no attempt at further interference.

The strength of the system in that country lies in the fraternal ties which bind the members to their societies. It was this which enabled reforms to be successfully introduced into many of them which, according to any commercial standard, were already bankrupt. The strength of the system in any country must depend on the fraternal character of the society in fact as well as in name. The chief weakness of the system lies in the temptation to divorce its twofold functions of benevolence and insurance, to regard the society either as a mere insurance organization for business purposes, or else as a brotherhood whose ties are strong enough to outweigh any defects in its insurance methods. When the fraternal spirit among the members is wanting, its work, to be a success, must be carried on along the business lines which characterize the ordinary insurance office. Such a change has actually taken place on a magnificent scale in the more recent development of these societies. It was from the fraternal society both here and in Great Britain that industrial insurance was evolved. It was just fifty years ago that the managers of such a society in London conceived a plan for abandoning its fraternal features and furnishing insurance to the poor on a strictly business basis. This was the origin of the famous British Prudential Insurance Company, whose policies are now found in the home of almost every workingman in that country. Such was the origin too some twenty years later of the Prudential Insurance Company of America, which started as a friendly society in New Jersey and whose policies along with those of its later competitors are to be found in millions of American homes.

The experience of Great Britain is being repeated in America. A similar insufficiency in the rates and ignorance of sound insurance principles have resulted in numerous failures and now threaten the solvency of many of our American societies. Similar efforts are now being earnestly made both by the more intelligent of the members and by state authorities to place fraternal insurance on a sounder basis.

With this preliminary historic review, I enter at once on the discussion of the more technical features of fraternal insurance. First let us examine the structure and legal character of these associations. They generally consist of one parent society with its constitution and by-laws and having numerous subordinate local branch societies termed lodges. These local societies are created by the parent, from which they receive their charters or right to exist. They are governed by its constitution and the laws which it lays down. In all questions of dispute the parent society has final jurisdiction. In a word, the local lodge, while it has separate existence as a society itself, and may within the limits allowed regulate its own affairs, remains subject to the parent society of which it is a part. This parent society is known as the grand lodge and is made up of representatives chosen by the local lodges. Sometimes a further subdivision is made and the parent society or supreme lodge is made up of representatives from a number of grand lodges each with its local lodges.

The membership of the society as a whole is thus made up of the members of these various local lodges. The government is purely democratic. Every member is entitled to a vote in his own local society and thus has a voice in the selection of the rulers and in making the laws for the whole. Initiatory rites and ceremonials are a common feature. Unlike the British societies, in which sick relief is a prominent feature, most of our American associations confine their insurance work to the payment of death and disability benefits. The funds required for this purpose are collected in the form of assessments by the local lodges and turned over to the officers of the parent society, by whom the insurance business of the whole is managed. Sick benefits when allowed are usually paid by the local lodges to their members out of their own separate funds. Expenses are generally met by dues and initiation fees. These local lodges thus act both as separate societies in the management of their own affairs and as agents of the parent society in collecting the common insurance funds and in securing the membership.

It will thus be seen that in their constitutions these societies resemble in many ways the ordinary social club and for certain purposes the law so regards them. The active fraternal or benevolent features of the society apart from its insurance work are chiefly confined to the local societies, where the individual members meet for business and social purposes and where the spirit of fraternity is fostered. They resemble too in certain respects some of our church organizations, with which the law frequently compares them. We have our individual church societies with their social and benevolent activities governed by representative bodies from the various churches and the whole united under one denominational form of government. These correspond to the local and grand lodges.

These societies are sometimes organized under corporate charters granted by the state, sometimes like the ordinary club they are mere voluntary associations. Most of our states now have general laws prescribing how these societies may be formed and carried on. When so formed the law itself becomes their constitution. Sometimes the parent society is thus incorporated while the inferior lodges remain voluntary associations. Sometimes it is the reverse. But in all laws regarding their formation their character as benevolent societies is insisted on. They are not allowed like ordinary companies to carry on insurance business for profit, and its benefits are usually limited to the relatives or dependents of the members. There are some important legal distinctions between those societies which are incorporated and those which are not, especially as to property rights, upon which I have not the time to enter. The courts endeavor in either case so far as the law allows to enforce the rules which they have made for themselves, if they are fair and reasonable. Nearly all these societies have their own judicatories for determining the standing and rights of their members, by whose decision the members must abide. These the courts will refuse to interfere with so long as they act honestly and fairly within their legitimate province. They are mutual societies in which, like churches, the members are expected to abide by the form of government to which they have subscribed. A local lodge may be cut off from affiliation with the parent society or may cut itself loose just as a church may cut loose from its denominational connection. In neither case is the society itself dissolved. It simply loses the rights which belonged to it as a member of the parent society and must surrender whatever is in its possession belonging to the parent. If it has a charter from the state, the state laws governing it as a corporation are superior to any rules of the association itself.

On one point, however, whether incorporated or not, the courts are insistent, that is, no rule or action of the society can deprive a local lodge or a member of insurance or other property interests which are already vested, that is, in which an unconditional ownership has been established. Where they are incorporated, like other corporations they are regarded by the law as artificial persons acting through their officers as their agents and with no personal liability on the part of the members except those imposed by the rules of the society itself. Where they are not incorporated their legal character is not so easy to define. They are often regarded as a peculiar kind of partnership qualified by the special purposes for which they were organized.

It will be seen from this brief sketch that these societies in their constitution and structure are strongly analogous to the ordinary social club or religious society, and bear all the earmarks of their historic origin.

But they also have another aspect in the eyes of the law. In respect to their insurance features they are regarded as business associations furnishing a peculiar type of insurance under contracts or agreements which are governed by the ordinary principles of the law of contracts. This leads us at once to the insurance features of these societies. As insurance associations they are treated as mutual companies regulated, of course, by their charter and by-laws, with which every member is assumed to be familiar. An application, much like that of the ordinary company, setting forth the age and health and other details regarding his desired insurance, is usually required of the applicant for membership. Instead of the ordinary policy he usually receives what is called a certificate of membership, reciting that he is a member of the society and entitled to its privileges, and to share up to a specified amount in its beneficiary fund, subject, however, to the laws and rules of the order, and conditioned on his compliance with them. This certificate in connection with the laws of the society is his insurance contract. It will be noted that unlike the ordinary insurance policy, which is a mere business agreement between the company and the purchaser for a specified consideration, these certificates are simply a recognition of the rights of the member which flow through his membership, to share in the benevolent fund. Unlike the ordinary policy which becomes the property of the beneficiary named in it, no matter who secured it or paid the premium, these certificates remain the property of the member, who can usually change the beneficiary at will.

The conditions on which those rights are to be enjoyed are not, as in the case of the policy, set out in the certificate itself, but are to be found in the rules of the society. Thus the mutual and fraternal idea of this insurance is adhered to. More than this, it is not allowed under the laws of most of the states to be a cold business agreement for the payment of a fixed sum of money for a definite premium. Either the amount must be capable of modification and adjustment according to the actual ability of the society to pay, or it must reserve the right to assess its members for enough to make up the required benefit. The societies are thus relieved from the obligation imposed on ordinary life companies to create and maintain a reserve fund which will be mathematically sufficient to pay their insurance obligations. In theory they can never become insolvent because never obliged to pay more than they are able or more than that they can collect from their members. As a matter of fact, they have failed disastrously at times because they had neither the requisite fund nor could collect the needed assessments.

Until very recent years it has been the almost universal practice to limit the actual funds of the society to the smallest amount which was deemed necessary to meet special emergencies. The constant inflow of new members, it was argued, would prevent serious deficiencies, and the fraternal spirit of the members would do the rest. The prime object aimed at was to give the insurance at the least possible outlay to the members in a work which was assumed to be benevolent in its character and not conducted for profit. The fallacy of these views is now being generally recognized, as we shall shortly see.

The payments made by the members are not, as in

ordinary life insurance, premiums paid for the purchase of a pure business contract, but are generally of two kinds, initiation fees and dues, used as in ordinary clubs for the expenses of the society, and assessments levied on its members as contributions to its insurance fund, and are provided for in the rules of the society itself.

In the earlier days of the societies these assessments were generally alike in amount regardless of age and were collected only on the death of a member for the payment of his benefit, thus, as you observe, carrying out still further the idea of fraternity. But as the societies grew older the fallacies of this method were taught the members by a hard experience. By simply dropping his insurance which he had already enjoyed a member could escape paying his share of the death losses. As the members grew older and the death losses increased, those that were younger were not long in discovering that they were contributing more than their share to the death losses, which were chiefly among the old. As a result these dropped their membership and joined younger societies. New recruits to fill their places could not be obtained. The average age of those that were left continued to increase and the assessments to grow heavier. This in turn increased the withdrawals, until at last few remained except the sick and aged. Assessments for losses could no longer be collected, and the society would dissolve, leaving a body of old and infirm deprived of the benefits for which they had so long contributed. This has been the story of scores of these societies in the past, and where otherwise honestly managed has been the cause of the numerous failures in this class of insurance. In spite of all the efforts to place assessment rates on a sounder basis, their inadequacy and inequity as between the younger and older ages still continues to threaten the permanence of a large proportion of our fraternal societies. As we have stated, most of the existing societies are less than thirty years old. In many of them the members have only within recent years reached the ages where these dangers in a serious form began to be felt. The members themselves were generally unfamiliar with the principles of insurance. The favorite argument was that a society of this kind was like any village community where the young continually take the place of the old and the community as a whole grows no older. Hence it was said that a scale of assessments which were sufficient for the early years of such a society would continue so. I emphasize this point. It has been in one shape or another the favorite argument and popular delusion among the members of these societies which more than any other has been, and continues to be, perhaps the greatest obstacle in the way of reform. To this day, when the need of large contributions on the part of older members is urged, some veteran will bring forward the old simile of the village or town community whose average age is no greater to-day than it was a score of years ago, and insist that all which the society needs is to increase its membership by securing new applicants in order to bring down the death rate and make the rates sufficient.

Let us see why this is not true, for it is a vital question in this business. The average ages of a village community remain unchanged only after that community has reached a normal average age and only so long as there are neither removals from or to the village and the birth rate just keeps pace with the death rate. But any change in these conditions will alter that average age of the inhabitants until a new normal age is reached. If the average age of the inhabitants is thirty years and the births should exceed the deaths, it would begin to drop to some lower age. On the contrary, if there should be an excess of deaths the average age would begin to go up. The removal from or to the village of younger members would have the same effect. Throughout New England you will find scores of towns made up almost entirely of elderly people. The young folks have emigrated and the children are missing. On the contrary, in the great West are hundreds of settlements made up chiefly of young settlers and their children, whose average will increase in the way described until a normal age is reached as the settlement itself grows older.

The process in these societies is the same. When first organized they are chiefly made up of younger members among whom the deaths are comparatively few. Rates may be charged that are not only enough to pay the claims as they arise, but to create a surplus in the hands of the society. This further helps to mislead the members, who point to the surplus as a proof of the soundness of the association. But gradually these members grow older and the deaths increase. For a time new members who are young can be procured to take their places. But the whole group is still young and unless the new additions are largely in excess of the death losses and withdrawals, the average age in such a society, and with it the death losses, will continue to increase until as in the village community a normal average age is reached. If the average age of the members in a new society was thirty, for instance, it might gradually increase to forty, although a new young member was added for each member that was lost. But this is not all. As the members of such a society grow older the death rate increases faster than the age. At forty it may be only one in a hundred. At sixty it will be three times as great. So that while enough new members may have been taken in to keep the average age in such a society down to the original figures, the actual losses will continue to roll up through the increasing deaths of these older members.

As the assessments for these losses grow heavier the difficulty of procuring new members will increase, and those who have already joined will continue to drop off and hasten on the ruin in the way already described. The society may really be likened to one of those Western village communities whose inhabitants are all young at the start, but from which the young and healthy are gradually drawn away to more attractive settlements elsewhere until the whole becomes like a New England village. As the membership dwindles the average age continues to increase indefinitely.

When the members of such a society have reached a certain age, the cost of insurance becomes too heavy to be borne by themselves unless aided by younger members. It has been found that the average member who has passed much beyond the age of sixty can no longer afford to pay the heavy cost of his own insurance.

In practice, these societies start with a limited membership which they increase year by year. The births as it were at first far outnumber the deaths and as a consequence for a while there will be no noticeable increase in the death rate. This growth may be rapid enough to conceal the real conditions for years. But there is another peculiar feature here. In order to keep down the death rate, not only must the society grow but the number of new members added must each year become greater. Now there is a limit to this rate of growth even under favorable circumstances. When it is reached, be it sooner or later, then the trouble begins. This is why some of the larger societies have gone on year after year with apparent success while their small competitors were in distress. They were able to increase their new membership at a faster rate than the others. And what is worse, this long-continued success makes the members skeptical about the insufficiency of their rates when the assessments finally become inadequate to meet their claims. They simply rely on their past experience.

It has been a favorite argument too on the part of these societies that the spirit of fraternity should be strong enough to overcome any feeling of injustice among the members and to induce them to make good deficiencies. In truly benevolent organizations this fraternal feeling has proved a valuable aid in sustaining societies that were financially embarrassed. Both in Great Britain and America, associations which, measured by ordinary mercantile standards, would be pronounced hopelessly insolvent, have been carried along for years through the loyal support of their members. Such was in fact the condition of many of those British associations which were finally rescued and placed on a sound basis through the adoption of correct principles.

And just here I wish to speak of a class of associations in this country which are often confounded with the fraternal society and whose disastrous records in the past have done much to bring reproach on these associations. I refer to a certain class of assessment companies, organized on somewhat similar lines, whose premiums were collected in the shape of assessments, but which were in reality nothing more than ordinary life companies, carried on for profit on the assessment principle. There were no real fraternal features in their make-up nor fraternal feelings among their members, who were solicited and joined solely for the purpose of securing insurance on what was claimed to be cheaper terms. Many of them were conducted in an honest belief that the principle was sound. As business institutions their history has been so replete with failures that they have evoked the severest condemnation on the part of state officials and called forth restrictive legislation. Their system has since been admitted to be fallacious by its most intelligent former supporters, and those of them which remain have for the most part abandoned or altered their assessment methods.

It is almost needless to say that they are not included in the subject of the present lecture. I refer to them chiefly as illustrations that the assessment methods of the fraternal society have proved fallacious when applied to mere business companies in which the principles of fraternalism were absent.

Another favorite argument has been that inequalities between the members on account of differences in age would in a measure correct themselves as each member in turn passed through the successive ages. But this is assuming that each entered at the same age and survived and retained his membership to the end, none of which are true. Experience has shown that ordinary selfish business instincts influence the members even in the most fraternal of these associations, and that new members can neither be procured nor existing members retained after finding that it is to their interest to drop their connection.

Various plans have been proposed or adopted by the societies from time to time in order to remedy these conditions. Assessments monthly or at other fixed periods have now been substituted for assessments on the death of a member. Emergency and mortuary funds have been accumulated to meet deficiencies, but generally wholly inadequate for the purpose. Diminishing benefits at the older ages have been proposed. Assessments graded according to the age at entry but remaining fixed thereafter have been tried, and this is the present method adopted by a large number of these societies. Assessments increasing with each age attained by the member have been proposed. As a compromise, assessments increasing with each ten years, known as the step-rate plan, have been recommended, as have assessments increasing with each age attained by the member and covering the cost of his insurance for that year, known as the natural premium plan; but the trouble with this last is that the cost becomes too heavy for the older members to carry. A few have actually accepted the better class of British friendly societies as their models and have undertaken, like the regular companies, to charge a level assessment rate fixed according to the age at entry and which will be large enough to accumulate a reserve that will meet the increased cost of insurance at the older ages, or that modified form of the same referred to as the step-rate plan.

This is the plan now advocated both by the most intelligent advisers of these societies and by state officials. It is the plan which many of the best of these societies are considering or proposing to adopt. It would seem to be the only true solution of the difficulty. Their insurance business in order to be permanent must be conducted on the same mathematical principles as that of ordinary life companies. This does not mean that it must in all respects conform to the methods applicable to the latter. The business of the ordinary company is carried on for profit. Its policy-holders are like the creditors of any other corporation. The contract is a rigid one and the premiums are fixed; its commercial security demands that both the premium payments and reserve funds shall be in excess of the probable needs, in order to meet the uncertainties of the future.

With the fraternal society the case is different. The insurance which it promises is either simply a maximum sum whose actual amount may be reduced by inability to pay, or additional assessments may be levied to make good the deficiency. The conditions which would make an ordinary life company commercially insolvent and lead to its closing may simply cause increased assessments or reduced benefits in the case of the friendly society. The fraternal ties of the members help to hold them together in case of adversity.

The great aim of these societies is to furnish insurance at the least possible immediate outlay to their members, and to avoid the expenses incident to insurance as a business. Hence their paid officers and agents are as few as possible. The salaries needed for expert talent are usually wanting. The work is largely carried on through the members themselves and their lodge system. Their equipment for conducting the society as a financial business corporation is limited. Surplus in the sense of business profits is regarded as foreign to their character, and the accumulation of funds beyond what is absolutely needed is discouraged as a temptation to extravagance as well as an additional tax on the members. Dividends of surplus profits to the members are not allowed. Any supposed excess of funds is met by reducing the assessments, and any interest which a member might have in those funds is lost on his withdrawal. He has no right to claim a surrender value as in the ordinary company on giving up his certificate.

You note how in all these features the idea of fraternalism distinguishes these societies from ordinary life companies. They enter directly into the question of the proper remedies for their defects. The failure on the part of many officials and life insurance experts to properly appreciate them has been one of the difficulties in the way of reform. A premium rate adequate to the risk and a reserve adequate for future deficiencies in the life insurance sense would seem to be essentials, if they are to furnish anything more than mere temporary or term insurance. But it does not follow that this rate must be computed on a table of mortality heavier than their own experience, nor that it must be loaded with a margin for contingencies and expenses like that of the ordinary life companies. Nor does it follow that their reserve funds as in the case of ordinary companies should be in excess of their obvious needs. It would seem essential too that, as in the case of our ordinary companies, official valuations of their assets and liabilities and balance sheets of their accounts should be required. It does not follow, however, that the same measure of supervision and control over their affairs should be exercised by the state authorities, since they are not ordinary business corporations nor subject to commercial insolvency in the strict sense of the word. It is held by many that the functions of the state are ended when, as in Great Britain, such valuations and balance sheets are published and the members are left with a knowledge of the facts to deal with their societies as they will. These are all controverted questions on which I hesitate to express any decided opinion. When, however, a society has become so mismanaged or its affairs have become so hopelessly involved that its ruin is inevitable, the state should at least have power to prevent a further increase of its membership.

In new societies the needed reforms are comparatively easy. But many of these societies have been years in existence. The increase of their rates to an adequate figure at the older ages means a heavy burden on their older members which some would be unable to bear. Hence these members are apt to favor the inequalities of present methods. Otherwise, they say, we shall be driven out. On the other hand, the young member argues that the societies are for the benefit of those with dependent families. The families of the old are no longer dependent, and the young should not be forced to pay for their insurance.

Most of the reforms thus far attempted have been a compromise between these two views. The rates have from time to time been increased, especially at the older ages when deficiencies arose that actually compelled it, but never to an adequate figure, and as the ages continued to increase new revisions were made. In some of the older societies such a system of compromise may be the only solution of the problem unless their old members are to be driven out or their ability to secure new members is to cease and the society is allowed to collapse. But even then the difficulty will be to so regulate the inequality between the groups that additions to the young membership can be kept up until such time as the rates can step by step be finally raised to an adequate basis.

The hardest task of all has been to educate the members up to these needed reforms, which mean to them heavier assessments and an insurance more costly than was promised when they joined. The insurance officials of our various states and the best representative men of these societies themselves are now earnestly striving both through legislation and through the education of the membership to solve the difficult problem. The laws regarding these societies heretofore have been little else than mere rules for their organization and management. No provisions for securing their permanent solvency are made as in the case of our ordinary life companies. In most of the states they have been left to run their own course. Their members as a body are exceedingly jealous of attempts by legislation to increase the cost of the insurance which they offer or in any way to reduce their popularity or their freedom of action. Through the ballot box they have stood ready by their numbers to defeat any attempted laws which they believe to be inspired by a spirit of antagonism. Any attempted legislation for the regulation of these societies to be successful must be framed in a friendly attitude with a recognition of their rights as mutual clubs to regulate their own affairs within proper limits.

A healthy change, however, has been gradually taking place within the last few years in the attitude of their own members as well as of the public. The opposition to legal interference of any kind has, in a measure, yielded to a growth of public sentiment favoring state regulation of insurance. This movement has been aided by the popular excitement which followed the exposures of mismanagement on the part of some of the regular life companies in 1905. Prominent fraternal organizations, which had long enjoyed a wide popularity, as well as smaller societies, have found themselves facing a threatened deficiency in the near future in consequence of a rapid increase of death claims. Investigations have shown their managers that a radical increase in their rates is essential to their continued existence. Such increase has been at times strongly opposed by those of the members who felt unable to carry the burden. The effect of the agitation has been a more general recognition of the fact that the rates must be fixed according to age and must be based, like those of ordinary life companies, on an adequate table of mortality. The National Fraternal Congress, an association made up of representatives of the best of the fraternal orders, earnestly took up the subject a few years ago and urged upon its members the adoption of such rates based upon the actual mortality experienced by the societies, and the maintenance of a reserve like that of ordinary life companies sufficient to meet the deficiencies of the older ages, but limited to the actual amount mathematically estimated to be necessary, allowing, however, no margins for contingencies or profits and leaving any resultant deficiencies to be cared for by assessments, as before. Under the supervision of this Congress the mortality of the societies, which it represented, was compiled and a mortality table was framed known as the Fraternal Congress Table. The rates computed from this table have, from time to time, been adopted by a number of these societies and in some states their adoption by new societies has been made compulsory by statute. They are not assumed to be adequate for societies that are in an unsound condition, but to be an essential aid in their restoration to strength by reducing the future assessments which will be required if the prospective death rate has not already become too excessive. Various states, too, during the past few years have empowered their insurance departments to exercise a measure of supervision over these societies and have compelled the latter to make returns regarding their business. But the supervision and returns have thus far been limited to publicity regarding the general conduct and condition of their business. No estimate is required of their actual liabilities and little light is thrown on their future ability to meet their obligations, except such as may be gathered from the facts presented. The theory that the state is concerned only with their proper conduct and existing status is still adhered to.

A special interest just now attaches to fraternal societies, in view of the popular agitation for a system of compulsory insurance, or protection for employees analogous to those now existing in Germany and Great Britain. The organization of mutual companies for the insurance of various classes of employees, similar in principle at least to fraternal orders, has been among the methods suggested in the United States.

Now a few words in conclusion concerning the character of the insurance offered by these societies. In essential respects it is widely different from that furnished by our regular companies. In the first place it is strictly benevolent in its character and limited to the members and their dependents. It aims to relieve the necessities of these in a way more effectual than the random charitable assistance furnished by ancient associations. It needs for its success that the members should be bound by a spirit of real fraternity to their association, and not use their membership as a mere cloak for ordinary insurance purposes. It needs that the members should be actively interested in the affairs of the society and should be ready to bear their share of the burdens in case of errors in its management. Their fraternal bonds are the chief substitute for the commercial security required of an ordinary business corporation.

To that large class in the community whose instincts and tastes lead them to seek insurance protection from such societies they aim to offer that protection at the smallest immediate cost. The work is done chiefly by the members. Expenses are reduced to a minimum. No dividends are provided for and the assessment rates are reduced to the lowest figures. These are the strong points urged by its advocates. Fraudulent claims too are less likely where the members take a personal interest, and for that reason these societies, in theory at least, should be peculiarly adapted to deal with sick and accident risks where fraud is a special danger.

On the other hand, this insurance must of necessity lack those elements of commercial security which attach to the ordinary life company as a business institution conducted by experts protected by large cash accumulations and regulated by laws enacted with a view to permanent solvency. Until at least the reforms referred to have been carried out, this insurance can hardly be regarded as of more than a temporary character covering the younger and more productive years of life, with the contingency that the cost at old age may prove too heavy to be borne or that inability to keep up its membership may cause default. In view of the fact that the whole machinery of these societies is organized on a benevolent rather than a business basis, it has been seriously questioned how far they should attempt to grant endowments or large life insurance benefits which involve investments of capital for the beneficiaries rather than a simple relief from misfortune.

I believe that their work should be confined within their legitimate sphere and that associations, whether incorporated or not, should not be permitted to organize and conduct their affairs as benevolent societies while they are merely seeking through this device to sell ordinary life insurance to the public. Those who wish to purchase life insurance policies as they would purchase ordinary stocks or bonds as a pure business investment, who desire insurance contracts which shall be commercial and marketable in their character and who care nothing for the institution which may furnish them, should seek their protection from the ordinary companies that deal with insurance simply as a business.

The numerous failures among these societies in the past and the disappointments resulting from the errors in their management have called forth severe criticism and even condemnation of the system itself from many quarters. This has been largely aided by the disastrous operations of organizations which were in reality life companies carried on for mere business purposes but employing the methods of the fraternal associations. Despite the failures it must be remembered they have furnished temporary protection to millions of families and have distributed hundreds of millions among the needy dependents of their members. It should be said too that, carrying small accumulated funds, the actual moneyed losses have been small compared with the failures. The gravest loss has been the disappointment of those whose protection failed at an age when they could no longer afford to purchase fresh insurance.

Despite their defects these societies are doing a great and responsible work among those who prefer the form of protection which they offer. The communal spirit which created the ancient clubs of Rome and the guilds of more modern Europe has been strengthened by the antagonistic spirit of selfish individualism which characterizes our commercial age. Fraternal insurance should be dealt with as an evolution of these more primitive societies that is here to stay, backed by the votes, if need be, of the millions who support it; but calling as in Great Britain for beneficent laws and the intelligent coöperation of its membership to remedy its defects.

CHAPTER XI

NET PREMIUMS[1]

AFTER a table of mortality and a rate of interest are designated, the method of calculating net values in life insurance is simple when carefully explained. The net premium is the amount that will, on the designated data — namely, rate of interest and table of mortality — exactly effect the insurance. In this calculation, expenses and profits are left out of consideration.

Life insurance calculations are made, first on the supposition that the amount insured is $1. Having obtained the net premium that will insure $1, the net premium that will effect similar insurance for $100, $1000, or any other named sum, is found by multiplying the net premium that will insure $1 by the sum actually insured. It is assumed that the payment of the premium is made at the time the insurance is effected; this is called the beginning of the policy year, and the amount insured is to be paid at the end of that policy year in which the insured may die.

Interest. — The first thing to be considered, in making calculations for net premiums, is the method by which we determine the amount of money that will, when increased by interest at a given rate per annum, compounded annually, produce $1 in any designated number of years. Suppose that the rate of interest is 4 per cent. per annum. The amount that will at this rate produce $1 in one year, when the principal and interest thereon for one year are

[1] By Gustavus W. Smith. Reprinted from pages 13–33 of "Notes on Life Insurance"; S. W. Green. New York, 1875.

added together, is expressed by $\frac{1}{1.04} = \frac{100}{104} = \$0.961538$, plus other decimal figures.

If the rate of interest is 4½ per cent. per annum, the amount in hand that will, at this rate, produce $1 in one year is expressed by $\frac{\$1}{1.045} = \frac{1000}{1045} = \$0.956938$. In general, divide $1 by one plus the rate of interest, in order to obtain the amount that will, if invested at this rate of interest, produce $1 in one year.

Having obtained the amount that will, at the given rate of interest, produce $1 in one year, in order to obtain the amount that will, at the same rate of interest per annum, produce $1 in two years, interest being compounded annually, we multiply the amount that will produce $1 in one year by itself. For instance, the amount that will produce $1 in one year at 4 per cent. being expressed by $\frac{\$1}{1.04}$, the amount that will, at the same rate of interest, compounded annually, produce $1 in two years, is expressed by $\frac{\$1}{1.04} \times \frac{1}{1.04} = \$0.924556$.

If the rate of interest is 4½ per cent., the expression becomes $\frac{\$1}{1.045} \times \frac{1}{1.045} = \$0.915730$.

The amount that will, at 4 per cent., produce $1 in three years is expressed by $\frac{\$1}{1.04} \times \frac{1}{1.04} \times \frac{1}{1.04} = \$0.888996$. Interest being 4½ per cent., the expression becomes $\frac{\$1}{1.045} \times \frac{1}{1.045} \times \frac{1}{1.045} = \$0.876297$.

In general, to obtain the amount that will, if invested at any given rate of interest, compounded annually, produce $1 in any designated number of years, the rule is: *Divide* $1 *by one plus the rate of interest, and multiply the quotient by itself a number of times equal to the number of years less one.* That is to say, for two years, multiply once; for three years, twice; for four years, three times, and so on.

These calculations have been made, and the results, at various rates of interest, have been placed in appended tables.

There is at present one table of mortality in quite general

use in the United States. The American Experience Table of Mortality is given below. It will be noticed that it is assumed that there are 100,000 persons living at age 10. In the column headed "deaths each year" will be found opposite age 10 the number that will die between age 10 and age 11. This will leave a certain number living at age 11. This number is placed opposite age 11, in the column headed "number living," and opposite age 11 in the column headed "deaths each year" is placed the number that die between age 11 and age 12.

American Experience Table of Mortality

Age	Number Living	Deaths Each Year	Death Rate Per 1000	Expectation of Life	Age	Number Living	Deaths Each Year	Death Rate Per 1000	Expectation of Life
10	100,000	749	7.49	48.72	35	81,822	732	8.95	31.78
11	99,251	746	7.52	48.08	36	81,090	737	9.09	31.07
12	98,505	743	7.54	47.45	37	80,353	742	9.23	30.35
13	97,762	740	7.57	46.80	38	79,611	749	9.41	29.62
14	97,022	737	7.60	46.16	39	78,862	756	9.59	28.90
15	96,285	735	7.63	45.50	40	78,106	765	9.79	28.18
16	95,550	732	7.66	44.85	41	77,341	774	10.01	27.45
17	94,818	729	7.69	44.19	42	76,567	785	10.25	26.72
18	94,089	727	7.73	43.53	43	75,782	797	10.52	26.00
19	93,362	725	7.76	42.87	44	74,985	812	10.83	25.27
20	92,637	723	7.80	42.20	45	74,173	828	11.16	24.54
21	91,914	722	7.85	41.53	46	73,345	848	11.56	23.81
22	91,192	721	7.91	40.85	47	72,497	870	12.00	23.08
23	90,471	720	7.96	40.17	48	71,627	896	12.51	22.36
24	89,751	719	8.01	39.49	49	70,731	927	13.11	21.63
25	89,032	718	8.06	38.81	50	69,804	962	13.78	20.91
26	88,314	718	8.13	38.12	51	68,842	1,001	14.54	20.20
27	87,596	718	8.20	37.43	52	67,841	1,044	15.39	19.49
28	86,878	718	8.26	36.73	53	66,797	1,091	16.33	18.79
29	86,160	719	8.34	36.03	54	65,706	1,143	17.40	18.09
30	85,441	720	8.43	35.33	55	64,563	1,199	18.57	17.40
31	84,721	721	8.51	34.63	56	63,364	1,260	19.88	16.72
32	84,000	723	8.61	33.92	57	62,104	1,325	21.33	16.05
33	83,277	726	8.72	33.21	58	60,779	1,394	22.94	15.39
34	82,551	729	8.83	32.50	59	59,385	1,468	24.72	14.74

AMERICAN EXPERIENCE TABLE OF MORTALITY — *Continued*

Age	Number Living	Deaths Each Year	Death Rate Per 1000	Expectation of Life	Age	Number Living	Deaths Each Year	Death Rate Per 1000	Expectation of Life
60	57,917	1,546	26.69	14.10	78	18,961	2,291	120.83	5.11
61	56,371	1,628	28.88	13.47	79	16,670	2,196	131.73	4.74
62	54,743	1,713	31.29	12.86	80	14,474	2,091	144.47	4.39
63	53,030	1,800	33.94	12.26	81	12,383	1,964	158.60	4.05
64	51,230	1,889	36.87	11.67	82	10,419	1,816	174.30	3.71
65	49,341	1,980	40.13	11.10	83	8,603	1,648	191.56	3.39
66	47,361	2,070	43.71	10.54	84	6,955	1,470	211.36	3.08
67	45,291	2,158	47.65	10.00	85	5,485	1,292	235.55	2.77
68	43,133	2,243	52.00	9.47	86	4,193	1,114	265.68	2.47
69	40,890	2,321	56.76	8.97	87	3,079	933	303.02	2.18
70	38,569	2,391	61.99	8.48	88	2,146	744	346.69	1.91
71	36,178	2,448	67.66	8.00	89	1,402	555	395.86	1.66
72	33,730	2,487	73.73	7.55	90	847	385	454.54	1.42
73	31,243	2,505	80.18	7.11	91	462	246	532.47	1.19
74	28,738	2,501	87.03	6.68	92	216	137	634.26	.98
75	26,237	2,476	94.37	6.27	93	79	58	734.18	.80
76	23,761	2,431	102.31	5.88	94	21	18	857.14	.64
77	21,330	2,369	111.06	5.49	95	3	3	1000.00	.50

Various other tables of mortality are sometimes used in making life insurance calculations, but it is not necessary to give them here. Mortality tables are all based upon statistical information, obtained by observation and experience. It is assumed that each insured person at any particular age has the average chance of living for one year that is indicated by the table at that age.

Manner of Using the Mortality Table. — In illustration of the calculation of the chance that a person may die during any given time, let us suppose that out of one hundred persons condemned to be shot on a given day, all are reprieved for the day, except one, and the one to be shot is to be the one who draws the black ball out of a box containing ninety-nine white balls and one black one. The chance, before the drawing, of any particular man's getting the black ball, and, therefore, his chance of being shot that day, is one only out of one hundred. If two men had to die that day, each individual's chance, before the drawing, of getting a black ball would be twice as great as it was before; for now there are two black balls and only ninety-eight white ones in the box. The chance in this case would be two out of one hundred; for three persons, three out of one hundred; and so on to the limit of one hundred out of one hundred — which would make it certain that each man would be shot.

To apply this principle to life insurance, and to show that the amount that will insure $1, to be paid certain at the end of any year, when multiplied by the fraction which represents the chance that the person will die during the year, gives what it is worth to insure $1, to be paid at the end of the year, in case the insured dies during the year: let us suppose that, out of one hundred persons alive at the beginning of the year, it is known that one of them, and one only, will die during the year. The value of $1, to be paid certain at the end of one year, in the particular case of interest at 4½ per cent., is $0.956938. The chance that the person will die during the year is one out of one hundred. To make it certain that his heirs will obtain $1 at the end of the year, he must advance $0.956938 at the beginning of the year. But the $1 is not to be paid certain; it is to be paid only in case he dies. Suppose the whole one hundred persons are insured; then, since there is but one to die, and but $1 to be paid, each person will have to give only the one hundredth part of $0.956938 in order to make up what is necessary to pay this $1 at the end of the year. Therefore, $0.956938 divided by 100 is what each man would have to pay. In case it is known that two persons out of the one hundred will die, the amount requisite to effect the insurance will be twice as much as before, because $2 must be paid certain at the end of the year. The chance that each person may die during the year is twice as great as in the first case, and is therefore two out of one hundred; and the amount that each person will have to pay for his insurance is $0.956938, divided by 100, and the result multiplied by 2. In case it is known that all of them will die during the year, the fraction which represents the chance that any particular individual will die becomes $\frac{100}{100}$, or unity. This represents the certainty; and to insure $1, to be paid at the end of the year to the heirs of the insured, in case he dies during the year, each person will now have to pay $\frac{100}{100}$ of $0.956938 — that is to say, each must, in this case, pay enough to make, with interest at 4½ per cent. added, the full amount for which he is insured.

To Insure $1 *for One Year at Age* 30. — The American Experience Table shows that out of 100,000 persons living at age 10, there will be 85,441 living at age 30. The number of deaths between age 30 and age 31 is 720. Therefore, $\frac{720}{85441}$ is the fraction which represents the chance that the insured will die before he is 31 years of age.

The present value of $1 to be paid certain at the end of one year has, in the case of interest at 4½ per cent., been found to be equal to $0.956938. Multiply this by the fraction $\frac{720}{85441}$ which represents the chance that the insured will die during the year between age 30 and age 31, and we have $0.0081064. This is the value of the risk on $1, or what it is worth to insure $1, to be paid to the heirs of a person at the end of one year, in case he dies during the year, the age of the insured being 30 years at the time he takes out the policy. It would require one thousand times as much to insure $1000 as it does to insure $1, and half as much to insure half a dollar as it does a whole dollar. We can obtain, by using the mortality table, the fraction representing the chance that a person of any given age will die during the succeeding year, just as we did in this case for age 30. We have, therefore, already determined the means for calculating the sum that will at any age insure $1, to be paid to the heirs of the insured in one year, in case he dies during the year; but we must know the age of the person, the rate of interest must be fixed, and a mortality table must be available for use in the calculations.

The following table shows the net amount that will insure $1000 for one year at different ages from 20 to 70 inclusive, the calculations being all based upon the American Experience Table of Mortality, with interest at 4 per cent.

Cost of Insurance on $1000 for One Year, at Different Ages — American Experience

Age	Cost of Insurance	Age	Cost of Insurance	Age	Cost of Insurance
20 ...	$7.504	37 ...	$8.879	54 ...	$16.727
21 ...	7.553	38 ...	9.046	55 ...	17.857
22 ...	7.602	39 ...	9.218	56 ...	19.120
23 ...	7.652	40 ...	9.418	57 ...	20.515
24 ...	7.703	41 ...	9.623	58 ...	22.053
25 ...	7.754	42 ...	9.858	59 ...	23.769
26 ...	7.815	43 ...	10.113	60 ...	25.667
27 ...	7.881	44 ...	10.412	61 ...	27.769
28 ...	7.947	45 ...	10.734	62 ...	30.088
29 ...	8.024	46 ...	11.117	63 ...	32.638
30 ...	8.103	47 ...	11.539	64 ...	35.455
31 ...	8.183	48 ...	12.028	65 ...	38.585
32 ...	8.276	49 ...	12.602	66 ...	42.026
33 ...	8.383	50 ...	13.251	67 ...	45.815
34 ...	8.491	51 ...	13.981	68 ...	50.002
35 ...	8.602	52 ...	14.797	69 ...	54.579
36 ...	8.739	53 ...	15.705	70 ...	59.608

In further illustration of the question of net premiums and net values of life policies in case the insurance is for one year only, we will suppose that the age of the person applying for insurance is 40, the mortality table used the Actuaries', the rate of interest is 4 per cent., the insurance to be for one year, the amount of the policy $10,000, and the policy-holder is a fair average of insured lives. What amount in hand ought to be paid to insure $10,000 as above, leaving out all consideration of expenses, and having neither gain nor loss represented in the chances of the transaction?

We will first determine the amount that will insure $1. The present value of $1 to be paid certain at the end of one year, interest being assumed at 4 per cent. per annum, is equal to $0.961538. From the mortality table we find that out of 100,000 persons living at age 10, there are 78,653 living at age 40, and that 815 of these will die during the year between age 40 and age 41. Therefore, $\frac{815}{78653}$ is the fraction which represents the chance that the insured will die during the year; and this multiplied by $0.961538, which is the present value of $1, to be paid certain at the end of one year, will give what it is now worth to insure the $1, to be paid in case the insured dies during the year, or $\$0.961538 \times \frac{815}{78653} = \$0.009963432$. This, multiplied by 10,000, makes $99.63, plus a fraction of a cent, which is the net premium that will insure $10,000, to be paid to the heirs of the person insured at the end of one year; provided he dies during the year.

If every one of the whole 78,653 had been insured for one year in the sum of $10,000 each, the heirs of the 815 who died were respectively entitled to, and were paid, $10,000 each. The aggregate payment of losses by death, for the year, amounted, therefore, to $8,150,000. The net annual premiums, $99.63 each, on 78,653 policies, when increased by 4 per cent. interest, amounted at the end of the year to $8,149,996.43.

It is seen from this, that the fraction of a cent omitted in each of the 78,653 premiums amounted, in the aggregate, to a deficiency of $3.57, in paying $8,150,000 losses by death. The 77,838 persons who did not die during the year, in this case receive nothing. They are not entitled to anything; they had their lives insured during the year; they each paid in advance a net premium amounting to

$99.63; the whole of this, and net interest on it, has gone to pay at the end of the year $10,000 to the heirs of each of the 815 policy-holders that died during the year.

Net Single Premiums for Insurance for Whole Life.— What sum paid in hand will, "*on the supposition that the mortality table and rate of interest designated as the basis of the calculations are correct,*" be the exact equivalent of $1 insured, to be paid at the end of any year in which the insured may die? In other words, we have now to determine the amount that, if paid in hand, will exactly insure $1 for whole life. The problem before us reduces to this, namely: *First,* calculate the present value of the amount requisite to effect the insurance each separate year that the insured may live, as indicated by the designated table of mortality. Then add together the respective amounts that are found to be necessary to effect the insurance each year, and their sum will give the amount that, if paid in hand, will effect the insurance for whole life.

Assume that the age of the person at the time he insures is 40, that he is a fair average of insured lives, the table of mortality is the Actuaries', and the rate of interest 4 per cent., compounded annually. We have already found that the amount necessary in this case to insure $1, to be paid to the heirs of the insured in case he dies during the first year — that is, between age 40 and age 41 — is $0.009963432. Now let us see what amount of money, if paid in hand at the time the policy is issued (age 40), will secure $1 to be paid to the heirs of the insured at the end of two years, in case he dies in the second year from the date of the policy. This problem is solved separately, and the amount we are now to find insures only against death in the second year.

Find the amount that will, if invested at 4 per cent. per annum, compound interest, produce $1 in two years. To do this, we have to divide 100 by 104; this gives $0.961538, and this is the amount that will produce $1 in one year at 4 per cent. per annum. Multiply this by itself, and we have $0.924556, which is the amount that will produce $1 in two years at 4 per cent., compounded annually.

Now, the question is, what fraction, at age 40 (the time at which the insurance is effected), represents the chance that the insured will die during the second year — that is, between age 41 and age 42?

By the Actuaries' Table of Mortality, we see that out of 78,653 insured persons living at age 40, the number that will die between age 41 and age 42 is 826. Therefore, the fraction 826 divided by 78,653 represents at the time this insurance is effected, age 40, the chance that the insured will die betweeen age 41 and age 42.

Multiply the amount, $0.924556, that will, at the designated rate of interest, produce $1 certain in two years, by the fraction $\frac{826}{78653}$ which represents the chance that the $1 insured will have to be paid, and we have $0.009705, which is the amount that will, if paid in hand at age 40, insure $1, to be paid to the heirs of the insured in case he dies in the second year.

In like manner, we can find the amount that, if paid in hand at age 40, will insure $1 to the heirs of the insured in case he dies in the third year — and for each and every year up to and including the table limit.

Add together these respective yearly amounts, and the result gives the net single premium that will, if paid in hand at age 40, insure $1 for whole life.

The amount in this case is $0.38104; multiply this by 1000, and we have $381.04, which is the net single premium that will at age 40 insure $1000, to be paid to the heirs of the insured at the end of any year in which he may die.

Detailed Calculation of Net Single Premiums for Whole Life Policies. — In illustration of this subject, we will assume that the age of the insured is 50. The amount insured is $1. The table of mortality used is the American Experience, and the rate of interest is 4½ per cent. per annum, compounded yearly. Opposite age 50 in the following table, in the column headed, "*Value in hand at age*

50, *of* $1, *to be paid certain at the end of each respective year,"* we find the amount $0.956938. This is the amount that at 4½ per cent. will produce $1 in one year, and it is obtained by dividing 100 by 104½. This is to be multiplied by the number of deaths during the year between age 50 and age 51; this number, as shown by the mortality table, is 962, and it is placed in the following table opposite age 50, in the column headed, "Number of Deaths." In the next column, which is headed, "Number living at age 50," we find the number 69,804; this, too, is taken from the table of mortality. The product arising from multiplying $0.956938 by 962 is divided by 69,804, and the result is $0.013188. This is the amount that at age 50 will insure $1, to be paid to the heirs of the insured at the end of the year, in case he dies between age 50 and age 51.

Opposite age 51, in the same table, in the column headed, "Value in hand, at age 50, of $1, to be paid certain at the end of each respective year," we find the amount $0.915730. This is the amount that will produce $1 certain in two years, when invested at 4½ per cent. per annum, compounded annually, and it was obtained by multiplying $\frac{1}{1.045}$ by $\frac{1}{1.045}$. Multiply this by 1001, which is the number of deaths between age 51 and age 52, and divide the product by 69,804, which is the number living at age 50, and we have $0.013132. This is the amount that, if paid in hand at age 50, will insure $1, to be paid to the heirs of the insured at the end of the second year, in case the insured dies in that year — that is, between age 51 and age 52.

In a similar manner, the calculations as shown in the table are made each respective year to include age 95, which is the limit of the table of mortality we are now using, and the sum of all these respective yearly values gives us $0.430037. This amount, if paid in hand at age 50, will insure $1 for whole life on the data assumed, — namely, the American Experience Table of Mortality, and 4½ per cent. per annum, compounded yearly.

In an entirely similar manner, the calculations can be

made at any age included in the table of mortality, and at any designated rate of interest.

Having found the net single premium that will insure $1 at any age, the net single premium that will insure any other amount at the same age is found by a simple proportion.

TABLE. — ILLUSTRATING THE MANNER OF CALCULATING THE NET SINGLE PREMIUM FOR A WHOLE-LIFE POLICY FOR $1; ISSUED AT AGE 50 — AMERICAN EXPERIENCE, 4½ PER CENT.

Age	Value in hand, at age 50, of $1.00, to be paid certain at the end of each respective year	Number of Deaths	Number Living at Age 50	Value in hand at age 50, of $1.00, to be paid at the end of each respective year, provided the insured dies during the year	Age
50 . . .	$0.956938 ×	962 ÷	69,804 =	$0.013188	50
51 . . .	0.915730 ×	1001 ÷	69,804 =	0.013132	51
52 . . .	0.876297 ×	1044 ÷	69,804 =	0.013106	52
53 . . .	0.838561 ×	1091 ÷	69,804 =	0.013106	53
54 . . .	0.802451 ×	1143 ÷	69,804 =	0.013140	54
55 . . .	0.767896 ×	1199 ÷	69,804 =	0.013190	55
56 . . .	0.734828 ×	1260 ÷	69,804 =	0.013264	56
57 . . .	0.703185 ×	1325 ÷	69,804 =	0.013348	57
58 . . .	0.672904 ×	1394 ÷	69,804 =	0.013438	58
59 . . .	0.643928 ×	1468 ÷	69,804 =	0.013542	59
60 . . .	0.616199 ×	1546 ÷	69,804 =	0.013647	60
61 . . .	0.589664 ×	1628 ÷	69,804 =	0.013752	61
62 . . .	0.564272 ×	1713 ÷	69,804 =	0.013847	62
63 . . .	0.539973 ×	1800 ÷	69,804 =	0.013924	63
64 . . .	0.516720 ×	1889 ÷	69,804 =	0.013983	64
65 . . .	0.494469 ×	1980 ÷	69,804 =	0.014026	65
66 . . .	0.473176 ×	2070 ÷	69,804 =	0.014032	66
67 . . .	0.452800 ×	2158 ÷	69,804 =	0.013998	67
68 . . .	0.433302 ×	2243 ÷	69,804 =	0.013923	68
69 . . .	0.414643 ×	2321 ÷	69,804 =	0.013787	69
70 . . .	0.396787 ×	2391 ÷	69,804 =	0.013591	70
71 . . .	0.379701 ×	2448 ÷	69,804 =	0.013316	71
72 . . .	0.363350 ×	2487 ÷	69,804 =	0.012946	72
73 . . .	0.347703 ×	2505 ÷	69,804 =	0.012478	73
74 . . .	0.332731 ×	2501 ÷	69,804 =	0.011921	74

75 ...	0.318402 ×	2476 ÷	69,804 =	0.011294	75
76 ...	0.304691 ×	2431 ÷	69,804 =	0.010611	76
77 ...	0.291571 ×	2369 ÷	69,804 =	0.009895	77
78 ...	0.279015 ×	2291 ÷	69,804 =	0.009157	78
79 ...	0.267000 ×	2196 ÷	69,804 =	0.008400	79
80 ...	0.255502 ×	2091 ÷	69,804 =	0.007654	80
81 ...	0.244500 ×	1964 ÷	69,804 =	0.006879	81
82 ...	0.233971 ×	1816 ÷	69,804 =	0.006087	82
83 ...	0.223896 ×	1648 ÷	69,804 =	0.005286	83
84 ...	0.214254 ×	1470 ÷	69,804 =	0.004512	84
85 ...	0.205028 ×	1292 ÷	69,804 =	0.003795	85
86 ...	0.196199 ×	1114 ÷	69,804 =	0.003131	86
87 ...	0.187750 ×	933 ÷	69,804 =	0.002509	87
88 ...	0.179665 ×	744 ÷	69,804 =	0.001915	88
89 ...	0.171929 ×	555 ÷	69,804 =	0.001367	89
90 ...	0.164525 ×	385 ÷	69,804 =	0.000907	90
91 ...	0.157440 ×	246 ÷	69,804 =	0.000555	91
92 ...	0.150661 ×	137 ÷	69,804 =	0.000296	92
93 ...	0.144173 ×	58 ÷	69,804 =	0.000120	93
94 ...	0.137964 ×	18 ÷	69,804 =	0.000036	94
95 ...	0.132023 ×	3 ÷	69,804 =	0.000006	95
	Total			$0.430037	

If the insurance is for a limited number of years only, the calculation is made for each year of the term, and the sum of these yearly amounts will give the net single premium that will, if paid at the time the policy is issued, insure $1, to be paid to the heirs of the insured at the end of the year in which the policy-holder may die; provided he dies before the expiration of the term. For instance, suppose the insurance at age 50 is to continue for ten years only; take in the above table the amounts for the first ten years, their sum will be the net single premium required.

If insurance is paid for at age 50, to begin only at the end of ten years from that time, and then continue for life; the net single premium is obtained by subtracting the amount that will at age 50 insure $1 until age 60 from the amount that will at age 50 insure $1 for life.

If insurance is paid for at age 50 to begin at age 60, and then continue for ten years only, subtract the net single premium that will at age 50 insure $1, to begin at age 70 and continue for life, from the net single premium that will at age 50 insure $1, to begin at age 60 and continue for life.

The net single premium that will at any age insure $1, to be paid at the end of any designated year, provided the insured dies in that year, is found, as before stated, by first determining the amount that will at the named rate of interest produce $1 at the end of the designated year, and then multiplying this amount by the fraction (obtained from the mortality table), which represents, at the time the insurance is effected, the chance that the insured will die in the designated year.

For purposes of comparison and general illustration, the following table is given, showing the net single premiums that will insure $1000 for whole life, at ages from 20 to 70 inclusive, at 4 per cent.:

NET SINGLE PREMIUMS — AMERICAN EXPERIENCE — FOUR PER CENT.

Age	Premium	Age	Premium	Age	Premium
20	$247.798	37	$343.088	54	$514.307
21	251.846	38	351.245	55	526.645
22	256.076	39	359.266	56	539.153
23	260.472	40	367.575	57	551.806
24	265.042	41	376.167	58	564.589
25	269.704	42	385.060	59	577.482
26	274.737	43	394.252	60	590.457
27	279.872	44	403.751	61	603.491
28	285.207	45	413.551	62	616.557
29	290.754	46	423.659	63	629.630
30	296.514	47	434.063	64	642.687
31	302.497	48	444.762	65	655.699
32	308.713	49	455.744	66	668.630
33	315.167	50	467.046	67	681.452
34	321.862	51	478.480	68	694.137
35	328.809	52	490.207	69	706.647
36	336.022	53	502.154	70	718.960

Net Annual Premium for Whole-life Policies. — Having shown how to calculate the net single premiums that will insure $1 for whole life at any age included in the table of mortality, it is now proposed to see how the exact equivalent can be determined when the payments are made by instalments instead of by one sum in advance. It is usual, in ordinary whole-life policies, for the companies to charge, and the insured to pay, equal annual premiums, the first in advance, and one at the beginning of each following year, as long as the insured is alive. When the net single premium at any age has been accurately calculated, the question arises, What is the net *annual* premium, under the conditions just named, that will be the precise equivalent of this net *single* premium at the time the policy issued?

When this net *annual* premium is accurately determined, it being the precise money equivalent of the net single premium, and the net single premium being just sufficient, on the data designated, to effect the insurance, it follows that its precise equivalent, paid in equal annual premiums, will also be just sufficient to effect the insurance.

To solve this problem, first find the value, at any named age, of a whole-life series of annual premiums of $1 each, the condition being that the first payment of $1 is to be made at the time the policy is issued, and that $1 is to be paid at the beginning of each following year, as long as the person is alive to make the payment. When this is done, the problem we wish to solve becomes simple, because, after we have found, at any named age, the value in hand of this life series of premiums of $1 each, *this amount will be to the net single premium at that age as* $1 *is to the annual premium required.* We will use the American Experience Table of Mortality and $4\frac{1}{2}$ per cent. interest.

The first thing, then, is to find the value at any age — say 50 — of a life series of annual premiums of $1 each, the first to be paid in advance, and $1 to be paid at the beginning of each following year, as long as the insured is alive to make the payments.

The first annual payment is to be made in hand, and its value, at the time the policy is issued, is $1. The value in hand of $1, to be paid at the end of one year, interest being 4½ per cent. per annum, is 100 divided by 104½; but this second payment is not to be made certain, but only on condition that the insured, aged 50, will be alive at age 51. The fraction which, at age 50, represents the chance that the insured will be alive at age 51 is equal to the number living at age 51 divided by the number living at age 50. From the table of mortality, we find the number living at age 51 is 68,824, and the number living at age 50 is 69,804. The fraction in this case is therefore $\frac{68824}{69804}$. The value, at age 50, of this second payment of $1 to be made at age 51, in case the insured is alive to make the payment, is equal to $\frac{1}{1.045} \times \frac{68824}{69804}$. In like manner, the value of the third payment, which is to be made at the end of two years, in case the insured is alive at that time to make the payment, is equal to $\frac{1}{1.045} \times \frac{1}{1.045}$, multiplied by the fraction which, at age 50, represents the chance at that time that the insured will be alive at age 52 to make the third payment. This fraction is equal to the number living at 52 divided by the number living at 50, which we see, from the table of mortality, is $\frac{67841}{69804}$; therefore the value in hand, at age 50, of the third payment of $1, to be paid only on condition that the insured is alive at age 52, is expressed by $\frac{1}{1.045} \times \frac{1}{1.045} \times \frac{67841}{69804}$.

In a manner entirely similar, we can calculate at age 50 the value in hand of the fourth and every payment of the whole-life series to the limit of the table. This has been done, and the sum of the respective values in hand, at age 50, of the whole-life series of annual premiums of $1 each, is found to be $13.235802.

TABLE. — ILLUSTRATING THE MANNER OF CALCULATING THE VALUE, AT AGE 50, OF A WHOLE-LIFE SERIES OF ANNUAL PAYMENTS OF $1 EACH — THE FIRST PAYMENT TO BE MADE IN HAND, AND ONE AT THE BEGINNING OF EACH FOLLOWING YEAR, AS LONG AS THE PERSON IS ALIVE TO MAKE THE PAYMENT. AMERICAN EXPERIENCE — 4½ PER CENT.

Age	Value in hand, at age 50, of $1.00, to be paid certain at the beginning of each year	Number living at beginning of each year *Numerator*	Number living at age 50 *Denominator*	Value in hand at age 50, of $1.00, to be paid at the beginning of each respective year, provided the person is alive to make the payment	Age
50 . . .	$1.000000 ×	69,804 ÷	69,804 =	$1.000000	50
51 . . .	0.956938 ×	68,842 ÷	69,804 =	0.943750	51
52 . . .	0.915730 ×	67,841 ÷	69,804 =	0.889978	52
53 . . .	0.876297 ×	66,797 ÷	69,804 =	0.838548	53
54 . . .	0.838561 ×	65,706 ÷	69,804 =	0.789331	54
55 . . .	0.802451 ×	64,563 ÷	69,804 =	0.742202	55
56 . . .	0.767896 ×	63,364 ÷	69,804 =	0.697051	56
57 . . .	0.734828 ×	62,104 ÷	69,804 =	0.653770	57
58 . . .	0.703185 ×	60,779 ÷	69,804 =	0.612270	58
59 . . .	0.672904 ×	59,385 ÷	69,804 =	0.572466	59
60 . . .	0.643928 ×	57,917 ÷	69,804 =	0.534273	60
61 . . .	0.616199 ×	56,371 ÷	69,804 =	0.497619	61
62 . . .	0.589664 ×	54,743 ÷	69,804 =	0.462437	62
63 . . .	0.564272 ×	53,030 ÷	69,804 =	0.428677	63
64 . . .	0.539973 ×	51,230 ÷	69,804 =	0.396293	64
65 . . .	0.516720 ×	49,341 ÷	69,804 =	0.365244	65
66 . . .	0.494469 ×	47,361 ÷	69,804 =	0.335490	66
67 . . .	0.473176 ×	45,291 ÷	69,804 =	0.307011	67
68 . . .	0.452800 ×	43,133 ÷	69,804 =	0.279792	68
69 . . .	0.433302 ×	40,890 ÷	69,804 =	0.253821	69
70 . . .	0.414643 ×	38,569 ÷	69,804 =	0.229104	70
71 . . .	0.396787 ×	36,178 ÷	69,804 =	0.205647	71
72 . . .	0.379701 ×	33,730 ÷	69,804 =	0.183475	72
73 . . .	0.363350 ×	31,243 ÷	69,804 =	0.162629	73
74 . . .	0.347703 ×	28,738 ÷	69,804 =	0.143148	74
75 . . .	0.332731 ×	26,237 ÷	69,804 =	0.125063	75
76 . . .	0.318402 ×	23,761 ÷	69,804 =	0.108383	76
77 . . .	0.304691 ×	21,330 ÷	69,804 =	0.093104	77
78 . . .	0.291571 ×	18,961 ÷	69,804 =	0.079200	78
79 . . .	0.279015 ×	16,670 ÷	69,804 =	0.066632	79

TABLE — *Continued*

Age	Value in hand, at age 50, of $1.00 to be paid certain at the beginning of each year	Number living at beginning of each year *Numerator*	Number living at age 50 *Denominator*	Value in hand at age 50, of $1.00, to be paid at the beginning of each respective year, provided the person is alive to make the payment	Age
80 ...	0.267000 ×	14,474 ÷	69,804 =	0.055363	80
81 ...	0.255502 ×	12,383 ÷	69,804 =	0.045325	81
82 ...	0.244500 ×	10,419 ÷	69,804 =	0.036494	82
83 ...	0.233971 ×	8,603 ÷	69,804 =	0.028836	83
84 ...	0.223896 ×	6,955 ÷	69,804 =	0.022308	84
85 ...	0.214254 ×	5,485 ÷	69,804 =	0.016835	85
86 ...	0.205028 ×	4,193 ÷	69,804 =	0.012316	86
87 ...	0.196199 ×	3,079 ÷	69,804 =	0.008654	87
88 ...	0.187750 ×	2,146 ÷	69,804 =	0.005772	88
89 ...	0.179665 ×	1,402 ÷	69,804 =	0.003609	89
90 ...	0.171929 ×	847 ÷	69,804 =	0.002086	90
91 ...	0.164525 ×	462 ÷	69,804 =	0.001089	91
92 ...	0.157440 ×	216 ÷	69,804 =	0.000487	92
93 ...	0.150661 ×	79 ÷	69,804 =	0.000171	93
94 ...	0.144173 ×	21 ÷	69,804 =	0.000043	94
95 ...	0.137964 ×	3 ÷	69,804 =	0.000006	95
	Total			$13.235802	

NOTE. — The remarks that follow the table illustrating the calculation of the net single premium that will insure $1 for life apply to the value, at any age, of a series of annual payments of $1 for a designated term of years.

Having shown, in the foregoing table, how we calculate the value, at age 50, of a whole-life series of annual premiums of $1 each, attention is called to the fact that the calculation of the net value at any other age of a similar series of premiums can be made, in a like manner, from any table of mortality, and at any rate of interest.

VALUE AT DIFFERENT AGES OF A LIFE SERIES OF ANNUAL PAYMENTS OF $1 EACH — AMERICAN EXPERIENCE TABLE OF MORTALITY — 4 PER CENT. INTEREST.

Age	Value	Age	Value	Age	Value
20 ...	$19.5579	37 ...	$17.0691	54 ...	$12.6280
21 ...	19.4520	38 ...	16.8676	55 ...	12.3072
22 ...	19.3420	39 ...	16.6591	56 ...	11.9820
23 ...	19.2277	40 ...	16.4431	57 ...	11.6530
24 ...	19.1089	41 ...	16.2196	58 ...	11.3207
25 ...	18.9854	42 ...	15.9884	59 ...	10.9855
26 ...	18.8568	43 ...	15.7494	60 ...	10.6481
27 ...	18.7233	44 ...	15.5025	61 ...	10.3092
28 ...	18.5846	45 ...	15.2477	62 ...	9.9695
29 ...	18.4404	46 ...	14.9849	63 ...	9.6296
30 ...	18.2906	47 ...	14.7144	64 ...	9.2901
31 ...	18.1351	48 ...	14.4362	65 ...	8.9518
32 ...	17.9735	49 ...	14.1507	66 ...	8.6156
33 ...	17.8056	50 ...	13.8583	67 ...	8.2822
34 ...	17.6316	51 ...	13.5595	68 ...	7.9524
35 ...	17.4510	52 ...	13.2546	69 ...	7.6272
36 ...	17.2634	53 ...	12.9440	70 ...	7.3070

To obtain the net annual premium. — When the net single premium that will insure $1 for whole life has been calculated, and the value at the designated age of a whole-life series of annual payments of $1 each is known, we obtain the net annual premium that will insure $1 for whole life at that age by the following rule: Divide the net single premium at any age by the value at that age of a whole-life series of annual payments of $1 each, and the result is the net annual premium that will insure $1 for whole life at that age. For instance (American Experience, 4½ per cent.), at age 30, the net single premium to insure $1 is $0.262609, the value at age 30 of the series of $1 premiums is $17.1238, therefore we have the proportion: $17.1238 : $0.262609 :: $1 is to the net annual premium that at age 30 will insure $1 for whole life.

NOTE. — It follows, too, from this general reasoning, that if it is desired to convert the net single premium into a limited number of annual premiums, or equal instalments, for a specified number of years, we first find the value at the age in question of a series of annual payments of $1 each for the designated term of years, and divide the net single premium by this value.

The following table shows the net annual premiums that will insure $1000 at different ages, from 20 to 70 inclusive:

NET ANNUAL PREMIUMS — AMERICAN EXPERIENCE — 4 PER CENT.

Age	Premium	Age	Premium	Age	Premium
20	$12.669	37	$20.124	54	$40.728
21	12.947	38	20.824	55	42.792
22	13.239	39	21.566	56	44.997
23	13.547	40	22.354	57	47.353
24	13.870	41	23.192	58	49.872
25	14.211	42	24.084	59	52.568
26	14.570	43	24.988	60	55.452
27	14.948	44	26.044	61	58.539
28	15.346	45	27.122	62	61.844
29	15.767	46	28.273	63	65.385
30	16.211	47	29.499	64	69.180
31	16.680	48	30.809	65	73.248
32	17.176	49	32.207	66	77.607
33	17.700	50	33.698	67	82.279
34	18.255	51	35.288	68	87.286
35	18.842	52	36.984	69	92.649
36	19.464	53	38.794	70	98.393

CHAPTER XII

PROVISION FOR EXPENSES[1]

THE more difficult problems of a science or art are naturally the last to be solved. The relations of interest and mortality to life insurance are comparatively simple factors, and well developed. But when we descend from the exact reasoning of these more exclusively mathematical subjects to the division of expenses, we encounter a confusion which makes it difficult to select and arrange a sufficient amount of controlling data for a basis upon which to erect a symmetrical structure for practical operations.

Too generally, when attempts have been made to construct a scheme for distributing expenses, the actual conditions imposed by competition and experience have been ignored with a vague hope that theoretical considerations might in some degree be made to govern custom. Or they have been restricted to too few elements of expense in an endeavor to minimize the labor of computations. While both of these considerations are entitled to recognition, they should not be allowed to handicap the search for a solution, by substituting deductions for inductions. At the bottom of the subject must be laid a fundamental classification of expenses themselves, derived from companies' financial statements.

It will aid us to summarize the discussions which have appeared. The original net premium seems to have been loaded by a constant percentage of itself to meet expenses and general contingencies; the latter, because the rates

[1] By William D. Whiting. Reprinted from pages 214–219, Volume V, "Transactions of the Actuarial Society of America."

of interest and mortality were considered more liable to fluctuation than are now feared by well-regulated companies. At present the assumed (3 per cent.) rate of interest is theoretically fixed low enough to cover the expenses and losses due to investments, and the assumed rate of mortality high enough to cover all contingencies due to the probability of dying, thus leaving the loading on premiums and discontinuance gains free to cover all other expenses without specification.

Finally a valuable suggestion came from Great Britain to the effect that, as the gross premium was irrevocably confined by competition to a uniform amount for each policy year, while the expenses of the first year from the same cause were irrevocably much greater than for any of its successors, the first year should be treated as term insurance, so as to obtain a larger loading therein by releasing it from the obligation of accumulating any reserve. Modifications of this idea have appeared by attaching liens to the policy equal to the first year's terminal reserve as additional first year's premium, leaving the character of the insurance undisturbed.

Although much has been written and said on the subject of providing for and assessing expenses, but little progress has been made, and it remains in so unsatisfactory a condition that an attempt, by another method, to contribute to its solution should be tried. I apprehend that a scrutiny of companies' statements will disclose five distinct kinds of expenses, which are independent and cannot be greatly modified, to wit:

1. New Business; consisting of examination fees, agents' first-year commissions, and advertising, printing, salaries, etc., incurred in getting new business; say, 80 per cent. of first year's premiums.

2. Collection; consisting of agents' renewal commissions, collection fees, exchange, taxes on premiums, etc.; say 10 per cent. on renewal premiums.

3. Settlement; consisting of the expense of investiga-

ting and resisting death claims; say $1\frac{1}{2}$ per cent. of face of death claims.

4. Investments; cost of making, handling, and protecting same, bad debts, losses over gains, taxes and repairs on assets; say, one-half of 1 per cent. per annum.

5. General; all other expenses, particularly those of general supervision, actuarial and clerical; say, $1 per $1000 of insurance annually.

How shall we provide for these necessary and independent expenses so as to charge them equitably upon each class of policies in proportion as they cause them, maintain consistency in computing reserves, surrender values, and dividends, and yet make no serious departure from present level office rates, without so complicating our processes as to render them unworkable?

The first expense item — for new business — should be met during the first year by each class of new entrants for themselves, so as to avoid a loss to persistent members being occasioned by the lapsing or death of one in arrears. The old members have built up the company at considerable cost to themselves and own it. It is unjust that new members should be allowed to participate in the benefits of an established plant without at least paying their own cost of entrance. It would be more proper, indeed they should be charged a bonus for the privilege of entering, to go to the old members in reimbursements of their early excess of expenses in establishing the institution. Old members should not need the new under a proper arrangement for future expenses; and any scheme which is not mathematically self-sustaining, until the last risk is disposed of, and requires "new blood" to support it, is insolvent by confession.

It is true that the old members, left to themselves, will gradually diminish in numbers and a certain class of expenses will proportionately increase thereby. Some arrangement among themselves must be made for this, and will be treated of later under item 5 of general expenses. The present contention is that each body of policy-holders must be wholly self-sustaining, as to mortality, interest and expenses, in order to work out a solvent scheme; and the fallacy of "new blood," which has been the excuse for so much extravagance and inequity, should be utterly abandoned. But how can the new entrant be made to pay the expenses incurred on his account during the first year, within that year? Ruling out the possibility of returning to the small initial expenses of twenty-five years ago, or of exacting a sufficient cash initiation fee, two methods are proposed:

First, subject the insurance to an interest-bearing note or lien equal to the extraordinary expenses of the first year, but not exceeding the terminal reserve of that year. The effect of this is the same as an initiation fee, not subject to agents' commissions. But it works awkwardly in so far as the sum payable as a claim is diminished by the lien if not canceled by dividends; and the interest continues payable annually after "limited premiums" have ceased. To avoid this it has been suggested that the lien be converted into an annuity in favor of the company, for the same term that the premiums run; and be counted as a diminishing asset or lien against surrender values. Neither of these forms, although mathematically sound, would be apt to be well received by insurance departments; and the notes or annuity liens (besides imposing considerable clerical labor) would run the risk of being disallowed as assets, notwithstanding being made so by the expressed terms of the contract.

Second, make the first year's insurance a preliminary one-year term risk, the permanent insurance to commence one year after the date of the policy at the premium rate for the then increased age. This method has come spontaneously into use on both sides of the Atlantic within a few years, on account of the necessities of the younger companies under the pressure of competition, and has proved successful with agents. It has the recommendation of high actuarial authorities, and no refusal to recognize it has yet appeared from state officials where the terms of the contract were stated so that the policy-holder could know the exact character of the insurance he was purchasing. This method of releasing the first year's premium from the obligation of a terminal reserve allows it to be wholly employed in meeting the heavy expenses and light mortality of this period, which should be confined strictly within this limit. This method works least advantageously on short, limited payment plans, as the permanent premium is not only based upon one year of age higher than entry, but the number of limited payments is lessened by one year.

With the new business made self-sustaining, in its first year, the renewal premiums need only be burdened (item 2) with the expense of their collection and renewal commissions to agents. This, with an allowance for taxes on premiums and occasional loss by misappropriation, is easily covered by an average loading of 10 per cent. added to the net premiums, which in the proposed distribution of expenses constitutes the only loading imposed upon the net premium. This readily permits the use of 3 per cent. as a basis for computing net premiums without exceeding materially the office rates now in use, except in the case of short limited payments as before mentioned.

The third item (settlement) of expense only occurs upon death claims, and a ready method for its provision may also be employed to correct a glaring defect in our present practice. Our computations of net premiums and reserves are made upon the incorrect assumption that death occurs at the end of the policy year, whereas claims are actually paid, on an average, about the seventh month and five months' interest on the face of the claim is lost to the company. This should be altered and death assumed to take place at the beginning of the policy year immediately after the premium is due. We would thus gain seven months' interest — about $17.50 per $1000 of claim — which would easily cover the expenses of investigation, litigation, and settlement in question. . . . The result would be an increase in all premiums and reserves, except endowments, of just 3 per cent. when the basis of 3 per cent. interest is employed. On endowments the increase would be only 3 per cent. of the term insurance portion thereof.

The fourth item of expenses exclusively concerns the care and investment of assets, including incidental losses and taxes and repairs on real estate. A small amount should be included for the time and expenses of officers and clerks employed in this branch of the business. This item is easily and naturally provided for out of the gross interest and rents earned on total assets, by assuming a lower rate of interest for computing net premiums and reserves. Thus, if $3\frac{1}{2}$ per cent. is the maximum gross rate which can be safely relied upon during a period of, say, thirty years to come, the net rate employed would be about 3 per cent., leaving a margin of $\frac{1}{2}$ per cent. to cover the various expenses included under item 4. There is a general agreement among actuaries concerning the propriety of this arrangement.

The residual item (5) is for general expenses which run with the entire duration of the policy. For this reason it cannot be loaded upon the premium (as was item 2) without establishing a new and burdensome side computation for future general expense reserves; as the premiums on a considerable portion of business stop short of the term of the insurance, and as this general expense (referred to in discussing new business, item 1), should *increase* somewhat as the original number of policies of its class diminish by *maturity*. That portion of diminution which is occasioned by lapsing should be offset by a surrender charge, and will be discussed later. Neither can item 5 be levied against the interest earnings of the reserve (as was item 4), because short-term insurance only has a nominal and erratic reserve, while reserves generally vary widely with the kind of insurance and usually increase rapidly.

We must therefore search for some basis which runs with the term of insurance increasing slightly, and yet may be easily handled as a measure for these small general expenses. The annual cost of insurance[1] offers such a basis, and has been warmly advocated for a much larger rôle in the distribution of expenses on account of its supposed equity, as already mentioned. By adding about 10 per cent. to a true q_x we would derive an additional annual cost of insurance, slightly increasing, but averaging about $1 per $1000 of insurance. Experience shows that this 10 per cent. is just about the difference between actual mortality and that expected under the Combined Experience (17 office) tables generally used in the United States, excluding first year's mortality. In other words, the mortality tables now in use may be considered to be equal to actual experience already loaded 10 per cent. so as to provide the extra "cost of insurance" necessary to meet these general expenses of item 5. Here, again, there is no occasion for alteration of present custom.

[1] The cost of insurance for the year is determined as follows: At age 56 the amount at risk on an ordinary life policy in the first year of insurance is $970.10. Of the 100,000 people starting in the hypothetical company at age 10, 63,364 survive at 56. Of these, 1260 will die during the year, making the net loss 1260 times $970.10 or $1,222,326, which is the total cost of insurance for the year. Dividing this amount by 63,364, the number living at the beginning of the year, we obtain $19.29, which is the pro rata cost of insurance per $1000 for the first year. In the fifth year of insurance taken at age 56 the amount at risk is $849.67, and multiplying this by 1546, the number of deaths, we get $1,313,589.82 as the total cost of insurance for the year. Dividing by 57,917, the number living at the beginning of the year, we obtain $22.68 as the cost of insurance per $1000, in the fifth year. At 90 the amount at risk is $127.82 and the total cost of insurance is that sum multiplied by 385 or $49,210.70. Dividing by 847, the number living at the beginning of the year, we obtain $58.10 as the cost of insurance per $1000 in the thirty-fifth year of insurance. (Editor.)

Thus, starting from practical conditions, a simple, consistent, and equitable theory for the provision and distribution of expenses as they actually exist, may be constructed, which will permit a company to go to a 3 per cent. basis for reserves and net premiums, without material alteration in present office rates, and which adds nothing to the ordinary labor of computations.

CHAPTER XIII

RESERVE[1]

THIS fund has by high authority been well styled "the great sheet-anchor of life insurance." By referring to the table of net single premiums (page 168), it will be seen that by the American Experience Table of Mortality, and $4\frac{1}{2}$ per cent. interest, the net single premium that will insure $1000 for whole life, at age 20, is $217.448. At age 21 the net single premium is $221.155. The latter sum is the net amount that must be charged by the company in order to insure a person who is 21 years old. This is the sum that the company must hold at the end of the first year, upon the policy issued at 20, after paying the net cost of insurance for the year. The net single premium $217.448 paid at age 20 will, when increased by net interest for one year, furnish the required contribution of this policy to pay death claims, and leave in the hands of the company the net single premium necessary to effect the insurance for whole life at age 21, in case death does not occur before.

At the end of the second policy year, when the policy-holder will be 22 years old, the net single premium that will then insure $1000 for whole life is $225.019, and this is the amount that must then be held by the company to the credit of this policy, if the insured is still alive. In like manner, each successive year, if the policy-holder survives, the company must have, in order to comply with its contract, an amount on hand to the credit of this policy equal to the net single premium that will at the age the

[1] By Gustavus W. Smith. Reprinted from pages 42–47 of "Notes on Life Insurance"; S. W. Green. New York, 1875.

policy-holder has attained be sufficient to effect the insurance.

Deposit or "reserve" in case a policy is paid for by equal annual premiums. — From the table it is seen that at age 42 the net annual premium that will insure $1000 for whole life (Actuaries' 4 per cent.) is $25.554. This premium is to be paid at the beginning of each year, as long as the person is alive to make the payment. At the end of the first year, or beginning of the second — supposing the insured to be alive — he pays the net annual premium, $25.554, and is insured for another year; but he is now 43 years old, and $26.585 is the net annual premium required to insure $1000 for life at age 43.

Why is it that the man who was insured at age 42, and who has been insured one year, and has paid for that insurance, can, at 43 years of age, be insured by the company for a less premium than is required to insure a man of the same age, 43, but who now takes out a policy for the first time in that company? Taking, for further illustration, a still greater age, we find that at age 65 the net annual premium that will insure $1000 for life is $74.718; and yet the person who took out his policy at age 42, supposing he is still alive, can be safely insured at age 65 by the company for a net annual premium of $25.554.

How is this? Why is it that a man 65 years of age can be insured safely by a company for a net annual premium of $25.554, and another man of the same age, probably in better health, because he has just passed a medical examination, can not be safely insured by the company for a less net annual premium than $74.718 ?

The net annual premium is calculated to provide against all the probabilities and risks of the insured dying in any year, and of his policy becoming due; and also the risk of his being alive, from year to year, to pay his annual premium. At the end of each year, after the net annual premium has paid its proportion of the losses by death for the year, there must be in the hands of the company, on account of *and to the credit of* each and every outstanding policy, an amount in money or securely invested funds that will be in present value the equivalent of a life series of annual premiums, each of which is equal to the difference between the net annual premium the insured paid on taking out his policy and the net annual premium he would now have to pay if he were taking out a new policy at his present advanced age. This amount that must be in the hands of the company at the end of each year's business, to the credit of the respective policies, is variously styled, by life insurance writers, "reserve" "reserve for reinsurance," "net premium reserve," "net value," "true value," "self-insurance," etc.

As before stated, the net annual premium to insure $1000 at age 42 is $25.554, and the net annual premium to insure the same amount at age 43 is $26.585. The difference between these two premiums is $1.031. The value at age 43 of a life series of annual payments of $1 is from the table found to be $15.374. We can find the value at the same age of a whole-life series of annual payments, each of which is equal to $1.031, by the proportion; $1: $1.031: : $15.374 is to the answer. Solving this proportion, we find that the value at age 43 of a life series of annual premiums of $1.031 is equal to $15.851.

If the company has the $15.851 on hand in deposit, which is the cash equivalent of this difference in the future net annual premiums, this amount of cash in hand, together with the smaller net annual premium due at the age of 42, is just the same value as the net annual premium due to age 43. This $15.851 is the amount that must be held on deposit in trust for the policy of $1000 taken out at age 42, at the end of the first year of the policy.

The net annual premium at age 44 to insure $1000 for whole life is found from the same table to be $27.682. The difference between the net annual premium due to age 44, and that which the person insured at age 42 will pay when he is 44 years of age, is obtained by subtracting

$25.554 from $27.682; this difference is $2.128, and there must be in the hands of the company a deposit at the end of the second year of this policy equal to the value at that time of a whole-life series of annual premiums, each of which is equal to $2.128, which is the difference between the net annual premium due to age 44 and that which the insured will pay. From the table, we find that the value at age 44 of a whole-life series of net annual premiums of $1 each is $15.119. We find the value at same age of a whole-life series of annual premiums, each of which is $2.128, by the proportion; $1: $2.128: : $15.119 is to the answer.

Solving this proportion, we find the value sought is $32.172. This is the fund on deposit, or the "reserve," for this policy at the end of the second year. In a manner entirely similar, we find the amount that must be on deposit at the end of each policy year; and if the company has it on hand, and keeps it securely invested at the net rate of interest, and regularly compounds the interest yearly, this "trust fund deposit," together with the present value of the future net annual premiums, will always keep the policy that is paying the smaller net annual premiums, due to the younger age at which the holder entered the company, just on a par with those policies that come in later, or at a more advanced age of entry, and pay the larger annual premium due to this advanced age.

The amount of this deposit may be calculated by a somewhat different process, as follows: At the time the contract is entered into, the value at that time of the whole-life series of net annual premiums to be paid for the policy is exactly equal to the net single premium at that age. Remember that the net single premium is obtained by direct calculation for insurance each separate year, and we convert the net single premium into an equivalent net annual premium. At the end of any policy year, find the net single premium due to that age, then find the value at that age of the series of net annual premiums the insured is to pay; this will be less than the net single premium that at that age will effect the insurance, and this difference is the amount that must be held by the company in deposit to the credit of the policy. For instance, at age 42 the net single premium to insure $1000 for whole life, actuaries' 4 per cent., is $399.184, and this is the value at that age of the whole-life series of ten annual premiums, $25.554, due to the age. At the end of the twentieth policy year, the insured, if alive, will be 62 years old. The net single premium required to insure $1000 for whole life at 62 is $623.826. Now the value at age 62 of a life series of annual payments of $1 each is $9.781; multiply this by the net annual premium the insured is paying, that is, $25.554, and we have the value at age 62 of the series of net annual premiums the insured is to pay. This amounts to $249.931, but direct calculation shows, as stated above, that the insurance on the assumed table of mortality and rate of interest can not be effected at that age for less than $623.826 net single premium. The difference between this sum and the value of the series at age 62 which the insured is to pay must be held by the company in deposit to the credit of the policy; therefore, subtracting $249.931 from $623.826 we have $373.895, which is the sum that must be in deposit at the end of the twentieth policy year belonging to a policy taken out at age 42 for $1000.

It is necessary to have the value of the net single premium at each age, and all that portion of this value not in the present value of the future net annual premiums must be on hand in deposit. Therefore, a company that charges a less net annual premium than that called for by the table of mortality and rate of interest designated by law must be required to add to what would be the legal deposit, in case the future net premiums are equal to those required by the law, an amount equal to the value at that time of a series of annual premiums each of which is equal to the difference between the net annual premium called for by the legal data and the net annual premium the company has agreed to receive.

Illustration. — To illustrate the manner in which the "deposit" must accumulate in the earlier years of a life insurance company, in order to enable it to meet its obligations when the death claims exceed the premiums, let us suppose that a company insures 20,000 policy-holders for $5000 each, at age 30. The net annual premium required for each person is $84.85. This, on 20,000 policies, would make the first payment of annual premiums amount to $1,697,000. The net interest is assumed to be 4 per cent., and, for the first year, it amounts to $67,880. The company has, therefore, at the end of the first year, $1,764,-880. By the table of mortality, 168 of the insured will die during the first year; to the heirs of each, the company must pay $5000. The losses by death are, therefore, $840,000; leaving on hand with the company, after all the death claims are paid, $924,880; which would be a handsome "surplus" at the end of the first year's business, but for the fact that every dollar of this sum belongs to the trust fund deposit, and is an already *accrued liability — a debt.*

At the end of the thirty-fourth year the deposit for each outstanding policy must be $2464.25. The table of mortality shows that 11,297 of the policy-holders will be living at the end of the thirty-fourth year; the company must, therefore, have on hand a trust fund deposit amounting to $27,838,632.25. We find that 11,742 policy-holders were living at the beginning of the thirty-fourth year, and their net annual premiums amounted, in the aggregate, to $996,308.70. There were 445 deaths during the year, and the aggregate losses by death amounted to $2,225,000. Thus, in this year, the death claims exceed the annual premiums by more than one and one quarter millions of dollars. But the company has on hand, in deposit, at the end of the year, $27,838,632.25, after having paid the death claims. The company, however, is not rich, nor more than able to pay its liabilities, because it will surely take the last cent of this amount, with all the future net annual premiums, and interest compounded regularly all the time, to enable it to meet and pay its now rapidly increasing death claims.

Let us look into the accounts of the company at the end of the fiftieth year. The "deposit" on account of each policy at the end of this year is $3708.20; and there are living 3080 policy-holders. The aggregate "deposit" for the outstanding policies at this time is $11,421,256. There were 461 deaths during the year, and the aggregate of policies that matured during the year amounted to $2,305,000. There were 3541 policy-holders living at the beginning of the year, and the aggregate of the net annual premiums paid by them amounted to $300,453.85. We see from this that the losses by death during the year exceeded the net annual premiums by more than $2,000,000. The "deposit" is reduced to $11,421,256, which is less than one-half the amount in "deposit" at the end of the thirty-fourth year. But the company has not lost money, it has only been paying its debts. At the end of the thirty-fourth year it had more, but it owed more. It had enough then, and only enough, to pay what it owed; it is in the same condition now.

At the end of the sixty-fifth year we find the "deposit" that must be in the hands of the company to the credit of each policy is $4560.87; and there are twenty of the original policy-holders living. The aggregate "deposit" for these twenty outstanding policies is $91,217.40. The $27,838,632.25 that the company had on hand at the end of the thirty-fourth year is now reduced to less than $100,000. But the company has only been paying its debts to policy-holders — not losing money. In fact, it had none to lose *of its own*.

At the end of the sixty-ninth year the "deposit" amounts to $4722.84; and there is one policy-holder living. He pays his regular net annual premium the day he is 99 years old. The premium is $84.85. This, added to the "deposit" on hand at the end of the preceding year, makes $4807.69 of this policy-holder's money in the hands of the company the day the policy-holder is 99 years old. At net interest, which is 4 per cent., the interest for the year will amount to $192.31; and this, added to the amount, $4807.69, on hand at the beginning of the year, makes $5000, with which to pay the policy of the last policy-holder in this company.

We see that the $27,838,632.25, which the company had in its possession at the end of the thirty-fourth year, belonging to policy-holders, has been paid to them. The policies were all paid at maturity; the company has nothing left. In fact, it never had a cent of its own during the whole time, although we have seen it the custodian, at one time, of nearly $28,000,000 of other people's money. It owed every cent, and it paid every cent it owed.

It is a marked peculiarity of life insurance business, as seen in this illustration, that the annual premiums exceed the death claims for the first 30 or 40 years; after which time the losses by death largely exceed the annual premiums. The trust fund deposit, after a table of mortality and rate of interest have been designated, is a fixed mathematical amount; it increases for each policy at the end of every succeeding year of the existence of the policy.

Deposit at the End of Each Year on a Whole-Life Policy for $1000, Taken Out at Age 45 — American Experience — Four Per Cent.

Age	Deposit	Age	Deposit	Age	Deposit
45	$17.24	62	368.46	79	$712.77
46	34.98	63	390.72	80	730.56
47	53.22	64	412.91	81	748.03
48	71.95	65	434.96	82	765.24
49	91.18	66	456.82	83	782.37
50	110.72	67	478.45	84	799.49
51	130.72	68	499.78	85	816.43
52	151.09	69	520.78	86	832.90
53	171.81	70	541.39	87	848.53
54	192.85	71	561.58	88	863.28
55	214.18	72	581.39	89	877.54
56	235.75	73	600.85	90	891.55
57	257.55	74	620.02	91	904.65
58	279.53	75	638.95	92	915.35
59	301.66	76	657.70	93	925.41
60	323.88	77	676.26	94	934.42
61	346.16	78	694.62	95	1000.00

CHAPTER XIV

NET VALUATION [1]

The insurance laws of the several states require every regular life insurance company to have on hand at all times cash or approved securities not less in amount than the *net value* of its outstanding policies, according to the *minimum legal standard of valuation.*

By *net value* is meant the amount of the reserve pertaining to the policy at any stated time. It is always the difference between the present worth of the net premiums to be paid on the policy, and the present worth of the benefits guaranteed thereunder — such as amounts payable at death, at maturity, on surrender, etc.

Net valuation is the process of determining the legal net value or reserve of a company's outstanding policies, the net premium only — not the gross premium — being considered. To understand what is meant by the term *minimum legal standard of valuation,* observe that, in the computation of the premium, it is assumed that the reserve will earn a specified rate of interest. In the case of most companies nowadays, the rate assumed is 3 per cent. On this basis, the required net annual premium of an ordinary life policy issued at age 56 was found to be $47.76. The reserve or insurance fund, consisting of the net premium receipts plus the interest earned thereon at the assumed rate, suffices for the payment of all existing policies at maturity.

[1] Reprinted by special permission from pages 78–87 and 114–122 of the "Educational Leaflets" issued by the Mutual Life Insurance Company of New York.

It is obvious that, in order to accumulate a specific sum within a stated time by means of small yearly deposits, the deposits must be larger if the interest to be added to the fund is at the rate of only 3 per cent. than if 3½ or 4 per cent. interest is to be received. It is, therefore, equally clear that, if the net premium receipts of a life insurance company were certain to earn 3½ or 4 per cent. interest, the rates necessary to provide funds sufficient for the payment of all policies at maturity would be lower than when only 3 per cent. interest is realized. In other words, when the reserve is to be accumulated at 3 per cent. interest, larger net premiums are necessary than when a higher interest rate is assumed.

In all cases, whatever the rate of interest assumed, the reserve at the attained age of 96 is equal to the face of the policy. The reserve at the end of the thirty-ninth year at the attained age of 95 is $923.11. That sum plus the next year's net premium, $47.76, plus 3 per cent. interest, amounts to $1000 at the end of the year at the attained age of 96. Had it been assumed in the computation that the funds would earn 4 per cent., the required net premium would have been only $45 instead of $47.76, and the reserve at the attained age of 95 would have been $916.54 instead of $923.11. Observe that $916.54, plus the next year's net premium of $45, plus 4 per cent. interest, likewise amounts to $1000 at the end of the year at the attained age of 96. Thus, as stated before, the higher the rate of interest assumed, the smaller will be the reserve pertaining to any policy. A 3½ per cent. reserve is larger than one computed on a 4 per cent. basis and smaller than a 3 per cent. reserve.

The laws of the several states prescribe the maximum rate of interest that may be assumed, and the mortality table that shall be used, in computing the reserve or net value of a company's policies. This requirement is termed the *legal standard of valuation*. The net value computed by the legal standard is termed the *legal net value* or *legal reserve.* In several states the rate of interest fixed by the *minimum legal standard,* or the lowest standard prescribed by law, is 4½ per cent. — in others 4 per cent. In New York, Massachusetts, and one or two other states, the minimum legal standard calls for 3½ per cent. interest, so that a company whose premiums are computed on a 4 per cent. reserve basis must, in order to do business in those states, submit to a valuation by the higher standard of 3½ per cent. Many companies have recently adjusted their premiums for new business to a 3 per cent. basis, and are accumulating 3 per cent. reserves accordingly, notwithstanding the lower minimum standard provided by law.

Knowing the ages of the several policy-holders, we may determine how many according to the mortality table will die in each year thereafter, and how many will be living at the end of each year, and hence the amount of claims to be expected in each year until all existing policies have matured, either by the death of the policy-holder or the expiration of the term for which the contract was written. Having these data we may compute the present worth or present value of all outstanding policies — that is, the sum which accumulated at a given rate of interest, say 3 per cent., will equal an amount sufficient to pay every policy in full as the latter matures.

In like manner, knowing how many policy-holders will be living according to the table at the beginning of each subsequent year, to pay the premiums called for by the several policies, we may determine the net premium income of each year until the last existing policy has matured. Hence we may compute the present worth of all future net premiums to be collected on outstanding policies.

Let us now take for illustration the case of a company issuing 100,000 policies, aggregating a total of $100,000,000 insurance. Assume that the present worth of those policies — that is, the present worth of the benefits to accrue under their terms, is found to be $37,055,000.

This sum then constitutes the present value of the policy obligations which the company has assumed. To pay these policies as they mature, the company has no other resource than the net premiums stipulated to be paid thereon plus the interest which those premiums will earn at the assumed rate, say 3 per cent. If now the present worth of these premiums is likewise found to be $37,055,000, it is obvious that the company is solvent and will — if 3 per cent. interest is earned and the mortality does not exceed that indicated by the table — be able to meet its obligations at maturity. A statement of its assumed condition would be as follows:

CREDIT SIDE

Present worth of net premiums to be collected on existing contracts	$37,055,000

DEBIT SIDE

Present worth of benefits under outstanding policies	$37,055,000

Such would be the exact status of a legally solvent mutual company the day it begins business, after a number of policies have been written but before any premiums have been collected.

Let us, however, take the same company after several years' premiums have been collected and a number of policies paid, a reasonable amount of new business having been written in the meantime. As some of the net premiums called for by existing contracts have been received and applied, the present worth of the premiums remaining to be collected will no longer equal the present worth of benefits under policies now outstanding. Assume, for example, the present worth of those benefits to be now $38,000,000, and the present worth of future net premiums $34,000,000. The present worth of benefits promised, or obligations assumed, will be larger than at first, because every existing policy is nearer maturity, while the present worth of net premiums to be collected in the future will be less than before, because some part of the premiums originally called for by every existing policy have already been collected. Our debits then in this case would exceed our credits by $4,000,000, and the statement would now be as follows:

CREDIT SIDE

Present worth of net premiums to be collected on existing policies	$34,000,000
Deficit	4,000,000
	$38,000,000

DEBIT SIDE

Present worth of benefits under outstanding policies	$38,000,000

The company is now clearly insolvent under the law, for the present worth of net premiums to be received — its only apparent resources — is $4,000,000 less than the present worth of the benefits to be paid. This deficit represents the *legal reserve liability* of the company — that is, the *net value* of its outstanding policies according to the legal standard of valuation, being the difference between the present worth of the benefits for which the company is liable under its policies and the present worth of all the net premiums to be received. If the company, however, after providing for the tabular mortality and matured endowments, has reserved from year to year the balance of its net premium and interest income, the funds so reserved will now aggregate exactly the amount of the computed reserve liability. In other words, it will have on hand the reserve required by law to maintain solvency, and the statement of its condition will now assume the following form:

CREDIT SIDE

Present worth of net premiums remaining to be collected on existing policies	$34,000,000
Reserve (Cash and Invested Funds)	4,000,000
	$38,000,000

DEBIT SIDE

Present worth of benefits contracted for in outstanding policies	$38,000,000

This suggests the definition of the legal reserve given above, to wit: "A fund equal in amount to the excess of the present value of benefits under outstanding policies over the present value of net premiums to be paid on those policies."

On the basis of the statement as last rendered, the company is technically solvent, since the credits and debits are equal. The form of the statement may be simplified by eliminating the two items, "Present worth of net premiums" and "Present worth of policies," and simply carrying to the debit side of the account the *difference* between the present worth of policy obligations and the present worth of premiums to be collected, which is, the company's *legal reserve liability*, or the *net value* of the benefits guaranteed under its outstanding policies. As the company holds cash and invested funds to the amount of this liability, the statement will assume the following form:

CREDIT SIDE

Cash, Invested Funds, and Credits (Assets)	$4,000,000

DEBIT SIDE

Net value of all outstanding policies (Liability)..........	$4,000,000

The comparison of a company's *admitted assets* — money, invested funds, and valid credits approved by the insurance authorities — with its total liabilities constitutes the legal test of its solvency. By the financial statement last above set out, the company in question is legally solvent — its assets being exactly equal to its liabilities; nevertheless, a company in just that condition would in fact be upon the verge of bankruptcy, for the loss of a small amount by depreciation of values, extra mortality, or other cause, would render it *insolvent* under the law. Such being the case, it is of the first importance for every company to maintain as a margin of safety an additional fund in excess of all legal liabilities, variously termed "surplus," "indivisible surplus," "unassigned funds," etc. Under the New York law this extra fund or margin of safety is called the *contingency reserve.* Assuming that the company in question has such additional funds to the amount of $1,000,000, a statement of its financial condition would then read:

ASSETS

Cash, Invested Funds, and Credits		$5,000,000

LIABILITIES

Net value of all outstanding policies	$4,000,000	
Contingency Reserve (Surplus)	1,000,000	$5,000,000

In the above case, a loss of assets in excess of $1,000,000 would sweep away the contingency reserve and render the company insolvent. The smaller the amount of such additional fund, the more imminent the danger. It is obvious, therefore, that the measure of a company's strength is to be gauged by the *amount* of extra or surplus funds which it holds in addition to the legal reserve or net value of its outstanding policies, as well as by the *percentage* which such extra funds are of the total liabilities, *i.e.*, the company's "*ratio of assets to liabilities.*" For example: According to the statistics for 1906, a certain company of well-known excellence had surplus funds at the end of that year of nearly $8,000,000, and a ratio of assets to liabilities of 108; that is, its assets exceeded its liabilities by only 8 per cent.

On the other hand, the assets of a smaller company of considerable prominence exceeded its liabilities by 29 per cent., yet its total surplus funds were less than $130,000. Assuming that the assets in each case were of the highest class, there can be no doubt as to the relative strength of the two organizations — the same being the reverse of what might be inferred if only the ratios cited were to be considered. A surplus of only $130,000 might be readily wasted or lost in a single transaction — far more readily, it will be conceded, than a surplus of nearly $8,000,000. A still more striking illustration of the misleading character of this ratio is afforded by the figures of a still smaller company with a ratio of assets to liabilities of 592 and a total surplus of less than $21,000. In another case, if the assets of a company were largely of real estate or of fluctuating securities, a surplus of 8 per cent. or less — however large in amount — might easily be swept away by a sudden depreciation of values, if current market quotations were to be taken as a basis of valuation.

Several modifications of the system of net valuation described in the foregoing pages have been established by recent legislation.

The statement may be safely made that the ordinary loading of a life insurance premium is never sufficient in the first year to meet the expenses incident to securing the business. To illustrate: If the gross premium of an ordinary life policy at age 56, American Experience Table, and 3 per cent. interest, is $63.68, we find by deducting the net premium of $47.76 that the loading is $15.92. The principal items of expense the first year will be the agent's commission, say 40 per cent., or $25.47, and the medical examiner's fee, $5, making for these two items alone $30.47, or nearly double the amount of the loading. As the net premium can not be trenched upon, the discrepancy of $14.55 is temporarily advanced from the accumulated surplus, the latter to be recouped subsequently from the saving in mortality or other gains accruing to the new policy.

In the case of new companies, however, and others which have accumulated but little surplus, the policy sometimes provides that the contract shall be valued in the first year as term insurance, the regular life insurance policy beginning one year later. Thus the entire first premium, less only the charge for the actual mortality of the year, is available as a loading for meeting the cost of new business. This method is variously designated as the *preliminary term,* or *first-year term* system, and has been adopted by most companies organized in recent years. In the case of a preliminary term ordinary life policy at age 56, the net premium in the first year would be merely the natural premium, or yearly term rate, that is, $19.31, as given above. The practice of preliminary term companies is, however, to charge the same *gross* premium in the first as in subsequent years. If the gross premium is $63.68, we shall have, after deducting the net premium of $19.31, a loading the first year of $44.37, or about 70 per cent. Deducting $5 for medical examination, there remains a balance of $39.37, or nearly 62 per cent., for commissions and other expenses.

In the valuation of such a contract the company is not, of course, charged with any reserve at the end of the first year, but during the second and subsequent years the net premium required will be that of an ordinary life corresponding to age 57, the attained age of the insured when the regular life policy begins. In this case, then, the net premium in the second and subsequent years would be $50.13 instead of $47.76 (the net premium at age 56), and if this amount be deducted from the gross premium of $63.68, the balance of $13.55 will be the permanent loading instead of $15.92. Thus it will be seen that by this system the loading is greatly increased in the first year, but is materially less than the regular loading in subsequent years. There will be no reserve at the end of the first year, and the reserve of the second policy year will be the same as the first year reserve of a regular ordinary life policy issued at age 57. In fact, from the beginning of the second year the policy will be valued as an ordinary life issued at age 57, or one year later than its actual date, as stated above. It follows that the reserve of an ordinary life policy issued on the preliminary term plan will always be less than it would have been had it been issued at the same age on the regular ordinary life plan, because always one year behind in the process of accumulation. This difference will continue until age 96, when the reserve in either case becomes equal to the face of the policy. It will be appreciated that smaller reserves mean smaller cash values, and also that smaller loadings mean smaller dividends.

We have heretofore defined the terms "level premium" and "net valuation." Under the preliminary term system the gross premium may be level from date of issue of policy, but the net premium is not so. For example, in the case just illustrated, the net premium in the first year is $19.31 and in subsequent years $50.13, though the gross premium is $63.68 for every year. On the other hand, we have seen that the net premium of the equivalent ordinary life policy on the regular legal reserve plan is $47.76, the same fixed amount for every year including the first. This is what is meant by a *net level premium*, and the valuation of policies on this basis is strictly *net level premium valuation*, though commonly termed simply "net valuation."

In the case of a "limited premium" policy the preliminary term plan varies somewhat from that illustrated. Let us consider its application, for example, to a fifteen-payment life. The net 3 per cent. premium of the regular policy at age 56 would be $60.17. If the gross premium is $78.16, the yearly loading will be $17.99. On a preliminary term basis, the equivalent contract would consist of a combined one-year term policy and a fourteen-payment life, the latter beginning at age 57. The net premium for one year's term insurance would be the same as before, $19.31. Deducting this amount from the gross premium of $78.16, we obtain a first-year loading of $58.85. The 3 per cent. net premium of the fourteen-payment life at age 57 would be $64.55, which leaves a yearly loading of $13.61, instead of $17.99, for the remaining fourteen years. As in the case of the preliminary term ordinary life, there will be no reserve at the end of the first year. At the end of the second policy year the reserve will be $46.14. This is larger than the first-year reserve of the regular policy, but much smaller than the reserve of the latter at the end of the second policy year, it being then $86.72. The preliminary term reserve at the end of each subsequent policy year approaches more and more nearly to the corresponding reserve of the regular fifteen-payment life until the end of the fifteenth year when, at the attained age of 71, both reserves are necessarily the same, since both policies are now fully paid up. In other words, on the regular fifteen-payment life the reserve of a fully paid policy is accumulated in fifteen years, while on the preliminary term fifteen-payment life the same reserve is accumulated during the last fourteen years.

The preliminary term system, as applied to an ordinary life policy, is not an unreasonable method of providing for the cost of new business in the case of a young company, notwithstanding the apparent injustice of charging a premium of $63.68 for term insurance during a single year, the net natural cost of which is $19.31. Indeed, only by the use of some such expedient would it be possible for a new company to establish itself at all on the mutual plan, since being in receipt of little or nothing from loadings on old business, and having no accumulated surplus, it would be unable to meet the necessary cost of new insurance and provide at the same time for the required legal reserve of the first year. Only on the stock plan, with the stockholders personally advancing extra funds for the purchase of new business, could a new company comply with the requirement to put up the full net level premium reserves on its policies beginning with the year of issue. The adoption of the preliminary term plan by an *old* company, however, is commonly regarded as a confession of weakness or of an extravagant management, since it is a virtual admission that the company is unable to keep its expenses within its aggregate receipts from loadings, and that it dares not trench upon its limited surplus.

If the application of the preliminary term plan to the ordinary life policy be defensible, it nevertheless becomes decidedly objectionable when applied without modification to limited payment and endowment policies, as illustrated in the following table showing the loadings of the first year:

Policy, Age 56	Gross Premium	Net Natural Cost	Loading
Ordinary life	$63.68	$19.31	$44.37
Fifteen-payment life	78.16	19.31	58.85
Ten-payment life	99.33	19.31	80.02
Twenty-year endowment	72.66	19.31	53.35
Ten-year endowment	121.06	19.31	101.75

The grotesque absurdity of such loadings sufficiently condemns the *full preliminary term system*, by which is meant the application of preliminary term without modification to all forms of policies.

In 1897, Miles M. Dawson, consulting actuary, introduced a modification of the preliminary term plan, which consists in limiting the loading of the first year on all limited payment and endowment forms to the amount available, on a preliminary term basis, on the ordinary life policy. For example, referring to the table above, while the gross premiums would vary on the different forms as indicated, the loading could in no case exceed that of the ordinary life policy, to wit: $44.37. From the balance of the premium on limited payment and endowment forms the company would put up a reserve in the first year, thus reducing the net premium and increasing the loadings of subsequent years. The tendency of this plan would be to encourage the sale of ordinary life policies rather than limited payment and endowment contracts. Several modifications of "modified preliminary term" have been legalized in different states.

The select and ultimate valuation method of computing reserves was likewise suggested by Mr. Dawson as a substitute for modified preliminary term. To a correct understanding of the system a knowledge of the several classes of mortality tables is necessary.

Assume, for illustration, that we wish to ascertain how many of 100,000 persons, all 30 years of age, will die within one year. If to that end we note the history for twelve months of 100,000 persons of the age stated, who have just passed a rigid medical examination for life insurance, we shall find a much smaller number dying than in 100,000 of the same age who were examined five years ago, at age 25. If we note the history of both classes during the succeeding year, we shall find a larger percentage of deaths in each instance than in the first year, and, as before, a smaller percentage of deaths in the first than in the second class, but the death rates of the two classes will now be nearer together than in the first year. In the third year, while the death rate of each class will again be higher than formerly, the difference between the two rates will again be less than in the second year. With each added year the difference in death rates of the two classes will diminish, until ultimately, after the benefit of medical selection has worn off, the two death rates will be theoretically the same. It is commonly assumed that this stage will be reached in five years.

Lives which have just been selected by a medical examination are called *select lives*, and a mortality table based on the subsequent history of such lives is called a *select table*.

As it is assumed that the effects of medical selection *ultimately* disappear, say in about five years, a mortality table based on the history of lives insured five or more years ago is called an *ultimate table*.

A mortality table based on the history of lives insured, some within the year, others within two or three or ten years or more, is called a *mixed table*.

The American Experience Table of Mortality, which is in general use in the United States, is supposed to be an "ultimate table," its compilation having been based upon the subsequent history of lives insured for five years or more. The rate of mortality indicated by this table, therefore, is materially greater in the first five years, at least, than that pertaining to select lives at corresponding ages. As a basis for establishing a minimum standard of valuation and for fixing a limitation of expenses in securing new business, the New York law assumes that the mortality of select lives in the first policy year immediately following medical examination will be 50 per cent. of the tabular mortality of the American Experience Table; in the second year, 65 per cent.; in the third year, 75 per cent.; in the fourth year, 85 per cent.; in the fifth year, 95 per cent.; and in the sixth and subsequent years, 100 per cent. On this basis smaller terminal reserves will be required during the first four years than by the American Experience Table, though they will be the same from the fifth year on, as illustrated in the following comparison of terminal reserves computed by the two methods on an ordinary life policy issued at age 56.

End of Year	Terminal Reserves	
	American Experience Table	Select and Ultimate
First	$29.90	$14.41
Second	59.94	50.84
Third	90.06	85.87
Fourth	120.21	119.13
Fifth	150.33	150.33
Sixth	180.36	180.36

This is the system of *select and ultimate valuation* prescribed by the laws of New York as a minimum standard. In this standard the new company, which might find it impracticable to put up the net level premium reserves in the first and immediately succeeding years, has a substantial measure of relief. The company collects during the first four years, as well as thereafter, the full gross premium. The margin in the first year's premium by reason of the smaller reserve required — the full reserve being made up in subsequent years by the saving in mortality — is available for other purposes and may be anticipated and expended in securing new business.

CHAPTER XV

POLICY CONTRACTS[1]

Life insurance practically had its origin in a contract between two or more parties that was in the nature of a wager. The payor of the premium would win if the insured died within a given period, and the insurer would win if the insured survived such a period.

The first record we have of such a life insurance contract shows that it was made June 18, 1583, in favor of Richard Martin, citizen and alderman of London. The subject insured was one William Gybbons, and the contract practically amounted to a wager between Richard Martin and thirteen merchants of the city of London. Martin paid the thirteen merchants about £30. If Gybbons died within twelve months, then the thirteen merchants agreed to pay about £400. While this was a wager transaction, and would now be void in law, it was, in a manner, the beginning of life insurance contracts.

A policy on the life of Nicholas Bourne, dated November 25, 1721, issued by the London Assurance Corporation at the request and expense of Thomas Baldwin, is the second authentic record we have of an early life insurance contract. An interesting feature of this contract is that it would meet the necessities of the Second Adventists, whose considerations of life insurance are disturbed by the prospect of being translated and thus leaving behind

[1] By L. G. Fouse, President of the Fidelity Mutual Life Insurance Company, Philadelphia. Reprinted with additions from pages 209–228, Volume XXVI, Annals of the American Academy of Political and Social Science.

them no evidence of death. The policy provided that "in case he, the said Nicholas Bourne, shall in or during the said time, and before the full End and Expiration thereof, happen to dye, or decease out of this world by any Ways or Means whatsoever, That then the above said Governor and Company will well and truly satisfy, content, and pay unto the said Thomas Baldwin, his Executors, Administrators or Assigns, the Sum or Sums of Money by him Assured, and here underwritten, without any Allowance, Deduction, or Abatement whatsoever." The only condition of avoiding the contract was going to sea or into the wars without written consent.

Another old contract of which we have a record is on the life of the Right Rev. William Carmichael, Lord Bishop of Clonfert, dated June 27, 1754. The insurance was effected by and for the benefit of George Cockburne at the rate of $5 premium for each £100 insured. Suicide, or death by the hands of justice, or going outside of his Britannic Majesty's dominions of Great Britain and Ireland without first obtaining license in writing, voided the contract.

A contract of life insurance must now be supported by a legal insurable interest. That is to say, when the insurance is effected by any person other than the insured, the beneficiary must have an interest in the continuance of the life of the insured and not merely a monetary interest in his death.

While it is not my province to discuss the actuarial and scientific questions involved, it is proper to say that the discovery of the law of mortality susceptible of mathematical calculation made it possible to supplant crude guesses at the chances of life and death by tables constructed from mortality observations.

The contracting parties under the policy are usually designated in this country as the insured, the subject upon whose life the policy is written; the insurer, the one who assumes the obligation to pay the insurance; and the beneficiary, the one to whom the insurance is paid in the event of death. There are, therefore, usually three parties to a policy contract.

Individuals under modern methods do not act as insurers. The laws of the several states have provided for the incorporation of insurance companies which have perpetual succession. Individuals die, but properly managed corporations are supposed to live always. The powers of a life insurance company under the statute usually consist of effecting insurance upon the lives of individuals, every insurance appertaining thereto or connected therewith, and the granting and purchasing of annuities. The companies are authorized to make by-laws for their government not in conflict with the laws and constitution of the state in which they are incorporated, or of the United States. Full liberty and freedom is, therefore, vouchsafed to the life insurance company in the making of contracts with a single requirement applicable only to companies known as old line or legal reserve companies. This requirement amounts to a standard of safety adopted by the state, which provides that whatever the policy contract may be the insurance company must always have in its coffers money or securities equal to the difference between the present worth of what it promises to pay, and the present worth of the net premiums the insured promises to pay, which difference is known as the reserve. Beyond this the state wisely does not undertake to interfere with or handicap the companies. While this latitude of license has probably in a degree been abused, it has given the public a great variety of policy contracts from which to select; and as the insuring public is becoming better informed and able to discriminate between the sound and unsound, such latitude or license is becoming less objectionable. Indeed, by reason of the ever changing conditions it is infinitely to be preferred to any attempt at circumscribing legal limitations to policy contracts.

The word policy means in general a course or plan of action or administration. During the Middle Ages it was used to designate memoranda. In England it has been applied to "a warrant or ticket for money in the public funds." In the United States it is applied to a gambling game. Among these varied definitions and uses has arisen its universal employment to designate comprehensively a written instrument embodying a contract of insurance involving, as it does, contingencies and probabilities. In life insurance a policy contract is, therefore, one involving the contingency of death, in which the minds of the parties thereto have met and agreed upon the terms and conditions of the underwriting.

The taking out of a policy of life insurance signifies a sense of responsibility, frugality, and thrift on the part of its owner. Under existing social and economic conditions the life insurance contract has become a necessity. The man who assumes the responsibility of a family and of engaging in business needs protection, in the event of his early death, for both. The insured or owner of the contract often derives substantial benefit from the self-denial and formation of the frugal habits acquired by the preparation to meet the periodical payment of premiums. He is also benefited by the consciousness that he is creating an estate to benefit his dependents, which, in the event of his death, becomes immediately convertible into cash without the intervention of administrator, executor, or attorney. It is generally conceded by the trust officers of our great trust companies that there are no securities left by decedents of as great general value, because of not being affected by market, etc., as are policies of life insurance. It is only in cases of gross fraud or where the rights of beneficiaries are disputed that any contest is made by the companies. For example; according to the sworn returns of 1902 and 1903 the total existing contested claims, representing an accumulation of years, amounted to only $668,200, while the claims paid during the same years by the legal reserve companies represented $367,-035,413. Thus the accumulated contests represented only one-fifth of 1 per cent. of the amount of claims paid in two years; or for every $1000 paid, only $2 were contested, and it is safe to say that currently not more than $1 out of every $1000 paid is contested.

For the beneficiaries of such contracts it signifies the means of support after the decease of the breadwinners; it means escape from the pittances or charities of the world.

To the state life insurance signifies a much reduced poor rate for the maintenance of almshouses and eleemosynary institutions.

. . . .

Motives in Framing Contracts. — In order to get at the motives we will take up the considerations involved in the framing of a policy contract. It is, no doubt, true that policies have been framed with temporary success, having quick returns to the managers as the principal consideration; schemes could be cited in illustration of this statement. I shall, however, not undertake to cope with or discuss dishonest schemes, but shall address myself to the difficulties involved under honest and legitimate projects.

The consideration of first importance is so to frame the contracts as to perpetuate the existence of the corporation. To this end due consideration must be given to equity and justice, and to protection against dishonesty and fraud.

A policy may be loaded down with unnecessary restrictions. In the earlier days of life insurance, when observations had not been made of the various supposedly hazardous conditions, it was attempted to avoid them by policy restrictions. Many of these have been found to be unnecessary. Some of them are needed, and in a modified form should be retained in the interest of a sound, wholesome public policy and of equity to all policy-holders.

While the motives involved in business getting cannot

wholly be ignored, they must be subordinated to the rules of good business, sound public policy, equity and justice. It will not do for those who have the framing of a policy contract to "play to the galleries" by a show of liberality, and thus secure public applause at the expense of policy-holders.

The beginning of a policy contract is a proposal in the form of an application for life insurance. In such application the applicant is required to make a detailed statement of his personal and family history, and such statements are usually made the basis of the contract. If the insured makes material misstatements, he is very much in the same moral position as any one who obtains a thing of value under false pretenses. Banks, business and manufacturing concerns, and individuals alike are protected under the laws against that class of people who do not hesitate to indulge in false pretenses. Notwithstanding these general facts, in some states life insurance companies have practically no protection. An applicant in such states may, with malice aforethought, misrepresent a material fact, and because of a prejudiced and pernicious public sentiment, which has invaded the courts of justice, the insurance management will sometimes pay rather than take the chances of greater loss in contesting a claim believed to be fraudulent. At best the binding obligations are all on the company, and both the insurance departments and the courts stand ready to enforce them, while the insured may at will discontinue the contract.

The public sentiment of which I have spoken largely ignores the fact that insurance is effected by the money of the policy-holders of the company; that, literally, the policy-holders are the company, and the officers are merely the managers. It is in part due to a condition which obtained after the Civil War in the seventies, when many companies were organized by men who knew absolutely nothing of the science of underwriting, and whose numberless blunders forced them to the last expedient of trying to perpetuate the existence of their companies by evading the paying of claims. While these companies ceased to exist many years ago, and while, if anything, the companies at present err on the side of liberality and promptness, the sentiment referred to remains in a modified form.

The application should and usually does contain a warranty clause in which the applicant warrants the truth of his statements that form the basis of the contract. If any material statements therein are found to be untrue, then the contract, according to its terms, may be voidable or become *ipso facto* null and void, and all payments, except as expressly provided therein, are forfeited to the company. The rule, however, is to make the policies incontestable, except for the non-payment of premiums, after from one to two years following the date of issuance. Under the head of policy restrictions I discuss in some detail the incontestable clause.

Before execution of a policy contract the medical and inspection departments of the company carefully investigate the statements made by the applicant. They determine whether the applicant is insurable, and if so under what conditions. The applicant's financial ability to pay the premiums is also considered. Upon proper certification the executive department executes the contracts. The policy, however, as a rule, does not become binding or operative until delivery to the applicant and acceptance by him during his lifetime and good health, and the actual payment of the required premium.

The title to the policy may vest in the insured or in the beneficiary, depending upon the terms and conditions of the contract. If the insured under the terms of the contract has the right to change the beneficiary, then the latter has a contingent interest only, which does not become vested until after the death of the insured. Hence, under such a contract the title vests in the insured because he can, at any time, substitute his own estate or another beneficiary for the one originally named. If, however, under the terms of the contract the insured cannot change the beneficiary, then the title to the policy vests in the latter and can only be transferred to another by assignment.

Under the laws of most of the states a policy of life insurance, made payable to wife and children, is not liable for the debts of the insured, and hence, though the insured may be insolvent at the time of death, the creditors cannot get any part of the insurance money unless it can be shown that the policy was contracted for after insolvency and that the contract was made to avoid the payment of debts and to defraud creditors.

A life policy is not consummated or completed until it either expires by limitation or by maturity at the end of a stated period, or by the death of the insured. In the last event proof of death and of claim, as required by the contract, must be made to the company. While many policies provide for the payment of the money within a limit of thirty or sixty days, it has become the custom of practically all the companies to pay the insurance money as soon as satisfactory proof of loss and claim has been made.

It is an established principle of the law courts to construe contracts against the framers or makers, on the ground that they are familiar with the technicalities of the law, and are presumed to frame the contracts in their own interest.

In construing contracts, in case of apparent conflict between written and printed clauses, preference is always given to the written clauses.

Notwithstanding the disposition of juries to favor individual claimants against corporations, and the disposition of the courts to construe the contracts against the makers, it is a fact worthy of note that more than 75 per cent. of the litigated cases are won by the companies. This is due to the further fact that the companies will only resort to a contest in most flagrant, fraudulent cases.

Variety of Life Contracts due to Method. — There are four methods legally recognized and mentioned under this section, each of which has its distinctive features. The distinctions between the methods are legal, mathematical, practical and, in part, due to prejudice and custom. Because of the distinctions mentioned, the form of contract adapted to one method would not be suited to another method. This has given rise to a much larger variety of policy contracts in life insurance than we should have if there were but one method. While the system of life insurance may be said to be one, the methods are many.

Ordinary Legal Reserve Methods. — This comprehends the classification of companies which are by law required to maintain a reserve at all times equal to the future deficiency in the premiums, so that the fulfilment of the policy obligations is guaranteed. There are probably as many as one hundred and fifty different varieties of policies issued by companies of this classification. It would be impracticable to attempt to enumerate them all, but I will mention the principal policies:

1. *The Ordinary or Whole-Life Participating Policy.* — Premiums continuous during the life of the insured; dividends applied to reducing premiums or increasing the insurance; insurance payable at death only.

2. *Limited Payment Participating Policy.* — Premiums limited to a term of years; dividends as in (1), or payable in cash at the end of the term; insurance payable at death only.

3. *Endowment Participating Policy.* — Premiums payable during the specified term; dividends as in (2); insurance is payable at the end of years specified or at death if prior.

4. *Non-Participating Policy.* — All of the several forms mentioned are issued at a low rate of premiums in lieu of dividends.

In addition to the several forms of policies referred to there may be mentioned joint life or partnership, renewable term, term, instalment, single premium or paid-up, tontine, semi-tontine, and a great variety of deferred dividend policies variously designated as accumulation, allotment, survivorship dividend, tontine dividend, etc.

Industrial Legal Reserve Method. — The variety is practically limited to the standard life and limited payment policies at premium rates considerably in excess of those charged by the ordinary legal reserve companies. This excess is due to the fact that the companies issuing industrial policies collect the premiums weekly — sometimes monthly — by collectors who go from house to house. By reason of the large premium charged, policies of the industrial variety contain but few restrictions.

Fraternal or Lodge Method. — These contracts are in the form of certificates of membership, and usually provide for suspension of a lodge in case payment is not made by the subordinate branches to the supreme body. Although the individual member may pay his dues and assessments promptly, if the lodge to which he belongs fails to pay he must suffer suspension. The rights of the individuals are subordinated to the conduct and will of the majority.

The contracts usually specify a maximum benefit, and are not in a legal sense guaranteed beyond the proceeds of the assessments collected from the lodges to pay the losses. The variety is usually limited to certificates in which payments of the member continue during the life of the contract.

As a rule very few restrictions are imposed.

Assessment or Non-Legal Reserve Method. — Under this method provision is made to effect the insurance by currently collecting from the members a specified or determinable amount to be paid periodically. Originally this form of contract usually specified that, in the event of the death of the insured, the beneficiary should receive the proceeds of an assessment not exceeding a maximum sum specified. Later the form was modified so that the sum payable at death should be fixed and certain, while the amounts to be collected from members become variable and uncertain, depending upon the mortality experienced. The variety is limited to the type of policies not requiring large accumulations for their fulfilment, and under which the payments of the insured are coterminous with the life of the policy. The restrictions and conditions, with the exception of the non-forfeitable and accumulation features, are in effect the same as in the policies of the legal reserve class.

The truth of the statements contained in the application must be a condition precedent to the issuance of the policy. The payment of the premiums when due is fundamental to the continuance of the insurance. Provision is generally made for the revival of the policy in case of default in the payment of the premium if the insured be in good health. The requirement of legal and proper proof that the contingency insured against has happened is also fundamental. The company that will pay a policy without due and proper proof of death and claim is recreant to its trust.

Sound public policy limits the insurable ages to the productive period of life, and requires policies to be non-forfeitable for any payments in excess of the current cost of insurance, allowing the companies a small margin for contingencies. It demands a clear and distinct statement of the respective rights of the parties to the contract with reference to the division and disposition of surplus. It requires policies to become incontestable within a reasonable time from date of issuance, except for failure to pay premiums when due, and imposes restrictions in the interests of the general public, such as will discourage and prevent fraud and crime. Suicide, which will be discussed under policy restrictions, is an important feature of life insurance as related to public policy.

Conditions imposed by equitable considerations require the policies which have been issued to be kept, as nearly as practicable, in the same classification of hazards. If the insured voluntarily assumes a hazard known to be great, and not originally contemplated in his contract, the burden of it must either be borne by himself or by other policy-holders. Equitable considerations require that every insured should bear his just proportion of such burdens. Hence in the case of military and naval service during time of war the extra premium involved by the war hazard should either be paid by the government served, or by the insured, or the policy should be proportionately scaled. Equitable considerations also demand that an extra premium should be imposed on persons who reside or travel in certain portions of the tropics where the death rate is fully twice as great as that upon which the premiums are based. A further and very important consideration, but much neglected, is that every policy should be made to pay its own way, including the expenses of writing and placing it. The policy should be so constructed that the premium loading the first policy year is sufficient to pay the expenses, and the loading in the subsequent policy years should be correspondingly reduced. The surplus belonging to those already insured should be apportioned to them, and should not be diverted to the payment of expenses incident to obtaining new business.

In a great many policy contracts conditions and restrictions are referred to as privileges. This use of the word privilege is rather difficult to reconcile with the general proposition of law that that which is not prohibited and comes within the purpose of the corporation is permitted. Therefore, unless a policy contract first limits and circumscribes, there is absolutely no significance to privileges. For example, to say, when there is no limitation as to travel, that the insured has the privilege of traveling or residing in any part of the known world signifies absolutely nothing, as that privilege is granted by its not being prohibited.

It may, therefore, be accepted as a guiding principle that within the limits of the powers of the maker of the contract, whatever is not restricted, forbidden, or prohibited is a privilege implied although not expressed.

I have classified the important conditions and restrictions of fifty-one companies. These companies are representative, and the result of the classification clearly indicates the principal policy conditions among the American life insurance companies:

1. Only eleven of the fifty-one companies formally announce accepting risks over sixty.

2. Thirty-seven accept women on the same conditions as men; thirteen require extra premiums or restrict them to certain policies, and one company refuses to insure them.

3. Thirty-eight companies voluntarily attach copy of application to the policy, thus giving to the insured a complete contract, and thirteen only do so when required or when the law requires it.

4. All companies have a provision in the policy that it shall not become effective and binding until delivered during the lifetime and good health of the insured and after the required premium is actually paid.

5. Seventeen have no restrictions with regard to occupation after the policy has once been issued; eight have a restriction imposing a penalty if the insured engages in a more hazardous occupation than the one stated in the application; twenty-six have restrictions limited by some to the first policy year and others to the first two policy years.

6. Thirty-five companies have restrictions in regard to military and naval service in time of war, requiring a permit for which an extra premium must be paid or providing for the scaling of policies; six have such restriction for either one or two policy years and ten have no restriction.

7. Nineteen have a suicide clause for one year; twenty-five for two years; three for three years; one without limitation, and three have no restriction.

8. In the matter of dueling and violating law thirty have no restrictions; six have them for one year; twelve for two years; two for three years, and one constant.

9. Forty-two have no provision against intemperance; two have it for one year; four for two years; one for three years; two for five years, and one constant.

10. Twenty-four companies have no restriction as to residence and travel; nine have it for one year; fourteen for two years, and four constant.

11. Two companies have no incontestable clause; two stipulate incontestability from date of issue; seventeen after one year; twenty-seven after two years; two after three years, and one after five years.

12. The policies of nine companies provide for no days of grace for payment of premium; those of forty-one companies provide thirty days, and one company six days.

13. Fourteen companies make no provision in policies for reinstatement or revival in the event of lapse, but reinstate merely as a matter of grace; sixteen companies make it a matter of contract without limiting the time; ten limit within a year; three two years; two three years; six five years.

14. All companies have some non-forfeiture provision after two or three years by way of loan, or paid-up or extended insurance; four provide cash surrender values after two years; twenty-nine three years; six five years; eight at periods specified in the contract; four no cash surrender values.

15. Six companies pay dividends annually; six annually after the second year; four annually after the third year; four annually after specified periods; nine annually after five years; twenty-two at stated periods or dividends deferred.

16. Forty-four companies provide for the payment of claims immediately after the receipt and approval of proofs of death, and seven specify payment within thirty or sixty days after proof.

I will consider the classes, as given in the above classification, in numerical order:

1. Insurance, as a matter of protection, should be limited to the productive period of life, or to between ages 15 and 70. If an aged man applies for insurance, and pays the premiums himself as a means of investment and a method of increasing his estate, then there is no special reason for limiting the age on the level premium, or reserve method, of life insurance. Unfortunately, however, a great many aged persons have allowed themselves to be used as subjects for speculation. The astonishing part is that a selfish, unnatural, and depraved desire should sometimes develop on the part of sons, daughters, and sons-in-law to insure their fathers and mothers under the assessment or cheaper method in the hope of financial gain from a speedy death.

Between the years 1880 and 1884, in the State of Pennsylvania, upward of two hundred assessment associations were organized for the purpose of speculating in aged human lives. Through the efforts of the legitimate life insurance companies and associations, the pulpit, the press, and the bench, public conscience was awakened, and a law was passed in 1883 which put the speculators in human life and the organizations through which they operated out of business within a year. This chapter in the history of life insurance has resulted in the refusal by most companies to insure persons over the age of sixty unless the policy be of the investment type, and the further refusal to issue a policy if any person other than the insured seeks to effect the insurance or to pay the premiums.

A man under proper policy conditions cannot, and would not if he could, speculate on his own life, and therefore, when he himself furnishes the money to pay the premiums the transaction is legitimate at any age and free from the suspicion of speculation.

2. Repeated mortality investigations have established beyond any question of doubt that, when the speculative

and moral hazards are eliminated, women are as good risks as men, if not better.

While there are still companies which charge women an extra premium of about $5 per $1000 insurance yearly, most of the companies overcome the hazards by limiting the beneficiaries to minor children and dependents. Such companies have had a satisfactory experience in insuring women.

3. Twenty-four years ago the Commonwealth of Pennsylvania enacted a law requiring a copy of the application, or any instrument referred to in the policy as a part of the contract, to be attached. Other states have done the same. This is a wise and proper provision and is being carried out voluntarily by many companies in states where it is not required. This law and practice are the outcome of litigation. In cases of contest claimants frequently have not learned until coming into court that a breach of warranty actually existed. It is true, however, that no company would have refused claimants a copy of the application prior to litigation; and it is also true that the knowledge of the contract given by the attached copy of the application does not deter ambitious attorneys from attempting to enforce payment of claim even in case of material breach of warranty.

4. The provision in all policies, that they shall not become binding until delivery during the lifetime and good health and upon actual payment of premium, has become, under the methods in vogue, an absolute necessity. Courts have even held that in the event of a change in the physical condition of the applicant between the date of application and the delivery of the contract the warranty is continuous, and that it is the duty of the applicant to give notice to the company of the changed conditions before accepting the contract.

Where no consideration has passed, where the agent has not given a binding receipt to put the policy in force as soon as the risk is accepted by the company, such decisions as referred to seem just and right. The applicant for insurance, until he has actually made payment of the premium, is in a position to temporize and procrastinate. He often does so, and as a matter of justice his delay should be at his own risk and not at that of policy-holders.

5. Restrictions with reference to occupations have been materially modified or entirely dispensed with during the last two decades. All companies at the inception of the contract take into account the hazards of occupations and impose conditions or rates to cover them, but it is so rare for men to change from less to more hazardous occupations that the majority of the companies, especially after the first policy year, have removed all restrictions, and this is particularly true under deferred dividend policies.

6. It has often been said, "In time of peace prepare for war." The long continued peace seems to have impressed a number of companies with the idea that there is no need of being prepared for war. Such companies have removed all restrictions with reference to military and naval service. In the statistics of war hazards there is no justification for doing this. In the late Civil War, as well as in European wars a generation or more ago, the proportion of the insured to the general population was so small as to produce no serious result to the companies, even if they had no policy restrictions. This condition has been changed; about one-half of the male population is now carrying insurance of some kind. In case of a general or extensive war the companies without restrictions might be wiped out of existence by a few battles. Hence, the removal of all restrictions is simply liberality gone mad. The people who insist on having a "wide-open" policy should realize that in several respects there is great peril and danger to them in such a policy.

It was my privilege, in the capacity of consulting actuary for the Army Officers' Association, to review the records of the United States War Department, from the institution of the department to the year 1893. From these records tables were constructed showing the war hazards as well as the mortality in military life. As a result I reached the conclusion that a company which entirely eliminates restrictions in time of war is recreant to its trust.

The clause in the policies with reference to military and naval service in time of war has, as a rule, been constructed on such equitable and reasonable lines as to render it unobjectionable. A clause which seems to me to be the most desirable is that which provides for the payment of an extra premium and a permit, and in the absence of the same provides for the scaling of the policy in the proportion of the war mortality to the tables upon which the premiums are based.

It is quite possible that with the increase of the insured population, in lieu of subsequently pensioning the widows of deceased soldiers, on declaring war the government might make provision for the payment of the extra war hazard premiums of the insured who enlist. The details of such a scheme could be worked out satisfactorily.

7. It has been assumed that a sane person will not commit suicide, and that therefore it should not be made a defense to a claim under the terms of the policy. This assumption has again and again been demonstrated to be a fallacy. While a certain proportion of suicides are no doubt irresponsible, the great majority are rational and thoroughly conscious of what they are doing. The proof of this lies in the statistical fact that companies and societies which have no suicide clause in the first few policy years have had from three to fivefold greater percentages of deaths by suicide than they have had in subsequent years. It is true that the deaths have not always been designated as suicidal, but the remarkable fact remains that the so-called accidental deaths have been much greater in the first than in subsequent policy years. If this is not due to a conscious selection against the companies, then how

else can it be accounted for? Again, some of the fraternal societies which have had no suicide provision, by adopting such a clause materially reduced the per cent. of suicides.

It is exceedingly difficult, in cases where suicide is suspected, to get the true cause of death properly stated in the proofs of loss and claim. Suicide at once becomes a sort of stigma upon the immediate family, and because of this and because a frank and honest admission might defeat the recovery of insurance, every means is resorted to to conceal the true cause of death.

In the interest of good morals and the elevation of the human race every policy of life insurance for at least the first two years should impose a penalty for death by suicide.

8. The restrictions with reference to dueling and violating law, or death by the hand of justice, have either been entirely removed or so modified as practically to amount to nothing. Happily, dueling is now regarded as an act of cowardice instead of bravery, and it is so seldom resorted to for the settlement of disputes or for the defense of honor as to make its elimination from the life insurance contract entirely practical. There is, however, a form of violation of law which has become quite serious in some states, and for which no remedy has been found. I refer to the feuds as a result of which a number of policy-holders have been murdered in cold blood at the expense of other policy-holders who had no part in the feuds. Indeed, there are sections of our country where the life companies for a time found it necessary to decline to do business. Feuds create conditions that cannot be met by policy restrictions.

9. The great care exercised by the companies generally in the selection of risks, excluding all persons of questionable habits, renders a policy clause against intemperance practically of no value. This is why a large proportion of the companies have no provision against intemperance.

10. The improvement in sanitary conditions and in the means of travel has justified the companies in eliminating most of the restrictions upon residence. About one-half of the companies have no restrictions whatever. A man can take out a policy in this country to-day, pay for it, and to-morrow travel to and reside in a country where the mortality is admittedly twofold. I fully agree, because statistics show that a restriction in the temperate zone is unnecessary, but I can find no justification for allowing persons to take out policies in the temperate zone at regular rates, and then permitting them to live in the fever-stricken sections of the tropics without requiring an extra premium. No argument against this is necessary beyond the statistics of our American companies which do business in the tropics. While it is true that they collect a larger premium, it is also true that about 50 per cent. of such larger current premium is required to pay the current losses, while in the temperate zone about 25 per cent. of a smaller premium is sufficient. Hence, conservatively managed companies incorporate some policy restriction which will neutralize the effect of residence and travel either in portions of the tropics or in portions of the frigid zone.

11. The public sentiment already referred to as due to unfortunate insurance conditions following the Civil War is responsible for a division of opinion among the life companies with regard to the so-called incontestable clause. One class — and this class is decidedly in the minority — favors what is known as the "open door" policy, which in effect provides that after the policy has been issued the company is precluded from raising any question as to the validity of the contract. This class of companies must of necessity employ a retinue of inspectors and detectives to learn all about the character of the risk before a policy is issued. This involves a large expense which must be borne by the existing policy-holders.

Another class of companies believes that every applicant should personally become responsible for the truth of his own statements for a limited time — usually two years — without entailing on the other policy-holders the expense incident to the special and searching investigations necessary in case a policy is incontestable from date of issue.

There are not only common law questions, but questions of public policy involved. As a common law principle fraud vitiates contracts. As a matter of public policy, no man should be allowed either for himself or his dependents to profit by his own fraud. Hence, 96 per cent. of the companies do not issue policies incontestable from date of issuance. Instead their policies become incontestable usually two years afterward. This gives a company the opportunity, in the regular course of business, of verifying the statements upon which the contract is based, and if it finds that untrue and fraudulent statements have been made, and the insured does not voluntarily surrender the policy when called upon to do so, equity proceedings are usually instituted to compel its surrender.

The courts of several states have held such policies, after the lapse of the contestable period, to be absolutely incontestable, because the company issuing such a policy has reserved to itself a period of time to investigate and discover any false or fraudulent statement that would vitiate the policy. If it fails to investigate and discover, the fault is its own and, therefore, it cannot avail itself of the common law principle which obtains in case the policy is made incontestable from date of issuance, viz., that fraud vitiates or renders null and void all contracts. It may therefore be contended, with considerable force, that the few companies which have no incontestable clauses are better protected against fraud than those which do have such clauses. On the other hand, if the fraud is of such a character as not to be detected within two years it cannot be serious and, by the express terms of the contract, should not be allowed to affect it.

12 and 13. The feature of grace in the payment of premiums had its origin in the desire of the companies to do all they could within the limits of safety to avoid lapses. Its principal effect is to postpone the last day of payment, or the final due date. Therefore, if a policy-holder, instead of using the days of grace as a margin to avoid lapse, should get into his mind that instead of the final day of payment being March 1 it is March 30, and should procrastinate accordingly every year, he would lose all the benefits of the feature.

Reinstatement should not be simply a matter of grace, but a matter of right under the contract, upon compliance with reasonable requirements to prevent those who purposely lapse their policies from coming back into the company after they have become afflicted with disease.

14, 15, and 16. The non-forfeiture and dividend provisions, as also those covering payment of claims, are features upon which there is such a degree of unanimity and such uniformity of practice that there is little to be said beyond what will be disclosed by the examination of the policies of any reserve company.

In a general way, however, I will say that cash surrender values are not only liable to defeat the very purpose of protection for which insurance stands, but to encourage selection against the company; and that the non-forfeitable values, through competition, have become liberal to a fault. A company that imposes penalty for discontinuance will best serve its persisting policy-holders.

The dividend clauses, whether annual or deferred, should be explicit, direct, unequivocal, and enforcible. A contract that does not clearly and distinctly draw the line between surplus and distributive surplus, and that without some governing, fundamental principle leaves the rules and directors of the company in the future to determine what surplus is or is not distributive, is objectionable.

The ideal policy stipulates the governing principle which

in the matter of distributing profits is binding both upon the insurer and the insured.

. . . .

The conditions[1] mentioned in the preceding sections under the laws as they existed in 1905 are referred to as not having been handicapped by legal restrictions, and although the liberty resulted in abuse, the public derived benefit from the great variety of contracts which could have been possible only in the absence of statutory policy provisions. What has been said in the preceding sections, therefore, has application to over five million life insurance contracts in existence. Conditions, however, have changed. In the year 1906, the legislature of the State of New York, following a legislative investigation into the methods of a few life insurance companies of that State, enacted various laws intended for the better regulation of the business of life insurance. Among such laws was one providing standard forms of policies to be used by the companies of that State. This has already been repealed. In its place, however, the legislature adopted statutory policy provisions substantially on the line of those adopted in fifteen other states of the Union.

Under the head of "Classification of Risks" will be found the classification then in use by fifty-one companies. The management of these companies classified according to the experience of the companies and the preconceived ideas of the managers. Such classification as to new business has been largely eliminated, and the following statutory provisions substituted, which must be inserted in the policies:

[1] The preceding paper on policy contracts was written by Mr. Fouse in 1905. The upheaval in the insurance world which was even then taking place produced so many changes in policy contracts that Mr. Fouse consented to add the following pages to his former paper. What appears in his former article applies to so many existing contracts, however, that students of insurance cannot afford to overlook it. (Editor.)

1. A provision that premiums shall be payable in advance at the home office of the company, or to an agent upon delivery of a receipt signed by one or more officers named in the policy and countersigned by such agent.

2. A provision for a grace of one month in the payment of every premium after the first.

3. A provision that the policy shall be incontestable after two years, except for non-payment of premiums and except for violation of the conditions of the policy relating to naval and military service in time of war.

4. A provision that the policy shall contain the entire contract and that all statements made by the insured shall be deemed representations and not warranties, and no such statement shall avoid the policy unless contained in a written application, a copy of which shall be attached to the policy when issued.

5. A provision that if the age of the insured has been misstated, the amount payable under the policy shall be such as the premiums paid would have purchased at the correct age.

6. A provision for ascertainment and distribution of surplus annually after the first policy year (in some states after third or fifth policy year), and that the owner of the policy shall have the right each year to elect to receive the current dividend upon the policy in cash; or to have it applied to the payment of premiums, or to the purchase of paid-up additions to the policy; or to be left to accumulate at a rate of interest to be specified, but withdrawable at any anniversary of the policy.

7. A provision that the owner of the policy may at any time after three years borrow on the sole security of the policy a sum equal to the reserve upon the policy at the end of the current policy year and any dividend additions thereto, less any indebtedness on the policy and interest in advance to the end of the current policy year, and that failure to repay such loan or to pay interest thereon shall not avoid the policy unless the total indebtedness thereon

shall equal or exceed the loan value at the time of such failure.

8. A provision whereby, in the event of default in premium payments after three years, the owner of the policy shall be entitled to extended or paid-up insurance, the net value of which shall be at least equal to the entire reserve upon the policy and any dividend additions thereto at date of default, less a sum not exceeding 2½ per cent. of the amount insured by the policy and any dividend additions thereto, and less any existing indebtedness to the company on the policy; also that the policy in such event may be surrendered for a specified cash value at least equal to the value of such extended or paid-up insurance.

9. A table showing in figures the loan value and options upon default in premium payments.

10. A provision for reinstatement of the policy within three years after default in premium payments upon furnishing evidence of insurability satisfactory to the company and payment of arrears of premiums.

11. A provision that when the policy shall become a claim by the death of the insured, settlement shall be made not later than two months after receipt of due proof of death.

12. A table showing the number and amount of instalments in which the proceeds of the policy may be payable.

13. A title on the face and on the back of the policy correctly describing the policy.

In addition to the statutory provisions as to what clauses the policy shall contain there have also been enacted laws prohibiting any of the following provisions:

1. A provision for forfeiture of the policy for failure to repay any loan thereon or interest on such loan while the total indebtedness on the policy is less than the loan value thereof.

2. A provision limiting the time within which any action at law or in equity may be commenced to less than

a specified period, varying from one to five years in different states.

3. A provision whereby the policy would provide for a premium rate at any age younger than age at date of application.

4. Any provision for any mode of settlement at maturity of less value than the amount insured, stated on the face of the policy, plus dividend additions, if any, less any indebtedness to the company.

The objections to statutory provisions are:

(*a*) They prevent development and improvement in life insurance in accord with the experience and progress of the age.

(*b*) The officials of every sovereign state, in obedience to the law of such state, are not always amenable to comity and, therefore, exact requirements that impose upon the companies and consequently upon the policy-holders excessive burdens that do not benefit the business and are in fact detrimental to it.

(*c*) In the absence of national supervision of insurance, standard policies and standard provisions are not practical, and sooner or later will be repealed, or national supervision will be adopted. Even though a reasonable degree of uniformity may be secured at one sitting of the legislature, at the next sitting it may be undone, and chaos and lack of harmony with other states created.

The advantages to be gained by the statutory policy provisions are:

(*a*) A greater degree of uniformity in contracts and less difficulty and expense on the part of the insured in interpreting contracts. This is evidenced by an examination of the classification of the restrictions of fifty-one companies as represented above, as compared with the restrictions and provisions set forth in this section.

(*b*) A careful examination will show that the provisions and policy conditions which obtained in the contracts of a majority of the fifty-one companies referred to above have been incorporated in the statutory provisions, and they are, therefore, in keeping with the best practice among the better class of companies. To this extent the enactment of the statutory provisions has been beneficial, and, upon the whole, will serve, educationally, a good purpose, even though such provisions should not, in the absence of national supervision, become a permanent feature of life insurance.

CHAPTER XVI

POLICY CONDITIONS [1]

IT is one of the characteristics of the American that when he takes up a fresh line of research or a new pursuit he is prone to concentrate his energies upon the particular subject which happens to engage his attention until he has exhausted its every useful possibility or developed it to such an extent that it seems incapable of further improvement. It is to this national characteristic that we owe much of our success as a people in practical pursuits, invention, commerce, and war. For the past ten years the architects of life insurance have been exhibiting this national characteristic in the development of special features in policy contracts. To such an extent has this tendency been carried that the good old-fashioned forms of life and endowment policies appear to be struggling for an existence amidst a mass of consols, debentures, bonds, and income policies.

These new forms of policies are generally produced by combining with the simpler forms of life and endowment policies a deferred annuity element guaranteeing to the insured after a specified period of years, or to a beneficiary on the death of the insured, an attractive income — usually, but improperly, called interest — upon the principal sum of the policy. In some instances an attempt is made to enhance the value of the policy by paying the income through a trust company or by attaching negotiable

[1] By John B. Lunger, Vice-President of the Travelers Insurance Company, Hartford. Reprinted from pages 178–211 of "Insurance, a Text-Book."

coupons to the policy. While the spirit of life insurance is keenly in sympathy with features intended to provide for old age or to guard the final effectiveness of the proceeds of a policy, care should be exercised in drafting contracts intended to subserve such excellent purposes to include only such benefits as are within the legitimate scope of the business. If an income (interest) is to be paid after the maturity of the policy, the rate assumed should be kept within the rate which the company makes use of in computing its policy liabilities, and the payments should be made direct to the insured or to the beneficiary. If the rate is made to appear larger than can be earned on a safe investment, or the deferred annuity element is merely a subterfuge to secure an extra loading on the premium, the policy is liable to become an instrument of deception.

The expediency of issuing policies with negotiable interest coupons is seriously open to question. It should always be borne in mind that the function of life insurance is to protect the family and to provide for adversity or old age; not to furnish securities to be bought and sold in the open market or passed from hand to hand, like railroad stocks or bonds. It is to be hoped that this particular feature will soon be numbered among the things of the past.

We might properly take exception to certain other of these basal features, but in the main the tendency has been in the right direction, and out of the many innovations, advantages will accrue which will prove of lasting benefit to the business.

There are no statistics upon which to base an estimate of the losses incurred through unwise investment of the sums paid to beneficiaries as death claims, but when one observes how very few have solved the problem of investing even small sums beyond risk of loss, it is not surprising that the officers of life insurance companies should feel great concern regarding the preservation of the sums paid to beneficiaries, especially when it is considered that such payments often constitute the only provision which the insured has been able to make for those dependent upon him. We should welcome, therefore, any feature which will protect the insurance after the death of the policyholder and serve to safeguard the purposes for which the insurance was taken. The plan of paying policy moneys in instalments is so in keeping with this thought that it is worthy of special mention and commendation. There are two ways in which instalment policies are made payable. The first form limits the payments to a specified period of years, generally ten, fifteen or twenty, and the second form, which is by far the more preferable, provides for at least twenty annual payments, and if the beneficiary is living at the end of this period, the payments are continued during the remainder of life. This latter method of payment is embodied in what is known as the continuous instalment policy, and when that policy is so drawn that the instalments cannot be assigned or commuted during the life of the beneficiary, it constitutes to my mind the ideal form of protective life insurance.

One of the prominent companies safeguards its insurance in another way. It will, at the request of the insured, attach to its policy a certificate, in which the insured may define his wishes as to the disposition of his policy. Generally a beneficiary is named to whom a stated income is paid as long as the proceeds of the policy will permit. Interest is allowed upon the fund remaining in the hands of the company, at a rate of about ½ of 1 per cent. less than the rate the company earns upon its investments. The proceeds of a policy to which this certificate is attached become a trust fund which is administered strictly in accordance with the wishes of the person by whom the trust was established. The payments made are free from taxation and all other charges.

I would venture to predict, as one of the outcomes of the present tendency amongst men of wealth to place their estates in trust, that a considerable number of the policies written in the future for large amounts will include either the instalment or the trust features which have just been described.

Among the special features wisely developed in recent years under the non-forfeiting tontine or accumulation policy is the privilege given the insured of making a choice among various methods of settlement at the end of the first dividend period. This feature has added greatly to the popularity of the form of insurance mentioned. The insured is no longer confined to one of two alternatives: (*a*) remain in the company and take insurance, (*b*) get out and take cash (often with a large discount); nor is he obliged to decide at the inception of his insurance what disposition he will make of his policy at the end of the first dividend period. At least three options are always given, namely, the privilege of withdrawing in cash the entire proceeds of the policy, consisting of the reserve and the accumulated dividend; or of applying the proceeds to purchase paid-up insurance at net rates; or to purchase an annuity. When the form of insurance permits, these three options are supplemented by others, which consist of combinations of cash and insurance, insurance and an annuity, annuity and cash, and so on; the options as a whole being so comprehensive that at the end of the dividend period the insured may adjust his policy to suit his then condition of life.

The practice of writing surrender values in dollars and cents in the policy, instead of merely giving the rule by which such values will be calculated, is helping to dissipate the idea that life insurance contracts are full of technicalities and pitfalls. It is to be regretted that some of our leading companies hesitate to adopt this practice, and for no other reason, apparently, than that it increases the liability to error in writing the policy, and puts them to a slight extra expense. Errors can be avoided by the proper checks, and the expense will be met many times over by the diminution in lapses, which is the invariable result of a clear and liberal policy. So far as I am informed, the first serious mistake in writing these tables has yet to occur. It is to be hoped that this feature will extend until all life insurance policies are so explicit that inability to read will be the only excuse that can be given for a failure to comprehend them in all their details.

The embodiment of cash loan privileges in policy contracts may be regarded as one of the most important new features in life insurance. The right of the insured to an equity in the reserve on his policy finds, in my judgment, its best recognition in the granting of loans at stated times upon reasonable terms and conditions. How often is it noticed that when the holder of a policy finds himself in trouble he hastens to apply for the cash value of his policy, although it is evident that at such a time life insurance is an urgent necessity and should not be abandoned without careful consideration. How much better for all concerned if the desired relief can be gained without the entire sacrifice of that which, in the event of death of the insured, may stand between those depending upon him and penury. The officers of companies granting cash loans will undoubtedly certify that in the panicky times of 1893–94 the relief given through loans on policies saved many thousands of policy-holders from serious financial trouble, while enabling them to continue the much needed insurance, and those benefited on their part will, no doubt, gladly testify to their appreciation of a plan which confers such important and timely advantages. In granting cash loans it is the practice in some companies to allow the loan upon application, without regard to the continuance of the payment of the premium on the policy. This practice is open to some of the objections that may be urged against cash surrender values. It is better to require that the premium for the ensuing insurance year shall be paid in advance, basing the loan upon the reserve in that year. By this plan the insured always secures a year, at least, in which to free himself from his financial difficulties and to make provision for the payment of the ensuing premium on his policy.

The premium lien note is but a modified form of the cash loan, and its use is to be encouraged when the financial difficulties of the insured affect only his power of paying his current premium. These notes are commonly drawn as a permanent lien on the policy, payable at the convenience of the insured. This convenient time, as is the case with most matters relating to life insurance when left to the discretion of the insured, is apt seldom to arrive, and the notes, therefore, generally become a permanent incumbrance on the policy. It has often occurred to me that if these notes could be drawn after the style of an ordinary note of hand, and made payable at the end of a stated period at a national bank, that a large percentage of them would be paid in cash. In event of non-payment they could be renewed for a further period, provided the policy was continued in force.

Among the new features introduced during the five years succeeding the Civil War was the first use of the return-premium idea in this country. Later it came into much wider use, and at the present time a considerable fraction of the life insurance contracts issued are in effect increasing insurances during the first twenty years of their existence, the annual increase being equal to the premium or to some proportion thereof. This appendix to the original contract has, in many cases, been the source of intense gratification to the heirs of the insured. It was Carlyle who pointed out that the mental satisfaction derived from any newly received possession depends on the ratio of what we receive to what we expected to receive. How often has it happened, in the settlement of death claims of policies which carried no return-premium attachment, that the deduction of unpaid fractional premiums from the understood amount, or in more serious measure of loans which the insured had obtained against the policy, has left the net result in the minds of the beneficiaries one of discontent, and how much more agreeable to all concerned are such settlements when that little return-premium attachment has provided the extra amount which covers all the company's claims against the insurance, and still leaves to the heirs some excess over the nominal face of the policy.

Our business has sometimes been referred to as one of risks, chiefly of death. Those who are familiar with the statistics know that so long as medical directors are restricted in their selection of lives by present rules and traditions, the "risk of death" may be forecast to an almost absolute certainty, and that the resulting deaths will be well within the tabular limits. The stringent selection of risks is chiefly due, in my opinion, to the pressure put upon the companies to pay large dividends. When this pressure is reduced, and the payment of dividends becomes, as it should be, a subsidiary feature of life insurance, the ratio of mortality will be somewhat nearer the tabular expectation, and there will have been a great addition to the usefulness of the business. In the meantime, many worthy applicants and their families must suffer because existing conditions demand low mortality ratios.

Until mortality becomes a more elastic factor, any plan which will give insurance to an under-average risk ought to be as welcome to the business as a breath of cool air to a fevered patient. Policies on under-average lives have been issued in England for many years, but the business has never assumed large proportions. Several small companies have been formed in this country for the purpose of making a specialty of this class of business, but those which have not failed have either drifted into regular channels or are still in the experimental stage. It is only recently that one of the prominent American companies has entered this very promising field. That company several years ago formed a special department for the collection of data pertaining to its declined risks. The information obtained was classified and special mortality tables were then computed upon which that company is now issuing policies subject to liens or extra premium, or both, to a large percentage of applicants who, under former conditions, would have been declined. Of all the new features in our business, this one is capable of the largest development and offers the best field for investigation and study. Life insurance should be a broad business of underwriting any reasonable contingency of life or death.

The practice of paying claims promptly, and of guaranteeing this in the policy, has blown away one of the clouds that formerly cast its shadow over life insurance, and may be fittingly referred to as a special feature. It is neither delicate nor prudent to force money on a beneficiary at a time when her mind is distracted by grief, but as soon as proofs of death are made out, both good taste and judgment dictate that payment of the claim should not be delayed. "Pay all debts promptly," is as good a maxim to follow in life insurance as in our private affairs.

There are a number of new features of minor importance in ordinary insurance that I might refer to if so disposed, but none of them seem to call for special comment beyond that they, together with the more important special features, the elimination of technical and objectionable conditions and the increase in surrender values, have aided to produce the policy of to-day, with its freedom from restrictions, its brevity, its clearness of statement, and its remarkable adaptability to every reasonable contingency.

. . . .

The fact that most life insurance companies are conducted on the mutual plan under which all profits revert to the insured, and the desire of the insured to secure the largest possible returns for the premiums paid, combine to make dividends and the methods of their distribution a subject of great importance; but it does not necessarily follow that so much stress should be laid on these features of the business as to lead one not familiar with life insurance to think that payment of dividends is the chief object of the business. More circulars were woven around, and more arguments based upon, the $18,000,000 of dividends that the companies paid out last year than upon the $80,000,000 that were distributed in death claims and endowments. Agents, in soliciting, fall into the same error, and discourse more eloquently upon the dividend which a particular policy will pay than upon all its other benefits combined; and when two agents meet in competition, one representing a semi-tontine company and the other an annual dividend company, many of the intrinsic merits of life insurance are lost sight of in the smoke that arises from the fiery arguments for and against these two methods of paying dividends.

. . . .

The inclination to mold the policy contract to the varying conditions of life has not been confined to the benefits secured by persistency, but is observable also in the development of plans whereby the rights of the policy-holder in case of the surrender of his policy are recognized. Surrender values were first allowed in the form of paid-up insurance. Subsequently cash surrender values were introduced, and more recently extended insurance has become a feature in policy contracts of several companies. At the present time the policies of a large number of the companies provide, in case of surrender, for a choice between paid-up insurance and extended insurance, or between cash and paid-up insurance, while the policies of several companies offer either cash, paid-up insurance, or extended insurance. Only two or three companies offer paid-up insurance alone, and it is but a question of time when these companies will yield to the pressure of the general practice. Each of the allowances made in case of surrender is computed on such a liberal basis that it would seem that the vexatious question of the proper charge or fine in case of surrender is being settled by requiring none at all. It is gratifying to find that this liberality has not encouraged surrenders, but has been rewarded by an increase in the tenure of life of the policy. In fact, we are led to the pleasant conclusion that the owner of a policy containing liberal and valuable benefits is as slow to part with it as he would be to sell any other valuable and profitable security.

As surrender values will be discussed analytically and at length in other papers to be presented to this Convention, I shall limit this section of my paper to a few brief remarks on the advantages or disadvantages of the three non-forfeiture benefits mentioned.

The especial applicability of either of these benefits can only be determined by a knowledge of the condition of the policy-holder at the time of surrender, taken with the standing of the policy. In the case of a policy which has acquired considerable value, it is advisable in the majority of cases for the policy-holder to take paid-up insurance, especially if he is well along in years and his income is uncertain or is growing less as time goes by. Paid-up insurance does not entail any obligation or impose any burden, nor is it brought to a close except by death or surrender. It is a security which can be filed away with the certainty that when it matures it will realize every dollar which it represents. Extended insurance, on the other hand, is the more advantageous benefit for those to take who are unable to pay their premiums, but who feel the need of a maximum of insurance, and expect within a reasonable time to be able to reinstate their contracts or to take new insurance. Extended insurance is generally granted without application; in other words, it is given automatically, thus protecting the policy in case the payment of the premium is overlooked during sickness or absence from home. Automatic extensions have this particular value — that no one is deprived of the equity in his policy through any technicality or through indifference or ignorance as to its value.

To my mind, in every policy issued, either paid-up or extended insurance should be made "automatic," and the companies should not rest content with merely granting this privilege, but should, in event of lapse, wait a reasonable time for the insured to apply for a surrender value, but if he does not appear within this time he should be followed up and a statement placed in his hands giving the value of the benefit to which he is entitled.

The arguments which I have advanced in favor of making provision in the policy for every emergency of life point to the advisability of granting liberal cash values after the necessity of protection may have passed away and provision for self may have become the first consideration, or after the policy has been in force for the period for which in the first instance it was advisedly taken out. While the propriety of allowing cash surrender values for the purpose which I have defined is apparent, there is little to justify the guarantee of annual cash surrender values in the early years of a policy, unless it is that we must take a very cold-blooded view of our business, and say that an equity in the reserve on the policy belongs to the insured, and that he should have the right to do as he pleases with this equity. I would contend that the insured having advisedly entered into a compact with the company to provide certain benefits for his family and for himself, such compact imposes on the company the obligation to protect the insured from a hasty or perhaps a foolish step that may defeat the good object he had in mind when he entered upon the contract.

A man is not likely to apply for a cash surrender value in the early years of a policy unless he has, through ignorance or prejudice, become dissatisfied with the company in which he is insured, or unless he is in such a tight place financially that he must secure cash at all hazards. A man who demands cash for the reason first given is entitled only to the same consideration that we would give to any impulsive or thoughtless request. In the case of a man whose affairs are so badly involved that he is obliged to resort to his policy for financial help, it is fair to assume that, by reason of his difficulties, he needs life insurance more at that particular time than at any other period in his life. It seems more in accordance with the spirit of life insurance to give him the desired assistance in the form of a loan and to extend with it the opportunity of continuing the life insurance. There are individual cases, of course, the circumstances surrounding which call for cash surrender values. Such cases should be taken up on their respective merits, but it does not follow, because cash values can with propriety be allowed in certain cases, that the interests of policy-holders or of the company require that they shall be given in all cases, irrespective of conditions.

In conclusion, I wish to express a thought that comes to me very forcibly as I write these lines. It is that the remarkable improvements and changes in our business in the past few years are influenced by motives more sincere and subtle than would be dictated by mere business policy.

Can we not discover in them evidence of a growing sense of conviction on the part of those to whom the administration of our companies is confided, that life insurance is a trust imposing moral as well as literal obligations which must be observed to the utmost degree?

We may not claim that life insurance has reached a state of perfection, but we may assert that the tendencies of the business are in the right direction, and that there are forces at work which will produce further and beneficial transformations as time goes by.

CHAPTER XVII

SURRENDERS AND LOAN PRIVILEGES [1]

WHEN we come to consider the matter of surrender values from the point of view of mutuality, we meet a situation involving opposing elements. The company has agreed for a certain premium to carry the policy for the lifetime of the insured or for a definite term of years, and, the premium being paid, it has ordinarily no option of discontinuance. Its calculations rest, and must rest, on the theory of the continuance both of its risks and of its premium income to their normal term. But it protects its theory by no contract to that effect from the insured. He is free to pay or stop paying, regardless of his family's need on the one hand, or his ability on the other. For some reason he stops. What considerations of duty should govern the company in its treatment of the case? To whom now does it owe duty; and, if to more than one person or group of persons, upon what several interests of these is this duty grounded; by what divergence of these interests or by what conflict between them is duty toward one or the other of them controlled or modified; which group is entitled to have its interests first considered?

There can be no question that the company's first duty is to those to whom it remains under contract obligation — its continuing policy-holders. It is first to consider how they are affected by a withdrawal of one of their number;

[1] By Jacob H. Greene, late President of the Connecticut Mutual Life Insurance Company, Hartford. Reprinted from pages 167–178 of "Insurance, a Text-Book."

how the sure basis of its operations, the solvency of its contracts, and the future cost of their administration stand affected. The elements of the problem are definite; the determination of their weight, the measurement of their operative force, is somewhat a matter of varying circumstances.

The effect of withdrawals is in three directions: they reduce numbers, thus narrowing the basis for averages, increasing the range of fluctuation, intensifying its effect, and prejudicing steadiness of operation; they presumably take out not only unimpaired lives, but the best lives, at least those having the strongest unconscious instinct of an enduring vitality; while this may not be and is not always the case under ordinary conditions inviting continued confidence, it would be unsafe to predicate any treatment of them upon any other assumption which there is no after opportunity of rectifying, an assumption which would be realized to an appalling degree under conditions which impaired confidence in corporate integrity; and, thirdly, surrenders for cash interfere, and may conceivably very seriously interfere, with that employment of the funds of the membership which is of the essence of financial stability and a most important factor in the reduction of current cost to continuing members.

On the other hand, it is to be borne in mind that in withdrawing the past member has exercised an unforbidden power, and that during his membership he has not only paid the current cost of his risk, but has also been making annual contributions to the reserve for the purpose of protecting the company against the future of his risk; a part of his increasing share in a future greater mortality contributed now because he is in theory expected to remain to share it without paying a correspondingly greater future premium. Against the greater future risk on his life as age increases the company has been laying aside each year a compensating sum out of a level premium. And now that future risk is eliminated by his termination of what was, at his option, and in the company's anticipation, a lifelong contract. The company is relieved of all liability for that future risk against which it has been reserving a sum from each premium paid.

The question now is: What in all-round equity — equity to him who has relieved the company of further liability, and equity to his associates from whom he has withdrawn the supporting vital and financial strength of his membership — shall be done with this man? How shall these dual elements of a situation which the company has left it in his power to create be held in just and true balance?

In general terms, the answer is and must be: do that which at once recognizes fully his free and legitimate right of withdrawal and the termination of the liability, but also that which is thoroughly conservative of every right interest of the membership from which he has withdrawn his support, of every interest, that is, which he, while a member, had in common with the rest.

If the withdrawal of members at any time, at discretion, did not affect the vital basis and therefore the sureness and steadiness of the company's operations, and did not so tend to introduce violent and dangerous fluctuations; and did not such withdrawals also tend to disturb and, under clearly probable conditions, to disturb very seriously those lines of financial management which the greatest good of the whole membership necessarily presupposes; and did not the duty of men to protect their families, which is the whole ground and aim of our proffered service to men and the reason for our existence, remain always the paramount fact and our primary point of view, and the one which should govern our treatment of every detail, and which gives to us the same plea to urge upon the old members for his continuance that we use in soliciting new members, and also lays upon us the duty to do what we justly and fairly can to see that those families which have been once committed to our care and sure protection are not lightly and easily exposed again to danger through any practice of ours, there would be no problem in the matter. We could freely give the departing member everything left from his past transactions with us. But every one of these propositions must be taken in the negative and taken seriously. The membership is the company, and the withdrawal of members narrows the basis of operation, and thus widens the range and intensity of fluctuation, and may be carried so far as to be destructive of a company's integrity. The company's investments are of funds held for a future; they must be made with a view to that future, and therefore of a character very different from those adapted to meet sudden and uncertain demands for which instantly and certainly available resources must be always in readiness. The scheme of life insurance proposes that its invested reserves shall be drawn upon only according to the foreknown and measurable operation of the law of mortality. The right of members to withdraw at any time, taking their contributions to reserve in cash, negatives the whole scheme, exposes the fund to be drawn upon at will, the draft upon it being, both in time and amount, dependent upon elements of motive which are unforeseen and incalculable, and of whose future operation nothing is known except that they exist, that they may be brought into great and most critical intensity of operation at any time by a variety of causes, and that they are uncontrollable by the company and have absolute free play against it. There is no defense against them except the blind hope that they may never operate.

The right of free surrenders for cash inverts the theory, and the only consistent, logical, and safe practice in life insurance, by making the reserve consist in effect of a mere group of individual deposits, subject to check at least once a year, and this feature of uncertain and precarious continuance of the insurance factor and of the right of withdrawal of invested funds becomes at once the dominant feature of the company's affairs and is the ultimate contingency to be kept always in view in every matter. The company, in effect, is no longer a life insurance company, treating all its affairs on a true life insurance basis, with withdrawal as a mere incident, subordinate in every respect to the integrity of its insurance operations, but a pseudo bank of deposit, liable to have all its funds withdrawn in any year, needing, therefore, to have its investments immediately convertible into cash without loss, while yet upon these funds are founded the presumably lifelong contracts for whose prosperous administration an entirely different theory of investment is essential and for the management of which a bank is utterly unfit.

So long as a company is rapidly growing and the average of its lives is still at a young age, and it has not reached that maturity necessary to complete its exposure to all the vicissitudes of mortuary and business experience, and its credit has escaped attack, the practical danger of these subverting factors will be at a minimum and their operation partly concealed, and hope may dwell in a fool's paradise. But the condition of growth is not an eternal one, no matter what energy, under what stimulus, be applied. To every company will come, ought to come, in time the condition when no pressure can make its inflow of new business exceed its outflow, and when its true normal will be a stable equilibrium in amount at risk, in assets, income, and outgo.

Consider a company in such a case — whether large or small does not signify — meeting those general business conditions which cause most men to take command of all available cash resources, with a membership which has been educated to regard their policies as tickets for cash practically on demand, and who have taken them in such a company because they were so available, who were willing to protect their families so long as they did not want to use the money themselves, but who, not having been educated to put family protection above every other interest and duty, would take that protection only where it would not interfere with their free use of the money when they wanted it, and what may that company reasonably, inevitably expect? It will suffer a withdrawal of its members, proportioned to the intensity of financial difficulty and pressure; in severe times a very great number, greatly reducing its vitality basis, certainly taking out its best and leaving its worst lives, and raising its mortality, and requiring the conversion of its best investments into cash at a most unfavorable moment for their sale, in order to enable it to pay out large sums to its outgoing members, thus destroying its own credit and furnishing strong reason to every sound life to get out.

The danger is an absolute, immeasurable, and most critical one. It has not yet appeared in full measure among American companies because few, if any, of those which are certainly exposed to its malign operation have yet reached the static condition which will leave no practical defense against its effects. But the conditions for a disastrous experience somewhere in the future are being fully prepared in many companies. The annual privilege of surrender for cash is now presented as a prime attraction; the bulk of the business is already exposed to be swept away by its exercise. The permanency of corporate life and uniformity of operation which are absolutely essential to the undertakings of a life insurance company are put completely at the caprice of members secured by an appeal to selfish interest, not to unselfish, paramount duty. In order to get new members the more easily, they are given unqualified power to wipe a company out of existence in any one year.

To do justice to the membership which remains, to protect the corporate life and integrity against capricious self-destruction or corrupt or malicious assault, to give still the family of him who withdraws of real necessity some remaining measure of that protection which is our function and their greatest need, and greatest when it cannot be longer paid for, and yet to recognize fully and equitably all that is due to the departing member whose future claim has lapsed, the only true, completely effective and safe method is to give paid-up insurance for the surrendered policy, for its unexpired term. This retains the member, minimizes the vital loss and the narrowing effect of withdrawal, and prevents disturbance, for the advantage to one, of the investments made for the common and equal benefit. Any other treatment of a withdrawing member ought to be rare and exceptional and governed in its detail by those special and rare circumstances which may rightfully constitute the exception for the individual as against the safety, profit, and general good of all the rest.

In a word, cash surrender values are false in principle, constantly destructive in tendency, expensive as calling for a maximum replacement of lost business, and dangerous to every operation by which a company proceeds to the fulfilment of its insurance obligations.

Concerning a proper surrender charge I wish to say only this: where paid-up insurance is given on a lapsing policy, the charge should have regard to the probable vitality loss on the amount of risk surrendered, and to the cost of replacing it by new memberships. These are variable elements, especially the latter. In the case of cash surrenders there is need of an additional charge in the nature of a safety fund or insurance against the destruction of the company or its reduction to perilous conditions by the free employment of the malign privilege. How much that part of the charge ought to be we have no means of knowing. We have only the conditions fairly set up for the future experience which will throw light on the matter. Some have already gone far enough to know that the danger is not imaginary and is something more than theoretical.

Akin to the annual cash surrender value in its destructive effect both upon the company's stability and existence and upon the protection of the family is the loan to the insured of the reserve upon his policy. Its sole virtue in comparison is that it does not at once and irrevocably destroy all the family's insurance, and leaves open the possibility of its restoration by the payment of the loan. But if it staves off the day of cash surrender it goes much more than half-way toward it. It gives the cash, leaves the full premium to be paid upon a reduced amount of insurance while the loan runs, and adds to the unreduced cost of a reduced insurance the interest on the loan. And, like the annual cash value, it has the abhorrent vice of teaching a man to consider himself first and his family last. Both in its suggestiveness and in the pressure of its conditions, it leads strongly toward lapse; and it is small wonder that so few loans are paid and so many lapses ensue.

I am aware — none better — that I have spoken to you, gentlemen commissioners, against an almost overwhelming drift of practices indulged in, not because they truly develop or conserve correct principles, but because they make it easy, for the moment, instead of hard, to get business; because in place of unselfish, persistent self-sacrificing duty, they present self-interest and a speculation; not because upon them one may build in assured soundness from the bottom up, but because one may thereby build rapidly and brilliantly, leaving to future storms the revelation of rock or sand in the foundation of these houses of hope for the families of our land. And I have so spoken to you because as the recognized and lawful guardians of the immeasurable public interest in these things, as those who are presumed and bound to know the true and to discriminate it from the specious, it is in your power to create a public intelligence, a public opinion, and a public conscience which will not always see the truth denied nor made of non effect.

CHAPTER XVIII

EXPENSES FOR AGENTS [1]

THE premium of a policy of life insurance is composed of two parts — the amount necessary to provide for the obligations assumed in the policy contract, and the portion added to meet the expenses of conducting the business. The net, or mathematical, premium is based on a mortality table and a rate of interest which it is assumed will provide for the final payment of claims whether they mature in the near or distant future. The expense portion may itself be divided into the amount required to meet the home office cost and that which is incurred in maintaining the agencies.

If it is proposed to start a new company, the question will naturally arise whether an agency force is indispensable in order to secure a sufficient number of members to justify the necessary cost of maintaining an office. Whether in the future such a company can be established on a permanent and satisfactory basis without agents may be a matter of opinion. It never has been accomplished in this country, and reference must, therefore, be had to foreign corporations of this character for information on this point.

Four English companies report that they pay no commissions. The oldest of these was organized in 1762, and the youngest in 1835. There is at this time no company organized since the latter date which is now in existence and attempting to conduct its affairs without

[1] By John M. Holcombe, President of the Phœnix Mutual Life Insurance Company, Hartford.

paying commissions for securing business and collecting premiums.

The oldest and best known of the British companies was organized in 1762. In 1839 it had about $70,000,000 of outstanding insurance and some $50,000,000 of assets. It has now about $41,000,000 of outstanding insurance and some $25,000,000 of assets. Its career has been a very remarkable one, especially in the low cost at which it has furnished insurance to its members. It is located in the heart of the city of London, within easy reach of some millions of people, and through its directors and policy-holders has a wide reputation for stability and for all those qualities which go to make up a mutual life insurance company satisfactory to its members. The largest number of policies it has issued in a single year in the past five years is 290, representing insurance to the amount of about $1,200,000. From a history of this company it appears that within the past seventy years it has very materially decreased its membership, outstanding insurance, and assets.

The other three companies referred to have made but little progress for many years. When these companies were organized and became firmly established the conditions were so different from those which now exist that no conclusions can be drawn from their early history which can be applied to the situation which would to-day confront those who would organize a life insurance company. So far as actual experience is a guide, it does not appear that such a corporation could, under the most favorable circumstances, secure a firm foothold without employing agents.

The consideration of an established company of considerable size may now be taken up. If its members are scattered over a large territory, it is for their advantage, as well as for the protection of the corporation itself, to have agencies at various points, in order that they may be accommodated in the payment of premiums and in taking advantage of the terms of policy contracts. If this is conceded, then a part of the agency expenses may fairly be said to pertain to outstanding business. But it still remains that in a modern and progressive life insurance company, which is growing in membership and resources, a considerable cost in procuring new business is incurred, not only in the agencies themselves but also in the conduct of the home office, from which point must emanate the materials for use in the field. Much has been said of late about the interests of policy-holders, and it is true that they should first be considered. Yet in this very question the fact must not be ignored that without new business a company will be in a condition of liquidation. It is clear that much of the new insurance which has been and is being placed upon the books of some of the companies has cost and is costing more, taken by itself, than it is worth to the old members. If, however, part of these expenditures may fairly be said to be incurred in the establishment of an agency force, looking to the future, it may still be for the interests of policy-holders that new business shall be acquired at what may appear to be an excessive cost.

It seems to be a well-established fact that even in a large community people will not to any considerable extent voluntarily apply for life insurance. If by education the people generally should themselves be led to seek life insurance, it must be considered what would be the result if applicants were to apply from considerable distances. In order to provide for absolute safety and equity, the members of a life insurance company must be chosen from a class so far similar in occupations, condition, and surroundings as to put them on a practical equality, or else the premiums must be graded according to the risks assumed. With one scale of premiums it is very evident that those persons who are below the average as risks would secure good bargains if they could get protection at the rates which were charged for select lives, and unless a company guards itself very carefully against the admission of under-average lives, there will be a marked inequality, and it is conceivable that disastrous results might follow. Competent and honest medical examiners must be chosen who will report the condition of applicants with accuracy. Moreover, deceptions can be practised even upon the most skilled examiners, and it is essential that a company shall guard itself against misrepresentations in stating the particulars called for in an application. Faithful and loyal agents, therefore, are necessary to produce those results which are in accordance with equity and even financial soundness; so that it is clear that if it is best for a company to secure business from a considerable territory, not only must agents bring the subject of life insurance to the attention of the people, but also they must guard the interests of the company in the applications which are made. Old policy-holders may well pay for a service which shall bring among their number new lives which shall experience a favorable mortality, and which shall share in the expenses of conducting the business.

It should not be lost sight of that in a company of considerable age, not only must the interests of the older policy-holders be guarded, but also that those who have lately taken insurance are entitled to the same consideration. In a condition of liquidation those who have been long insured might not suffer materially, but for the sake of the younger members the distant future should be foretold as accurately as possible. If an agency force is desirable in the interests of policy-holders, then it is also important that a company should be so organized as to make it attractive for young men to engage in agency work to take the places of those who will from time to time drop out. This can be accomplished only by maintaining a strong financial condition, by issuing attractive policy forms and by so compensating agents as to make the business lucrative. It is true that allowances to agents may be carried to such an extent as to prejudice the rights of policy-holders, but a well-established and satisfied body of agents is of very great importance to the permanency and the well-being of such an institution.

That the spread of life insurance protection among the people is beneficial not alone to those who enjoy this protection, but also to the community at large, cannot well be doubted. It should be kept in mind, however, that life insurance companies are not benevolent institutions and they have no right to use the funds of their members except for those purposes for which premiums are paid.

The reasoning which should be brought to bear upon this whole question is from the standpoint of the policy-holders, and while it is not practicable to fix definitely a limit for agency and home office expenses which have to do with acquiring new business, it may be said that these are legitimate if they do not go beyond the point where reasonable returns can be fairly expected.

The cost of establishing a new company is of necessity greater than that of maintaining an old one. In the first these expenditures are necessary. On the other hand, it may be that an old company will be benefited by the enlargement of its business, in which case an investment, so to speak, for an agency plant may be made within reasonable limits. No definite rule can be laid down on this subject, for each case must be considered in connection with the circumstances which surround it.

Altogether it cannot be gainsaid that an agency organization is necessary to the establishment of a new company or to the perpetuation of an old one. Whether in any particular case a wise investment can be made cannot be told with certainty by mere inspection of an annual statement. The best results in this business are often slow in coming. A larger inflow than can be thoroughly cared for may appear like prosperity, but may have in it elements of inequity or danger. The obligations imposed by a policy contract should not be evaded or postponed, and expenses of all kinds should be limited to those sums to be available after the insurance liabilities are fully provided for. Within this limit sound principles will not be violated by wise investments in intelligent and reliable agency forces, to which an increased revenue may be expected at a decreased ratio of expense.

CHAPTER XIX

DISTRIBUTION OF SURPLUS [1]

THE ideal of the contribution method for the distribution of the surplus of a mutual company is the return to each member of such share of the surplus as has been contributed by him. To this ideal no exception can be taken. Those who question the value of the method do so, not because they question the equity of returning to each member what his payments have contributed to the surplus, but because they do not admit that by the application of this so-called contribution method, as usually practised, this ideal result is reached with essentially greater accuracy than by other, and perhaps simpler, methods.

The application of this method, as usually explained, viz., to credit each member annually with the reserve or previous accumulation from his payments, the premium paid and the interest earned, and to debit him with his share of the losses and expenses of the company and with the reserve or sum which must be set aside to provide for a deficiency in the premium or the maturity of the policy in future, seems sufficiently simple; and so it is, merely as a book-keeping direction. But the determination of the equitable amount to be so debited on account of expenses is one of the most perplexing questions with which the actuary has to deal.

It is of the very essence of the contribution method that no member or class of members shall be made to pay for

[1] By Daniel H. Wells, Actuary of the Connecticut Mutual Life Insurance Company, Hartford. Reprinted with additions from pages 361–368, Volume II, "Transactions of the Actuarial Society of America."

the insurance furnished to any other member or class of members; that the cost of insurance shall not be increased to any individual or class because of the insurance of any other individual or class. Thus the reserves of the paid-up business should not be burdened with the expense of premium collections, nor the expense of handling such reserves assessed against the margins or loadings of premiums on premium-paying business. Newly selected lives should not be required to share the heavier death cost of those longer insured, nor the old members the reasonable cost of bringing the benefits offered by the company to the notice of new members.

We shall, perhaps, all agree that the expense of caring for investments should be paid out of the income from investments. I do not think it necessary to discuss this point at length, but only to emphasize it, that it may not appear as a disturbing factor in the remaining discussion. All forms of insurance which involve a reserve, or accumulation of assets, are necessarily and inseparably connected with investment. But this does not seem to me to warrant, certainly not to require, that the expense attending the investments should be paid otherwise than out of the earnings of such investments. The man who chooses insurance as an investment, or a form of insurance which involves large accumulations, has no right to ask that the expense attending the handling of funds held for his benefit shall be paid, in whole or in part, by those who insure under other plans. On the other hand, his funds should not be taxed for the payment of expenses other than those chargeable to their care, on the plea that from the nature of the business the company is able to make long or permanent investments, and so, perhaps, to realize somewhat better returns than investment companies generally. Such conditions are not inseparable from insurance contracts, and if one chooses to invest under such limitations he is entitled to any advantage to be derived from them.

Dismissing now the matter of investments and investment expenses, let us consider those expenses which have to do with what we may, for convenience, call pure insurance. In common with all insurance, life insurance is but a device for the wide distribution of losses, so that the loss which would embarrass or crush the individual, being distributed among the multitude, is borne by them without serious inconvenience. The service rendered is measured by the risk covered; the amount of the loss insured against multiplied by the probability of the occurrence of the loss — the death cost. If the expense incurred were proportional to this benefit, there would be no room for question as to the proper assessment of it. But to assess the expense in proportion to the benefit, wholly without regard to the cost of rendering the service, seems to me to be an abandonment of the principle of the contribution method (the return to each member of such share of the surplus as has been contributed by him) altogether. We are bound to assume that the expense incurred is reasonable, and necessary to the conferring of the desired benefit. Why, then, should others be taxed to pay it?

Disregarding for the present the distinction between old and new business, we note that certain items of expense — expenses incurred for the general supervision, care, protection, and extension of the business, such as salaries of officers and of a considerable part of the clerical force, legal expenses, most of the cost of advertising and supplies, a part of the expense for postage, telegraphing, etc., and, perhaps, a part of the taxes and fees paid — are dependent, in a general way, upon the magnitude of the interests at risk, rather than upon the number of individual policies, the amount insured under individual policies, or the premium rates. That is to say, the larger the interests at risk, the greater the labor and expense which must necessarily, or may profitably, be devoted to such matters; although such labor and expense are not directly dependent upon the number of the insured or of the policies upon the company's books, as are in large part, for instance, the expense of medical examinations and the clerical labor of keeping the agency accounts; nor upon the premium rates, as to a large extent agency commissions are. There is no controlling reason for the assessment of such general expenses pro rata of the membership, the policies in force, the amount insured, or the premium income. As investment expenses, which depend in a like general way upon the magnitude of the investments, are properly assessed pro rata of the income, the benefit earned, and not of the individuals interested, so it would seem the most equitable way to assess these general insurance expenses pro rata of the insurance benefit received, the death cost, or "cost of insurance."

I am aware that it has been urged against the assessment of expenses on the death cost, that it makes the expense on some forms of policies increase with the age. Probably this has had something to do with the introduction of the more usual practice of assessing such general expenses pro rata of the amount insured. But if the death rate at age 65 is four times the death rate at age 40, it is certain that, assuming the same amount at risk on each life, the company assumes four times as great a risk on, renders four times the service to, a life aged 65 as to one aged 40. The insurance of a given number of lives at 65 would involve as great a probable loss, with double the probable fluctuation, as the insurance of four times that number of lives aged 40. Would not essentially as great care and expense in the supervision of the business, in the selection of territory, of agents, of forms of contract, in the investigation and settlement of the equally numerous claims, in all the varied expenditures required for the replacing of the business lost by death and otherwise, be as necessary or advisable in the first case as in the second? And finally, while we cannot justly disregard the cause or origin of the expense, it is better to err in the assessing of it by making it follow more closely the benefit rendered than to err in the opposite direction.

Certain other items of expense, such as collection fees, the bulk of agents' commissions, exchange, and taxes on gross premiums, are based upon the premiums collected, and may, properly, and without serious practical difficulty, be so assessed.

Medical examinations and a part of the expense for clerical labor attach to policies, with but little or no reference to the amount insured, the premium, or the risk. If such expenses cannot be assessed against the individual policies, and such a course is impracticable under existing conditions and perhaps undesirable under any conditions, the death cost furnishes the best basis for their assessment. The medical examination, while exacted as a necessary condition of membership, and so properly to be assessed against the applicant, is intended to protect the members of the company against the introduction of under-average risks and an increased death rate; and so is for their protection and benefit in proportion to their proper share of the death cost. The expense for such clerical labor as has direct relation to individual policies is but small, and may be assessed on the death cost at least as equitably as on the amount insured or the premiums.

It seems to me, therefore, that the equity which is the aim of the contribution method, is most nearly attained by an assessment upon the investment income to pay all investment expenses, upon premiums to cover such expenses as are determined by the premiums, and upon the death cost, or what is technically called the cost of insurance, to cover all other expenses.

The cost of procuring new business has been increased by excessive competition until it has become a very serious tax upon the companies. I do not attempt at this time to set a limit to the expense which may be legitimately incurred for the procuring of business. I have to do only with the proper assessment of such expense. Whatever may be the cost of bringing insurance to the attention of the public, or the value of the new insurance placed, its value is to those insuring or their beneficiaries, not to those previously insured. It is true that some slight advantage may accrue to the existing membership from the broadening of the field for the operation of the law of average; and, in theory, some slight decrease in the expense rate might be possible later from the increase in volume of business. But certainly any such incidental advantage to the existing membership is more than offset by the advantage to the incoming member. He cannot in fairness ask that the special expense involved in bringing the benefits of the company to him should be shared by the existing membership on the plea that his incoming broadens the field, when the existing membership *constitute* the field to which he only adds his mite; when the benefits to him from the existence of such a membership are a hundred thousand times any benefit he can confer upon them. It is certainly sufficient that he be admitted to the common advantages of a more stable experience and a decreased expense ratio, if such result, without requiring that others be taxed to pay the cost of giving him these advantages. The assessing upon the old business of the expense of procuring new business cannot then be justified either upon the ground that the expense is due to, or is for the benefit of, the old business.

It is a difficult matter to analyze the expenses of the company with which one is officially connected, and with whose operations one is personally familiar, and arrive at a fairly approximate estimate of the expense directly or indirectly due to the writing of new business. It becomes an impossibility in the case of other companies. Yet I think I am warranted in saying that the average expense cost of new business, other than term business, as now written by our life companies, including, so far as chargeable to new business, commissions, salaries of managers of agencies, superintendents and special agents, traveling expenses, salaries of medical directors, medical examinations, advertising, rents, salaries of officers and clerks, etc., is probably over rather than under $30 per $1000 of new business on which a full year's premium is collected. Against this, the cost of caring for old business, exclusive of investment expenses, is probably considerably under $3 per $1000, and the saving from the lighter mortality on the new business for the first three or four years after its issue does not exceed an average of about $7 per $1000. Deducting the sum of these from the expense of new business, we still have a balance of at least $20 per $1000, to be provided for before the new business would be entitled to share on the same basis as the old in the distribution of surplus. These figures are in the rough, but they will serve the purpose of illustration.

If, now, a company writes $100,000,000 of continuing new business, on the average not less than $2,000,000 is sunk, planted if you prefer, for the time being, in excess of all that will be recovered from a reduced mortality, and under the present method of valuation the surplus is decreased by at least that amount to the injury and loss of the existing business. This sum is only recovered through a decrease in future dividends on the business so written, through future expenditures for the procuring of other new business. The existing membership is continually taxed for the procuring of new business, and no corresponding tax laid upon such new business in the future can ever adjust the injustice done to the continually changing existing membership. Further, the cost of new business is so large that no matter what may be assumed to be its value to the company or to the insured, a limit is put upon the amount a company can afford to write, varying with the size and surplus of the company.

The most satisfactory, and indeed the only satisfactory way of dealing with the matter seems to me to be to make the initial expense (and all the expense) of the business an element of our computations. A necessary and reasonable expense in the securing of new business, as well as every other necessary expense, may as properly be taken into account in the computation of premiums, reserves, surrender values, surplus, etc., as may death claims, and should be so taken into account. It is time to do away with the idea that all expenses and contingencies are to be provided for by a more or less arbitrary loading or margin added to the computed premium, and, lest that should prove insufficient, by further holding an enormous undivided surplus; and to provide for them in a more rational manner by suitably modifying our fundamental assumptions and computations.

A life insurance company has two sources of income: the premiums paid by its members, and the earnings of its investments. These must suffice to provide for the policy claims and the expenses of the business; the latter as truly and as certainly as the former. If all investment expenses, and all taxes and losses on investments, are to be charged against the earnings on investments, as they should be, the rate of interest assumed in the computations should be such as the company, so far as human foresight can avail, will be certain to realize, net, over all such expenses, taxes, and losses.

As ample provision should be made for investment expenses in the assumption of the interest rate, and not by an arbitrary addition to the premium, so ample provision should be made for such of the ordinary and continued insurance expenses as are properly assessable upon the death cost by a loading of the death rate or mortality table. For the ready and equitable distribution of the surplus, the mortality table should express the relative probabilities of death at different ages. It is not necessary that it should express the actual probability of death, but only that the actual probability should bear a fixed and known ratio to that given by the table. The table used should, then, represent a fixed per cent. of the probable mortality at each age, such per cent. being taken high enough to provide amply for all the ordinary expenses properly assessable upon the death cost as well as for the death cost itself. An addition of 25 per cent. to the probable mortality after the expiration of the first five years of insurance should be more than sufficient. To the premium computed on the basis of the assumed interest rate and the modified mortality table should be added, as a provision for the first cost of new business, an annuity, contemporaneous with the premium payments, the present value of which is equal to the necessary first cost of such new business in excess of the subsequent annual expense and of the gain in the first two or three years from a favorable mortality. The sum so found should be increased by a small per cent. to provide for such continued expense as may be assessable against the premium.

In the computation of the premium we have provided, in what seems to me a rational way, for (*a*) the first special expense of the business, (*b*) a percentage charge against the premium year by year to cover expenses so assessed, (*c*) a margin of income from investments to cover investment expenses, (*d*) a percentage of the death cost to cover other expenses, and (*e*) policy claims. If it is thought more equitable to assess general expenses upon the amount insured rather than upon the death cost, it is only necessary to add to the premium computed upon the unmodified mortality table and the assumed rate of interest an annuity for the premium-paying term, the present value of which is equal to the present value of an annuity equal to the expense to be provided for and running through the term of the policy, instead of increasing the assumed mortality.

The proper reserve would be the single premium for the insurance, less the present value of the future premiums receivable, if any, deducting from such premiums, however, for purposes of valuation, the final percentage loading, which was added to provide for certain continuing annual expenses, and presumably will be needed for that purpose, which loading is not offset by any corresponding loading of the single premium. The computation should be based upon the modified mortality table and the assumed rate of interest. A reserve so computed would take account of the necessary cost of new business, so that such cost would not be at the expense of the existing membership, and would also provide for all the expense attending paid-up business. Under such a computation of premiums and reserves there should be no need of any considerable amount of undivided surplus. Contingencies and expenses are otherwise provided for. Sufficient surplus only is needed to serve as a balance-wheel to enable the company to pay a uniform dividend undisturbed by temporary fluctuations of values and mortality.

The foregoing is a very simple statement of what seem to me the principles which should guide in the distribution of the surplus and the determination of the requisite reserve of a mutual life insurance company. In applying these principles in practice all sorts of difficulties will be met with. I venture to refer to some of them.

Investment income earned will vary in rate in case of an established company but slowly, and can be to some extent forecast. Death claims may vary irregularly by considerable amounts year by year; but it is to be remembered that it is the risk of death the company insures against, and just as in the case of an individual the company does not make the cost to him dependent upon his living through a given year, so in the case of 100,000 individuals it should not necessarily vary the cost to them of the risk assumed according as more or less of them die in a given year. The number dying in any year may assist in determining the risk of death age by age, but does not determine it. A reasonable surplus should be carried to provide against fluctuations, and serve as capital for the prosecution of the business.

Again, a uniform or slowly decreasing cash payment is very desirable. The desirability of a fixed income from a given investment is recognized by almost every reliable and well-established financial corporation in existence.

The shares of any railroad or other corporation would very quickly decline in value if the dividends of its stockholders varied year by year according as the year chanced to be more or less prosperous. So it is desirable that the cost under a life insurance policy should not vary greatly from year to year but should be substantially uniform. A carefully determined scale of dividends should not, therefore, be lightly thrown aside because for a given year the business has been more or less prosperous.

The method of distributing its surplus in case of a mutual company should also take account of the history and traditions of the company. What method have its members been led to expect? What method has been tacitly agreed upon among themselves by the past history of the company and the results with which they are familiar under different classes of policies? Do not hastily substitute your individual opinion of what is right and proper for the custom of years past approved by the bulk of the members.

Competition, too, is to be considered. It may be that a given kind of business must be done at a given cost or not at all, and one may be driven to consider whether it is wise to do a certain class of business at the price at which it can be done.

Freedom in the choice of methods of distributing surplus may be limited by legal enactments. If such enactments do not meet your views of what is right and proper you may strive for their repeal or modification, but so long as they remain as legal enactments it is the duty of a good citizen to conform to them.

The above are by no means the only difficulties that beset the path of one who endeavors honestly to determine to whom and in what proportions the surplus of a mutual life insurance company belongs, but they will perhaps serve as illustrations. Remembering, then, that the preceding is only a statement of general principles to be applied to each particular case as circumstances permit, we may proceed to apply it to an assumed case.

Let us assume that the company earns a net income, after providing for the cost of its investments, of 4¼ per cent.; that its death losses, less the liability from which it is relieved by the payment of them, are 75 per cent. of the tabular cost of insurance or contribution to death claims; that it reserves on the basis of the American Table of Mortality and 3 per cent. compound interest; and that it is required to find the tenth annual dividend per $1000 on 20-payment life policies issued at age 35 at a premium rate of $36.20. For convenience of reference we add that the reserve at the end of the ninth year upon such a policy is $226.31 per $1000, and that at the end of the tenth year is $255.78 per $1000; and that the cost of insurance for the tenth year is $8.06. Let us assume, also, that the cost of new business less the saving in mortality is $20 per $1000 in excess of the subsequent cost. This $20 equals an annuity of $1.42 a year through the premium-paying period, which, having been appropriated already, reduces the effective premium to $34.78. Let us assume that the expenses chargeable to the premiums upon the business as a whole are 7½ per cent. of such premiums, and those chargeable to the cost of insurance are 20 per cent. of such cost. The dividend, then, may be found as follows:

Reserve at the end of the 9th year	$226.31	
Plus the effective premium	34.78	
Plus interest for a year.........................	11.10	$272.19
Less reserve at the end of 10th year	$255.78	
7½ per cent. of the premium	2.72	
95 per cent. of the cost of insurance..............	7.66	$266.16
Leaving a dividend of..........................		$6.03

The mathematical work may be somewhat abbreviated, and the form of it will depend somewhat on the means at hand, and is, of course, immaterial.

The method suggested of determining the reserve which a company should make has not come into use, and may be dismissed with very brief reference. It substantially regards business on the books as an asset. In view of the first cost of such business it is such. By distributing such first cost as an annuity through the premium-paying period, it to that extent equalizes the expenses and so the annual cost of the insurance while still making it a charge against the individual policy on account of which it was incurred. In the event of the surrender of the policy, any balance of such cost still remaining as a charge against future premiums should be collected as a part of the surrender charge.

CHAPTER XX

DEFERRED DIVIDEND POLICIES [1]

THE Blank Life Insurance Company is prepared to insure lives upon a *method which has never before been practised by any life insurance company,* and which, it is thought by those who have given it the most study and reflection, *will render life insurance popular to a degree hitherto unknown.* Government bonds and bonds and mortgages on real estate are considered by many persons the safest kind of investment. They regard money paid for insurance of any kind rather as an expense than as an investment adding value to their estates. To obviate this in the fullest degree, the present method has been devised, which is now *for the first time presented to the public.*

Tontine annuities, which were first made attractive by Lorenzo Tonti about the middle of the seventeenth century, have become exceedingly popular throughout Europe and in some parts of South America. A tontine is quite the reverse of life insurance, it being, in fact, a combination of persons who contribute to a common fund which shall be enjoyed by the survivors only; so that as years roll on and the numbers surviving diminish, the income is, of course, constantly increasing to those who live, until the last members of a class enjoy most extraordinary advantages from the system. In 1689 the last survivor of the

[1] Reprinted from a circular issued in 1869 by a life insurance company, announcing a new scheme of declaring dividends. Since so much controversial discussion has taken place over deferred dividends, it has been thought best, since it detracts nothing from the value of the pamphlet, to omit the name of the company which issued it.

tontine in France, a widow, just before her death, enjoyed an income equivalent to about $20,000 of our money for her original subscription of about $80. So popular has this system been in Europe, that governments have used it for the purpose of raising money for national support. Those who invest in tontines care little for leaving money to those who may come after them (who — they may consider — have little or no claim upon them), and prefer to enjoy while living a large annual income, which, combined with entire safety, their money could not produce, in the shape of interest, in any other way. Life assurance, as has already been observed, is quite the reverse of the tontine principle, and the arguments which induce persons to invest in securities of this character appeal to higher and more unselfish motives than those which influence investment in tontines. The apprehension arises in the minds of many persons who are asked to assure their lives, but who have not given life assurance much study, that in case of a long life the investment may prove a bad one; but a careful investigation will prove that this objection is not well founded. We have before us a policy in one of the leading mutual companies, issued more than twenty-five years ago, taken out originally for $5000, on which, when the policy became a death claim, more than $10,000 was paid by the company, the excess over the original amount of the policy being more than 7 per cent. interest on all the payments received by the company. It is proper to state that this result was due not only to the marvelous power of compound interest, but also to the fortunate increase in the value of investments, the large return of surplus premiums, and other gains incident to the business. The case cited is not an isolated one; the same thing has been often repeated and may again be repeated. At the same time, it must be acknowledged that the gain from investments in life policies is greater in the case of early death; and the popular mind seeks for some simple method by which an equalization of the benefits of life insurance can be secured, whether the insured die soon or late. The system now under consideration, though differing from either tontine or life assurance, combines all the advantages of both, and has been brought out under the supervision of two mathematicians, Mr. George W. Phillips and Mr. Sheppard Homans, author of the contribution plan of dividends. This system is known as the "Tontine-Dividend System," under which, by a skilful adjustment of the dividends, a recompense is given to those life assurants who live nearly up to or beyond the period known among actuaries as their "expectation" of life. If a person at the age of 35 insures his life in a company for $25,000 and pays a premium of $659.50, and dies during the year, while theoretically as much profit is made by the company from insuring his life as from insuring the lives of those who are long lived, because the tables are adjusted to meet this exigency, still, in a practical sense, certainly no money is realized from the individual transaction. It would appear exceedingly equitable *that the person who dies early,* and whose family receives the face of his policy, equal to a profit of 100, 500, or even 5000 per cent. on the money he has invested, *should not receive a further sum in the shape of dividends,* and that *those who continue to pay* their premiums through a long series of years should have the benefit of the accumulated dividends, in addition to the face of their policies respectively, *giving them a profit on their outlay somewhat approximating to that of those dying early.* The "Tontine-Dividend System" aims, among other things, to accomplish this equitable distribution of surplus. And it is thought by the Superintendent of Insurance of the State of New York, Hon. Wm. Barnes, and many of our most prominent business and financial men, that *it will popularize life assurance to a degree hitherto unknown.*

The plan as applied to a particular case is simply this: If a person at the age of 35 years insures his life for $25,000, and pays the annual premium of $659.50, interest on these annual premiums is to be theoretically compounded at the rate of 10 per cent. per annum, until such premiums, with interest as specified, amount to the face of the policy, which, at the age mentioned, would be in 15.5 years. During the intervening period the company issuing the policy makes its annual dividends on this and all other tontine policies, keeping the profits on the same separate from the rest of its policies, and setting them apart as a fund belonging to the tontine class, but not payable in any case until the end of the specified period of 15.5 years, and then only on such policies as shall be actually in force, those policies terminating in the interval receiving no dividends. The person holding the tontine-dividend policy above mentioned will, at the end of the 15.5 years, begin to benefit by the dividends already declared; and further dividends will be made annually thereafter throughout the remainder of the term of the policy. These dividends will be payable in cash, thus reducing or canceling the annual premiums, and afterwards yielding a constantly increasing cash annuity as well. It has been calculated by the best actuaries that the dividends on such policies will be three or four times greater than have hitherto been declared by any company. The same principle is applied to policies on lives at other ages; *the distinctive feature being that there is no participation in profits until the premiums paid, compounded at* 10 *per cent. interest, equal the face of the policy, and then the survivors receive the whole accumulation of profits.*

Persons dying during the non-dividend period receive the amount secured by their policies respectively without further profits.

Persons discontinuing their policies prior to the dividend period receive no surrender values therefor.

Policies are to be issued at the rates charged in the "*Ordinary Life Table*" or in the "*Endowment Table*" (*with twenty years or more to run*), payable in either case by premiums continuing during the whole term of the policy. These premiums may be paid annually, semi-annually, or quarterly.

This plan will admit of a number of variations; for instance (1), the division of profits may begin at the end of an arbitrary period of ten, fifteen, or twenty years; or (2), a separate class of policies may be issued on either of the foregoing plans, upon the surrender of which paid-up policies will be given for the value thereof, in case the same are allowed to lapse by non-payment of premium before the dividend begins, but on which no dividends will be paid in case of death before the dividend period. It is not to be expected, however, that the dividends will be as large as in the previous classes, because one of the material sources of profit is diminished.

In order to carry out the views above suggested, the Blank Life Insurance Company has determined to establish for its assurants tontine-dividend classes, which any, who may hereafter assure, may enter on giving due notice of their election so to do.

Class A

In this class (designated in "*application*" and "*policy*" as Class A), policies are to be issued at the rates charged in the "*Ordinary Life Table,*" or in the "*Endowment Table*" (*with twenty years or more to run*), payable in either case by premiums continuing during the whole term of the policy. These premiums may be paid annually, semi-annually, or quarterly.

No dividends will be *paid* until the premiums, with compound interest thereon, at the rate of *ten* (10) per cent. per annum, shall amount to the sum assured by the policy.

In case of death before the dividend period begins, the assured will receive the sum secured by the policy.

The society will allow no surrender value to those who *give up* their policies, or dividends on those policies that may become death claims, before the dividend period begins; but will reserve all profits resulting from such sources, as well as the profits accruing upon the policies of those who persevere in paying their premiums, until the premiums paid by the latter, with compound interest thereon, at the rate of ten (10) per cent. per annum, shall have amounted to the face of their policies respectively.

The dividends *then* are to be equitably adjusted on the contribution plan accordingly as each class and age has contributed to the surplus, and paid on such policies as are actually in force; of course allowing for irregularities incident to a small number of policies in any sub-class, but faithfully regarding the general course of mortality at different ages and in different classes, and the growth of profits as affected by the difference in the length of time for which the division of profits at the various policies shall be deferred.

The dividends will be applied to the reduction of subsequent premiums falling due during the continuance of the policy, and in case of a surplus after doing this, as is probable, the excess to be applied to the purchase of an annuity to continue up to the termination of the policy.

Annual dividends, thereafter, will swell this annuity, so that the policy, which was a burden in its early years, will yield an increasing income, payable yearly in cash. It is estimated by the most competent actuaries in this country, that dividends on policies in this class may be more than three times as great as have hitherto been declared by American companies.

Class B

In order to meet the views of those who may not desire to lose the privilege of receiving a value for their policies, if obliged to give them up before reaching the dividend period, the society will establish another class (designated in "*application*" and "*policy*" as Class B), in which the original policies will be exchanged for paid-up policies according to the rules of the company.

As in the previous class, no profits will be paid on policies which may become death claims before the dividend period begins. Although the final dividends in this class will not be as great as in the first, still they will be much larger than those which have been hitherto declared by any life insurance company.

Class C

Again, as some persons may prefer to have their dividends come due at the end of a stipulated term of ten, fifteen, or twenty years, policies will be issued containing such a stipulation, but in other respects not differing from those issued in Class A. (This class will be designated in "*application*" and "*policy*" as Class C.)

Class D

Policies will also be issued on which the dividends will become due at the end of a stipulated term of ten, fifteen, or twenty years, but in other respects not differing from those issued in Class B. (This class will be designated in the "*application*" and "*policy*" as Class D.)

The profits on each of these tontine classes (namely, those in which neither surrender value nor paid-up policies are given for policies surrendered before the attainment of the dividend period, and those in which a paid-up policy for a certain amount is given) will be kept *separate*, so that those who bear the *greater risk* will receive a GREATER RECOMPENSE.

In the payment of premiums on all policies in the tontine classes, a grace will be allowed of as many months (not exceeding six) as will correspond to the age of the policy in years; thus the payment of any premium for the first year of the policy may be deferred for one month, of any premium for the second year, two months, and so on, — provided that in all cases when this grace is availed of, a fine at the rate of ten (10) per cent. per annum will be exacted. Thus there need be no accidental forfeiture of a policy, and the greater the value of the policy, the longer is the grace allowed for the payment of premiums upon it.

Such is the proposed system of tontine dividends. What are its advantages?

It will be seen that by this system, if an assurant dies at any time, even on the last day, before the period is reached when participation in profits begins, *his representatives will receive more than ten* (10) *per cent. compound interest upon the money paid into the society for premiums.* If he dies within the first few years of his assurance his representatives will receive many times 10 per cent.; if during the first year it may be 5000 per cent. At the age 35, on a life policy, the dividend will commence in 15.5 years; an assurant therefore on this plan may secure in case of death during that time a 10 per cent. investment at least. And afterwards, it is probable that on such a policy the dividend will not merely pay the premium in full, but secure a very comfortable annuity besides to the assurant during his life.

Now, is not this just what many men in the community need — something to protect their families in case of sudden early death — an investment which is certain to pay ten (10) per cent. compound interest at least for, say fifteen years (at the average age of asssurance); then afterwards the requirement of no more premiums, the assurant receiving instead a considerable annuity, commencing just at the time *when age begins to impair the faculties?*

Does not this plan do in effect what the policies payable in ten, fifteen, or other limited number of annual payments, aim to do — the complete paying up of the premiums during the productive years of life, and the securing of an income from the policy at middle life and in old age. And though the tontine-dividend policies receive no dividend for some ten or fifteen years, yet as the ordinary life premium at the average age is but half the ten-year premium, the result in actual outgo on a tontine-dividend policy will be more satisfactory than that on a ten-annual payment policy, at the same time that the lightening of the pressure of the payments required will be often very desirable during the first year or two of the policy, when the policy-holder, perhaps just starting in business, can spare with difficulty the amount required by the lowest tables.

Again, to compare the tontine-dividend system with the stock system without profits, is it not better to pay a somewhat higher mutual premium for, say fifteen years, with the expectation that after that time not only will no premiums be required, but that *a very considerable income* will be received from the policy, rather than to pay up to the very end of a long life — as a penalty, it would seem, for superior vitality — a stock premium, somewhat lower indeed, *but without the least abatement in old age?*

It would seem that this plan, while it gives the class who pass the dividend period all the advantages of the mutual plan, also gives them all the benefits of the stock plan as enjoyed by the holders of stock in companies of that kind; the class who pass the dividend period obtain their insurance at the net rate, *while the profits of those policy-holders who fail to pass the dividend period go to swell the annuity of the former, which same profit in a stock company would contribute to enlarge the dividends of the stockholders.*

It is claimed by the Blank Company that the system of tontine dividends is adapted in a most remarkable manner to the *wants of those persons who have mortgages upon their real estate* which they may either *not care* or *not be able to pay off.* Their unwillingness may be owing to the fact that the money borrowed is more valuable to them in their business than the current rate of interest which they pay for its use; their inability to the fact that their necessary expenses make it difficult for them to save enough money to make very rapid progress in removing the mortgages. In either case the apprehension may weigh heavily upon their minds that in case of their sudden death the mortgages might prove unfortunate, if not disastrous encumbrances, at a time when all available moneys are needed in winding up their estates; as many a time a mortgage made during the lifetime of an owner proves, in case of his death, *the loss of the entire property to the family.* So great have been the changes produced during the last ten years in the prices of living and the general expenses of the man of family, that many persons have been anxious to buy homesteads rather than pay the large rents and suffer the inconveniencies and uncertainties incidental to the rental of houses. This proceeding would in all cases probably prove a wise one provided the persons in question could be guaranteed a long life, but they have frequently been obliged heavily to mortgage these homesteads in order to carry out and fully perfect their plans. The reflection which is sure to come over their minds of the trouble that would result to their families in the event of their sudden death often causes *untold anxiety;* and the difficulty they experience in saving from their incomes a yearly sum sufficient to give promise of a liquidation of such mortgages within any reasonable time fills them with *evil forebodings for the future.* Now it is proposed in a most easy and simple manner to obviate all this trouble. Let the person so situated insure his life on the tontine-dividend plan for the amount of his mortgage. While the sum, as before mentioned, which may be saved year by year, is small as compared with the amount of the mortgage, it may still be enough and more than is necessary to pay the annual premium required to cover the entire *amount of the mortgage.* Having done so, the person may *dismiss this anxiety entirely from his mind,* and devote himself to his business with a heart free from care, for he then knows that in case of death at any time, even the very next day, *his policy would pay off his mortgage.* And as years roll on and he reaches the period when the dividends commence, his premium will be almost if not entirely extinguished, and the annual dividends thereafter will soon yield him a cash annuity, at first almost, and then entirely *sufficient to pay the interest on his mortgage.* So that the policy, which was first and during the producing years of his life an annual expenditure to him, may in the end, as fully as a government bond, produce a yearly revenue sufficient not only to pay the premium on the policy but interest on his mortgage and prevent the same from being any burden to him. If the person should be able to spare a slightly increased premium, it would be wise for him to take a "twenty-year endowment policy" instead of an ordinary life policy. The same advantages would then be gained with the additional feature that the person would in twenty years, if then living, himself receive the amount of his policy, and the mortgage could then be discharged, instead of waiting until the time of his death.

The same principle which has been thus described in regard to the owners of mortgaged premises applies with equal force to the case of those persons who may have incurred debts which they are at present unable to pay with convenience, but for the satisfaction of which they consider it both *their duty and pleasure to provide, if possible.*

The arguments supporting the tontine-dividend system address themselves with peculiar force to many persons who are in the possession of large incomes. These may be divided into two classes: (1) those who are possessed of large assets, and who enjoy large incomes as well, and (2) those whose large expenses during their business life have prevented their accumulating much, but who are, nevertheless, earning large incomes by the exercise of their hands or brains.

Let the first class remember that their estates, as a whole, *are worth much more to-day, if they are living, than to-morrow, if they are dead.* No one can settle an estate, and disentangle the meshes in which a man's business is oftentimes entwined, as well as the owner. It is well known to most business men that, in the majority of their investments, living they gain, dying their representatives lose. It is now proposed to such persons to cast an anchor to windward. Let them wisely hedge themselves in at least one of their investments. Now the characteristics of life insurance are, in some respects, directly the opposite of those we have described, as peculiar to most other investments. For the sake of the parallel, we will assume (what nevertheless is untrue), that life insurance will prove a loss to the person who lives long; for no one will deny that in the event of his dying soon it will be a large gain; and it is a demonstrable fact that this gain may be as great as 100, 1000, or even 5000 per cent. on the actual outlay. *Thus the business man, who, dying early, will lose to his family a portion of his investments, may by the same stroke make a gain to them of a sum quite as large.* The tontine-dividend system brings this argument home to business men with greater force than it could be presented by the ordinary system of life insurance, from the fact that the profits upon the policies of this class, as specified above, will probably be three or four times as great as have hitherto been declared by any life assurance company; and, in the opinion of the most competent judges, *a policy of this kind will pay a remunerative rate of interest, in the end, upon the whole investment.*

To those having large incomes, but who have not accumulated sufficient to make them independent, policies of this class present strong attractions. There are few men possessing the ability and industry to earn annually large sums of money, and having great and constantly increasing experience and knowledge in the pursuits to which they devote themselves, who do not feel a confidence (provided their lives are spared) that they will be able to maintain, and even enlarge, their power to produce the same results during the early and middle portion of their lives, if they can only keep their minds free from anxiety in regard to the future prospects for their families. Such, however, may be their love of luxury, and their determination to surround themselves and their families with present comforts, that they may not see any practicable way of rapidly providing an independent competency for those they leave behind them. But they can easily save a sufficient amount from their annual incomes to insure, as the case may be, for either 10,000, 25,000, 50,000, or 100,000 dollars, and, having done so, feel quite as great a certainty that their families will be provided for in the event of early death as if they were possessed of an equal amount in United States bonds, or other marketable securities. Such persons might hesitate before using the sum of money which would be required to pay the premiums, in any way which they might consider an expense, but it would seem a most wise and commendable thing for them to *invest* such money in a tontine-dividend policy, which will be in the end an investment as profitable to them as a government bond could be, and which possesses the power (to be found in no other kind of security) of providing for their families a sum much greater than the amount paid in *whenever they may die.* There is no kind of investment, excepting life insurance, in which present payments of trifling amount, and the promise of future payments while the investor lives, are received in full satisfaction for the amount deemed necessary for the support of a family, which is paid down in cash, whether the death occurs early or late.

To those who may already have policies upon their lives, issued upon any of the plans hitherto practised by life insurance companies, it is thought that this tontine-dividend plan presents strong arguments for taking additional policies. The profits on such policies (which, upon any of the ordinary plans, would be enjoyed by the general mass of the policy-holders, and are on this plan given only to those who pass the period when the dividends begin) are, by the power of the tontine principle, augmented to such a remarkable extent that, while the taking of the additional policies is wise in itself as a new security, the annuity ultimately to be derived from the same may most opportunely aid in the payment of the premiums of the policies already in force, and thus "make assurance doubly sure."

CHAPTER XXI

ECONOMIC ASPECT OF LENGTHENING HUMAN LIFE [1]

CONCERTED action by life insurance companies to lengthen human life would mark, I believe, one of the greatest steps, if not the greatest step, ever yet taken toward the improvement of human longevity. The nearest analogy is perhaps to be found in the work of fire insurance companies in reducing the number of fires. But it is a general truth that the best success of any movement is found only when, in a sense, it reaches the commercial stage — in other words, when it is made to pay in some tangible way. Philanthropy is keen to lead the way to reform, but becomes a broken reed if depended upon for its support continuously or on a large scale.

The insurance men whom I have consulted as to whether it would pay to engage in the saving of lives have been unanimously affirmative in their answers. So obvious does this seem that the question arises, why have insurance companies never attempted it before? There seem to be three explanations:

First, the continuance, until recently, of the tradition that human mortality follows a nearly invariable law, and a law which cannot be appreciably affected by any act of man.

Second, after it became known to experts that human life is greatly extensible through public and private hygiene, this knowledge was possessed by so few, that the general

[1] By Irving Fisher, Professor of Political Economy in Yale University, President of the Committee of One Hundred on National Health. Reprint of a speech delivered before a meeting of the Association of Life Insurance Presidents.

public, and even the rank and file of the medical profession, remained of the contrary belief, and the inertia of their conservative opinion prevailed.

Third, it seemed too large a task for any one company to prolong life for the whole country, and there seemed no way to prolong the lives of its own policy-holders alone, so long as unsanitary conditions prevailed throughout the communities in which these policy-holders lived, while finally there seemed no way of bringing the various life insurance interests to agree on concerted action.

It seems now, however, that the time has arrived when all three of these objections can be removed. I assume that before this audience there is no need of presenting evidence or arguments to prove that human life may be lengthened by hygienic measures, and shall therefore merely run over very briefly the most salient and general facts, as introductory to the formulation of a practical plan of action.

It has long been known that there is no iron law of mortality, but that mortality depends on the hygienic state of the community. Baines, in a recent paper in the Journal of the Royal Statistical Society, has calculated that the average duration of life in India is only twenty-three years for males and twenty-four years for females, or less than half the life span in the advanced countries of Europe. The estimates of Finkelnburg show that in Europe human life has probably doubled in the last 350 years. More recent and more reliable figures show that life is lengthening to-day more rapidly than ever. If we take life tables for different periods for England, France, Prussia, Denmark, Sweden, and Massachusetts, we find that human life lengthened during the seventeenth and eighteenth centuries at the rate of four years per century; that during the first three-quarters of the nineteenth century it lengthened at the rate of about nine years per century; that at present it is lengthening in Europe generally at the rate of seventeen years per century, and in Prussia (which is perhaps the home of preventive medicine) at the rate of twenty-seven years per century. For this country the rate can only be judged from the statistics for Massachusetts, which show that life is lengthening by about fourteen years per century, or approximately half of the Prussian rate. These rates may not continue in the future, but the opinion of our best authorities on longevity, such as Ray Lankester and Metchnikoff, is that there is still great room for improvement, especially after middle life. Hitherto almost all the improvement has applied to ages before 50, and only the most recent figures show any tendency toward improvement beyond that age. It is significant that backward India — in spite of the enormous room for improvement — shows during twenty years no rate of improvement whatever.

The statistics of insured lives show that the insured poor, as represented by the industrial companies, have a mortality from 50 to 80 per cent. higher than the insured rich or well-to-do, as represented in the ordinary insurance companies. The unsanitary districts of Glasgow and Paris show a mortality more than double that of the sanitary districts, while cities in general show a much higher mortality than the open country. A fall of the death rate always promptly follows sanitation. Colonel Gorgas cut the death rate in Havana in two, bringing it down to between 20 and 24 per 1000. The New York death rate responded at once to Colonel Waring's clean streets, and that of Rochester to Dr. Goler's milk crusade. And now it is announced that the death rate of New York is 16.5, the lowest on record — a result, in all human probability, due to the hygienic work of Dr. Darlington, the efficient health officer, Mr. Nathan Straus, the milk reformer, and the public agitation for health prosecuted by the *New York Times*, the *Journal*, and other media, allied with the health work of the Committee of One Hundred on National Health, the Tuberculosis Association and Committees, and other organizations.

These and other facts and the mass of detailed figures which they represent show conclusively that human life is long or short precisely according to the hygienic conditions under which it is lived; that human life can be prolonged as these hygienic conditions are improved, and that there is still enormous room for improvement. Farr, twenty years ago, in his masterly work on Vital Statistics, stated that any community could attain an average duration of life equal to that in the so-called "healthy districts" of England, where the average duration of life was then fifty-one years. To bring all England up to this level would at that time mean a lengthening of life by one-fifth, or 20 per cent.

A report which I have recently prepared for the Conservation Commission, based on data contributed from acknowledged American authorities, shows that human life in America could, by the adoption of hygienic reforms already known and entirely practicable, be lengthened by over one-third — that is, over fifteen years. This calculation has been made very conservatively and is probably several years inside the truth. The statistics and estimates on which it is based have been taken from published sources, as well as contributed by some score of American authorities — medical, actuarial, and hygienic.

A safe minimum estimate was made of the degree of preventability of the deaths from each of the ninety principal causes of death in the United States. For instance, for typhoid fever, experience in Lawrence, Massachusetts, has shown that the introduction of a public water filter reduced the typhoid mortality by 80 per cent. In Munich the cleaning of cesspools and other hygienic measures reduced the mortality from typhoid by 97 per cent. On the basis of these and other facts, it was conservatively estimated that 85 per cent. of the deaths now occurring from typhoid fever in the United States could be easily prevented. Professor Sedgwick recently announced the truth of Hazen's theorem — that for each life saved from typhoid, two or three lives are saved from other diseases. This cumulative effect, however, was not taken into account in the calculations, nor was account taken of the constant advance being made in preventive medicine.

For these and other reasons, the calculated estimate of the improvability of human life is regarded as ultra-conservative. Tuberculosis is known to be preventable. In my table, it is entered as only 75 per cent. preventable; pneumonia as 45 per cent. preventable; typhoid as 85 per cent.; diphtheria, 70 per cent. These conservative figures are among the highest allowed. Many diseases, such as cancer, are recorded in the table as zero per cent. preventable, although the best expert opinion would allow some degree of preventability, if prevention begins early enough in life.

On the basis of these ratios of preventability, or rather *postponability* of death, has been computed the possible extension of the average human life by saving lives now lost by preventable diseases. The calculation is made on the assumption that those thus saved from death enjoy as their new lease of life only the expectation of life now belonging to their respective ages. This assumption is very conservative, for it means that lives once saved shall receive no further benefits from improved mortality, but shall die off at the old rates of mortality.

Even on these safe premises of partial postponability of deaths, we find that about two years of the possible lengthening of human life would be due to the elimination of preventable tuberculosis; .6 of a year to the elimination of preventable typhoid; .5 to the elimination of preventable diphtheria; .9 to the elimination of preventable accidents. It is estimated that at least eight years could be added to human life merely by securing reasonably pure air, water, and milk.

A grouping by ages will bring home these figures to life insurance companies. It was estimated that for diseases of infants under one year of age, such as broncho-pneumonia, diarrhœa, and enteritis, at least half of the deaths were preventable — that is, postponable. For diseases of childhood such as meningitis, diphtheria, and scarlet fever the same is true; for diseases of middle life, such as typhoid fever, tuberculosis, pneumonia, and accidents, over one-third are postponable; and for diseases of late life, such as Bright's disease, heart disease, and apoplexy, at least one-fourth of the deaths are postponable.

These ratios may seem high at first glance, but only because no one has previously attempted to assemble all ratios of preventability. Each investigator has seen clearly the preventability within his own special sphere, but assumed that outside that sphere the preventability was less. One specialist knows that tuberculosis is, for the most part, preventable; another, typhoid; a third, diphtheria; a fourth, infantile diarrhœa. And yet each clings to the idea that disease in general is unpreventable. Some of the very experts of the Yale Medical School and state and federal health officers who contributed the individual estimates — and these experts include eighteen of the best and safest authorities in the United States — have been surprised to find how large in the aggregate the resultant preventability is. It shows that over a third of all deaths which now occur could be prevented — that is to say, deferred. Every precaution has been taken to make these figures so safely within the truth as to avoid the possibility of any reasonable criticism. I will add that those who contributed the statistics, estimates, and expert guesses on which these aggregates are based were especially urged to be conservative. The eighteen estimators included Drs. Flint, Blumer, Swain, and Osborne of the Yale Medical School; Dr. Wilbur, Chief of Vital Statistics of the United States; Health Officers Townsend of Connecticut, Baker of Michigan, Wright of New Haven, Woodward of Washington, Chapin of Providence, etc. These gentlemen made their estimates independently, but they agreed remarkably well. This would indicate that they were correct. These gentlemen are not given to exaggeration, but even if their estimates are three times too great, the preventable deaths still exceed 10 per cent.

By working out the ratios of preventability for each of the principal causes of death, it is possible to construct an ideal survivorship table which may then be compared with existing survivorship tables. Actuaries' tables show that a reduction of one-third in mortality would enable the premium to be reduced by over 15 per cent. Even if only a third of this possible reduction were obtained, or 5 per cent., the insured in the United States would be saved many millions annually. Of course whatever saving is possible can not be secured without effort or cost. Not all of it can be obtained at once, and some of it can be obtained whether insurance companies take a hand or not. But by so doing they can greatly accelerate the improvement. While it would be manifestly impossible to estimate exactly what returns could be made on the investment, it is clear that even if the most meager returns could be secured, the gain would pay.

It can scarcely be imagined that the companies would lose anything. I understand that $200,000 a year is about two cents per $1000 of insurance carried. It would be strange if $200,000 could not be expended in such a manner as to secure a saving of a postage stamp a year on each $1000 policy! As one of your actuaries, Mr. Messenger, has shown, $200,000 is only one-eighth of 1 per cent. of present annual death claims.

The chance of failure is further reduced when we remember that the effect in reducing mortality is progressive or cumulative, while no cumulative effect is needed to return the money invested.

The conclusion seems safe that here is a rich unexploited field for saving money. And the beauty of it is that these gains bring with them gains far more precious to the nation than dollars — immeasurable gains of longevity, vitality, efficiency, and happiness. Life insurance is not philanthropy, but it is a beneficent business. Though at first glance it might seem that to prevent the pollution of streams, to improve the milk supply, to obtain pure foods, and freedom from accident is no part of the business of life insurance, yet it is easy enough to see the very vital connection. By far the larger part of the cost of the insurance business is not management nor agents' fees but cost of mortality. It is the right, if in fact it is not the duty, of any business to reduce its cost. To pare down salaries might not save the policy-holder 1 per cent. of his premium, but to reduce mortality cost might save him many per cent.

Another point may be emphasized. The mere announcement that insurance companies intended to improve health conditions would have an effect in improving those conditions. This effect would be felt in two ways: First, it would convince millions of the ignorant and indifferent that the public health movement must have substantial merit to be an object of interest by life insurance companies. People are easily led by those whose opinions they respect. In spite of the great progress of the health movement, there are still vast hordes of our people who know nothing of it. Knowledge of its merits is largely confined to scientific and medical men, who constitute only a small fraction of the population. The actuaries and medical boards and other insurance officials constitute a still smaller class. Yet these classes can easily sway the whole. The second way in which the mere announcement of your purpose to labor for health would have immediate effect is in spurring numerous officials and firms to reform. Every health officer, every food manufacturer, every milk dealer in the United States that heard of the intention of the insurance companies to improve health conditions would become ambitious to make a good showing. Local pride in every community would result in efforts to keep abreast of the best records and avoid the reputation for being an unhealthful place in which to live. Insurance companies sometimes charge, I believe, higher rates for policies involving tropical residence, but in the United States are not allowed to make local discrimination. There is, therefore, all the more reason why they might properly endeavor to lower the mortality in say Mississippi — if the mortality is high there — in order that they might be enabled to do business there.

In the history of fire insurance, the mutual companies first made the effort to reduce fire risks. When the importance of exercising the function of preventing fires, as well as indemnifying against fires, once entered into the plans of stock companies, they soon overtook, if they did not outrun, the mutual companies in the success of their efforts. It is estimated that the risk from fire in certain particular classes has been reduced, through the fire insurance companies, some 70 per cent. In New England seventy years ago the rate on cotton and woolen mills averaged three or four dollars per hundred. To-day these mills are being insured at a total cost per annum of seven cents per hundred. In some cases the cost has been reduced to 1-100 of the former amount. This enormous decrease has been accomplished by slight expenditures. In some factories the cost of improvements has been more than paid for in the saving of premiums for fire insurance in one year. The stock companies were forced by the competition of the mutual companies to take up preventive measures. They now employ fire insurance engineers to maintain a laboratory in Chicago which is well equipped for the purpose of studying fire-resisting materials, fire-resisting devices, new apparatus, and fire prevention in general. Many fire insurance men believe that this laboratory is their best investment. No reduction in rate is guaranteed until fire-fighting devices are approved by the laboratory. Now that the stock companies have gone into this work of fire prevention systematically, they are regaining the ground that they lost by allowing the mutuals to get ahead of them.

In employers' liability insurance, the idea of prevention has made great headway. Here the companies are all stock companies, but they have learned that their function is not simply to distribute losses, but to lessen them as well. So also accident companies have aided in passing laws which tend to prevent accidents to life and limb. Here they have reached the very threshold of public health. It is manifest destiny that if insurance companies now aid in legislation to save the arms and legs of workmen, they will soon aid in legislation also to save lives. In fact, protection from accidental injury is also protection from accidental death; and if you strive to reduce the deaths from accident, why not reduce the deaths from other causes? If casualty companies work for improved safety, why should not life companies work for improved sanitation and improved hygiene in general? In fact, the Industrial Department of the Metropolitan Company has just announced that if prevention of tuberculosis and reduction of the death rate will give cheaper insurance, the company hopes to coöperate with existing agencies for the eradication of this and other diseases, and to place at their disposal its machinery and the statistical material which it has gathered since its organization.

According to the plans which I have in mind, the money to be invested in life-saving would be largely in the education of the public and especially policy-holders in health matters, and coöperation in every legitimate way to improve the public health offices and service in the municipalities, states, and the federal government. In this latter way, the result of the expenditure of money by the insurance companies would be to induce the government to spend much larger sums, and the money invested by the insurance companies would be multiplied in efficiency several fold. If, for instance, by the expenditure of $200,000 a year the public throughout the country could be made to appreciate the importance of clean streets, pure water supply, etc., sufficiently to result in municipal expenditure by the cities of the United States for public health of an additional $20,000,000 which would otherwise not have been made, every dollar invested would be multiplied a hundred-fold. In other words, the insured lives would not have to carry the entire load, but could induce the tax-payer to do his share. Our public health laws and administration leave vast room for improvement. As Dr. Welch has said, neglect of public health is a disgrace to the nation. Some states have no boards of health. Few have good ones. A minority have accurate registration of deaths and not one has accurate registration of births. We therefore lack even the first step toward efficient national health protection — good vital statistics.

Just as fire insurance companies endeavor to secure in municipalities adequate fire protection, so life insurance companies might properly endeavor to secure adequate municipal health protection, and they might likewise bring their influence to bear in securing the passage of model health laws by our states in respect to slaughter houses, pure food, and other health reforms. The present great and needless waste of human life brings its heavy financial weight largely on insurance companies. The Prudential Company pays out annually $800,000 for death claims on account of tuberculosis alone, a disease which is known to be preventable.

As to a practical plan for participation by the life insurance companies in the health movement, two methods suggest themselves. The first is for the life insurance companies, in combination, to establish their own machinery for disbursing funds intended to improve the public health. The second is to contribute to one or more organizations already existing for this purpose. I shall speak in favor of the second, and in particular of the advantages to be obtained by using the Committee of One Hundred on National Health, of which I am president, as the agent for this distribution. I will say at the outset, however, that I think our committee would be willing, if need be, to stand aside in favor of any plan which the insurance companies should prefer. We have been interested in this work from a philanthropic point of view only, and have borne its burden because no other organization was doing the work. It has been a tax on our time and purses, and we should, if the same work could be done by others without this tax, be only too ready to hand it over. We believe, however, that there would be a distinct advantage to the insurance companies in utilizing our agency, instead of creating a new one. Since the work is largely one of educating and convincing public opinion, it seems an advantage that the movement should have a scientific as well as a commercial flavor. Our committee was appointed by the American Association for the Advancement of Science, and consists, for the most part, of men of national reputation.

As to the methods of expending the proposed fund to be created by the insurance companies, details can be submitted to the committee appointed to consider them. This would include the enlargement of our magazine, the pressing of health bills before Congress and the legislatures of the several states, the publication and distribution of leaflets of information in continuation of the series of twenty-six which we have already published, a campaign of newspaper publicity and education, especially through plate matter prepared and given to 10,000 country newspapers. It would also include efforts to enlarge the American Health League so that it may fulfil two functions: first, create an interest in a large number of people in healthful individual living, and, second, create and formulate public opinion which shall secure public health legislation.

CHAPTER XXII

CONTROL OF LIFE INSURANCE COMPANIES[1]

FROM the standpoint of control, there are three classes of life insurance companies: stock companies, mixed companies, and mutual companies. The stock companies were the first in the field, writing a small amount of purely nonparticipating business. About 1840, companies began to be organized on a mutual basis, and these soon drove the three old stock companies out of the life insurance field. In the twenty years following 1840, practically all the prominent mutual companies of to-day were organized. Following the organization of these successful mutual companies came the formation of a large number of stock and mixed companies, as a result partly of the desire on the part of capitalists to engage in an apparently profitable business, and partly of the enactment of state laws, which from that day to this have made the formation of a mutual company difficult.

Control of stock companies is, of course, lodged in the hands of stockholders, and problems connected with their management would be no more serious than those arising in the management of any joint stock company, if it were not for two conditions. In the first place, these companies are permitted to write participating as well as nonparticipating policies; that is, they are allowed to solicit business on promise of a division of profits among purchasers of their product. This differentiates a stock life

[1] By Lester W. Zartman, Assistant Professor of Political Economy in Yale University. Reprinted from pages 531–541, Volume XV, *Journal of Political Economy.*

insurance company from any other joint stock concern. Although some of the leading stock companies may have paid nearly as large dividends to their participating policy-holders as have been paid by mutual companies, it is still true that the privilege granted these companies is of doubtful advantage to the best interests of the business. If the dividends upon the capital stock are limited in amount, there is no added incentive to the officials through the existence of the capital stock to manage the company well, and the capital stock remains as a dangerous weapon by means of which men can obtain control of the company. If the dividends are not limited in amount, there is the possibility that the participating policy-holders will be mulcted to the advantage of the stockholders. If, as in the case of some companies, the dividends beyond a certain amount which the company can pay upon the capital stock are limited to the profits made from the non-participating policy-holders, the division of the fixed charges of the company can be so arranged as not to do substantial justice to the participating policy-holders. For these reasons the state is justified, if not in prohibiting stock life insurance companies from writing participating policies, at least in exercising much more control over their affairs than is exercised over other corporations.

The second peculiarity differentiating stock life insurance companies from other corporations is that the stockholders of the life company soon come into nearly absolute control of much larger assets than the capital originally invested. To be sure, this is true in a way also of banks and other fiduciary institutions, but the insurance company differs radically from a bank in that its reserves, unlike deposits, cannot be withdrawn at the will of those to whom they belong. No matter how inefficient the management of a stock company, there may be no weeding out of incompetent men. The policy-holders, who are the most interested, have no redress. They cannot withdraw their savings, thus showing their disapproval of the management, without a considerable financial sacrifice. They cannot change the management. The men in control own the capital stock, and to displace them it is necessary that a controlling interest in the capital be purchased. Not always have owners of a majority interest been willing to sell; only an aroused public opinion has forced them to part with the control of a company.

Furthermore, stock-life insurance companies are at the mercy of designing financiers who may seek to control them. All the stock companies are subject to this danger, and many have suffered already. The American Life of Philadelphia was wrecked in two years by men who surreptitiously purchased a controlling interest.[1] These men never had any intention in purchasing the stock other than to possess themselves as quickly as possible of the American's valuable assets. A similar disaster to the Phœnix Life of Hartford, which at one time had a guarantee capital, was averted only by a special session of the Connecticut legislature, which passed an act changing the Phœnix into a purely mutual company.[2] The Equitable and the Washington of New York are at the present time under the domination of one man. The Prudential of New Jersey is controlled absolutely by a small group of men who, in 1902, tried to avoid the necessity of keeping even six million dollars invested as a controlling interest in Prudential stock. The scheme for effecting this release was as follows: The Prudential Insurance Company was to purchase a controlling interest in the Fidelity Trust Company, and a contract was entered into between the Fidelity and the majority interest of the Prudential stockholders, in which the latter contracted to sell their holdings of Prudential stock to the trust company.[3] In this way the directors of the Prudential could have perpetuated their control without any financial

[1] *The Insurance Spectator*, 1890, p. 305, and the *Pennsylvania Life Insurance Report for* 1889.

[2] P. Henry Woodward, "History of Insurance in Connecticut," p. 97.

[3] *Massachusetts Life Insurance Report*, 1902. Preface.

outlay whatever. The plan was defeated by an appeal to the courts, brought by the Massachusetts Insurance Commissioners,[1] but President Dryden has since announced that the "good" results of such a merger have been secured in an unobjectionable manner.[2] A New Jersey investment company controls the Bankers' Life of New York,[3] while a few years ago a coterie of New York financiers purchased a controlling interest in the United States Life of that city. It is not asserted that all the companies which have here been enumerated have suffered through the control exercised by the capital stock; on the contrary, some of them have been most excellently managed by stockholders. Some, however, have already suffered seriously, and it is believed that all in which the control is lodged exclusively in a few hands are in a precarious position. The assets which the stockholders control really belong to the policy-holders, and yet the policy-holders cannot withdraw that which belongs to them, since they have entered into long-time contracts.

Certainly the problems connected with management of stock life insurance companies are serious; so serious, indeed, that it is urged in many quarters that the state should not allow such companies to be organized. All insurance is essentially mutual in principle; the mutual system has demonstrated its fitness in dealing with life contingencies, and if the states would amend their laws, capital stock would be unnecessary in starting a life insurance company;[4] legislatures might not be entirely unjustified in prohibiting the formation of stock life companies.

[1] *The Insurance Spectator*, 1902, p. 223.

[2] *Massachusetts Insurance Report*, 1903, p. xxxix.

[3] *The Insurance Age*, 1904.

[4] Nearly all states insist upon a system of net valuation of policies. Under such a system it is practically impossible to start a new life insurance company, unless capitalists stand ready to make up deficiencies during the early years. In other ways, state laws have been so framed as seriously to discourage the formation of any but stock companies.

As regards control, a company which is mixed — that is to say, a company which has capital stock but which allows policy-holders to vote — possesses no considerable advantage over a purely stock company. The restrictions placed upon the policy-holders' voting powers are such in most cases that the concession has little practical value. For instance, the Michigan Mutual is a mixed company with $500,000 of capital stock. Each share of stock has a vote. In addition, policy-holders insured for life for $5000 in amount may vote in person only.[1] The management can rest assured that 5000 persons carrying $5000 policies of a particular kind will never present themselves in Detroit to cast their ballots in person. In the Metropolitan of New York there are 40,000 shares of stock. Policy-holders paying $100 premium per annum may vote, but two-thirds of the directors must be stockholders, so that the privilege granted to the policy-holders is worthless.[2] The Manhattan has a thousand shares of stock, each share entitling its owner to one vote. Policy-holders paying an annual premium of $75 on a life policy may vote, but half of the directors must be stockholders.[3] Half of the board with the president is all that is needed for control, even if the policy-holders should elect all the directors to which they are entitled. The Home is likewise a mixed company. Policy-holders paying $80 annual premium may vote.[4] The testimony before the Armstrong committee showed that the Home has never been troubled with policy-holders voting; in the forty-seven years of its existence, only one policy-holder has appeared to cast his ballot.[5] It does not appear that mismanagement has been so common in the history of mixed companies as in the case of stock companies, and this is due, perhaps, to the latent

[1] Article IV of Constitution.

[2] New York Laws of 1868, Chap. XLVIII, §§ 6 and 11.

[3] Charter, §§ 5, 8, and 9.

[4] Charter, Art. V.

[5] Testimony of George E. Ide, *Armstrong Report*, p. 3587.

possibility that policy-holders will assert their rights; nevertheless a mixed company would seem to be, for all practical purposes, a stock company, and as regards control it presents most of the problems and dangers inherent in a stock company.

Nor is the question of management and control solved when companies are made mutual in their organization. The system of mutual life insurance contemplates a management elected by the policy-holders and responsible to them. This theory of government has, however, never been worked out in practice in the United States according to the spirit of its constitution. The long distances and the expenses of traveling have made it impossible from the beginning for policy-holders to cast their ballots in person. Resort has been made to proxy voting, and the result of proxy voting, as allowed by most of the states, has been to make the management of mutual companies as certain of tenure, and hence as careless of the rights of policy-holders, as have been the managements of stock companies. State laws have placed few restrictions on the collection and voting of proxies. In some instances policy-holders have even signed a proxy when making application for a policy; in many instances they have given their rights to the officials for long periods. A part of the agents' work each year has been to gather proxy votes, and send them in to the home office, so that the management should have at all times a sufficient number of proxy votes to defeat any movement of opposition on the part of dissatisfied policy-holders. The companies have always gone about the gathering of proxies quietly, for they have not cared to remind members of their rights, yet they have succeeded in keeping a large number always on hand.

Whoever in the company controls the proxies, controls the company. In 1870 there was an internal conflict in the Mutual Life. On the day of the election a considerable number of policy-holders appeared in person to vote. President Winston of the company controlled ten thousand proxies. In the afternoon, with the outcome of the election in doubt, Winston appeared with several thousand of the proxy votes, cast them in favor of himself, and the day was won.[1] The same thing has happened often enough to show the policy-holders the futility of opposition. Policy-holders have come to take no interest in the active management of companies, and certain officials have stayed in power so long that they have come to look upon their company as a personal asset, the sense of private property becoming so strong in some cases that they have felt that control of a company ought to be inherited.[2]

Officers of all the companies are practically unanimous in declaring that the present system of voting in mutual companies, or rather what was the system a year and a half ago, should not be changed. That section of the Armstrong law which changed the method of voting in mutual companies was vigorously opposed by the New York companies, and during the past winter similar legislation in other states has met the opposition of the mutual companies in those states. Many of the officials recognize that the old system is far from ideal, but they believe that the proposed reforms will lead to worse conditions in making an annual contest for the control of the companies a probable event. They hold that any changes in the laws calculated to make such yearly contests for control inevitable will do more harm to the insurance business than the present system has done. They urge that it is not fair to subject a company, which has been brought to a successful stage of its existence through efforts of its officers, to annual contests for control. Such contests, it is believed, will surely follow the adoption of the proposed reform methods of voting. They point out that men are always willing to listen to evil reports regarding anybody in power; and

[1] President Winston's circular letter of April 16, 1877, to the policy-holders of the Mutual Life. See also, Julius Wilcox, *Scribner's Magazine*, Volume XIV, pp. 382, 383.

[2] *Wisconsin Life Insurance Report*, 1903, Preface.

that the greater the ease with which a change in administration can be secured, the greater the chance of success for selfish and unjust methods which will be used for securing a change. As a final objection, they maintain that the expense attendant upon an annual repetition of such a demonstration as has been witnessed in New York during the year past is a greater strain on a company than is a good sized "graft"; while the annual throwing of mud and the staining of a company's reputation, with the consequent loss of policy-holders and trouble in getting new members, entail far greater expense and loss than any sort of extravagance. On these grounds, the officers oppose the changes in insurance laws revising methods of electing trustees.

If such conditions as indicated would result from any method enabling policy-holders easily to express their desires, then we should unite with the companies in opposing the new laws. However, it seems that the officials of the various mutual companies have become unduly alarmed. With complete power in the hands of the policy-holders and an easy method of voting devised, it is not at all probable that there would be an annual contest for control. A management which is capable and conscientious may be sure that policy-holders will have sense enough to keep it in power. Crafty financiers may seek to get a board of trustees elected of their liking, but they will soon learn the folly of going to the heavy expense of a campaign to oust an efficient management. It is almost safe to say that it will be many years before we shall witness another campaign like that carried on during the past year for control of the two large New York companies.

Some of the officials have expressed the fear that in a campaign for control of a mutual company, policy-holders will not know what is to their advantage. They, therefore, are afraid to trust the issues to them. Such statements remind one of the arguments in favor of an autocratic form of government. An autocratic form of government is good if the autocrat is wise and beneficent. But since autocrats in the past have not always been wise and beneficent, a government responsible to the people has worked better. So it will be in life insurance corporations. Policy-holders are the company, its gain is their gain, its injury is their injury, and they will soon, if not immediately, begin to examine closely the men who are seeking their votes to oust an existing management.

Besides the natural conservatism of investors which will work in favor of the management in power, there is still another advantage which the officials possess. It will practically always happen that the agency force will work in favor of the administration party, and with the agency force so disposed, the men in power will have such an advantage in a campaign that even better men will have a hard task in defeating an administration ticket. This is as it should be. The end that is desired by those who see the evil of the old system is not an annual scramble for control of the companies, but such an easy method of removal that the officers will at all times be forced to keep in mind their responsibility to policy-holders.

A more fruitful question for discussion to the man who desires a change from the old system is whether an easy and effective method of voting in mutual companies can be devised. New York has made a serious attempt to put the policy-holders in control. In the revision of the insurance laws of the state, in 1906, it was provided that two lists of policy-holders' names and addresses should be filed by each mutual company with the Superintendent of Insurance at Albany, and two similar lists with the general agents in each state and foreign country in which business is transacted; that the tickets be nominated by the administration five months prior to the election, and by an opposition party at least three months before the election; and that policy-holders should be allowed to vote in person, by mail, or by proxy.

One election has already taken place under the New

York law. Some criticism may be offered of the method adopted. In the first place, the companies are bitterly opposed to that section of the law which provides for public listing of the names and addresses of policy-holders. The New York companies would rather have this provision repealed than any other of the so-called Armstrong laws. Officers of mutual companies in other states will make no compromise on this subject. The contention of the companies in this respect is well grounded. Such a public posting of names does a serious amount of damage to the companies compelled to obey the law. Agents of rival companies prize a list of policy-holders in another company very highly, not only for the purpose of twisting the policy-holders into their own companies, but also because the best purchasers of insurance are those who already have policies. For this reason, the companies regard this provision of the law as a violation of their rights not to be condoned.

Yet such a measure, or some substitute for the measure, is absolutely necessary if there is to be any appreciable opposition to the administration party. In the past when there has been among policy-holders wide-spread dissatisfaction with a management, opposition has been ineffectual because it never could be united. If such opposition is ever to accomplish its ends, it must be concentrated, and no sort of coöperation is possible unless the policy-holders have some means of communicating with each other. So long as the administration alone possesses a list of the voters with their addresses, it has an advantage which a scattered opposition cannot overcome. All that is left to the opposition under these circumstances is communication by means of advertisements in the papers, an expensive method, as well as one of doubtful utility. Therefore, unless some method is devised of allowing the opposition to communicate freely with voters, the system of control by policy-holders fails. However, it is not necessary that the list of names should be open to public inspection. It might be practicable to have all the literature which any opposition ticket may wish to send out addressed by the state at the expense of the opposition, or even sent out by the administration under the supervision of the state, but still at the expense of the opposition. Company officials do not take kindly to either suggestion, holding that the opposition has no right to this advantage of intercommunication. In doing so, they are carrying their opposition too far. The officials have no inherent right to hold their positions irrespective of the wishes of the policy-holder, and the latter rightly insist upon some means of close coöperation.

Insurance men are further opposed to the enactment of laws similar to those of New York, on the ground that the carrying out of such a system of voting entails a very heavy direct expense. They point to the situation in New York where the cost of counting the ballots alone reached $50,000 for each one of the large companies. They assert that such an annual expense is a heavy burden to place upon the policy-holders, when, in most cases, it is not necessary. Without desiring to criticize too strongly the men who were in charge of the counting of the ballots in New York, it seems that the work was unnecessarily drawn out. As a matter of fact, if the inspectors of election appointed by the officials of the two large companies, and paid by the companies $25 per day for their services, had counted ballots as rapidly as do the judges of elections in our political contests, the votes would have been counted in perhaps a third of the time it did take to count them. As the ballots in the insurance election were the simplest possible to count — there being no split ballots and practically only one office for which to count, and in one case only two tickets, and in the other three, in the field — it does seem that the suspicion raised in some quarters that the contest was drawn out for political effect is well grounded.

If this is true, the heavy expenses of the present election cannot be used as an argument against the proposed changes. If the suspicion is without truth, and the elections are really expensive, it has been already pointed out that few elections will be carried out on the scale that the present contest has been waged. Admitting, however, that annual elections will cost from thirty thousand to fifty thousand dollars for each company, it is no conclusive argument against the reform measures. The states might well relieve the companies of taxation, and make them have annual elections for the sake of securing the gain that will accrue from such a change.

It should be noted that the reformers, as well as insurance officials, criticize the New York law. The Armstrong law still allows proxy voting. The application of proxy voting in mutual life companies is a misapplication of a system working fairly well in joint stock concerns. Under the old system of electing trustees, it was necessary to allow the officers to collect proxies, but when policy-holders are allowed to vote by mail, the system cannot be justified. The man who under the reformed conditions gives his proxy is the man who is not interested enough to care what the outcome is, and gives his proxy as a personal favor to the first one who solicits it. The administration is the only party which has the machinery necessary to solicit these proxies, therefore the disinterested or indifferent policy-holders control the outcome of the election rather than the men who are interested and have informed themselves. That administration tickets won the New York elections was largely due to the work of agents in soliciting proxy votes. While not desiring to express any opinion upon the outcome of the New York elections, as a general principle it is wrong that the careless and indifferent policy-holders should dominate the situation. Therefore, the right of proxy voting should be abolished.

Company officials need not be alarmed if such a system of voting as is here advocated be carried out. It will not mean frequent changes in management because such changes will be unnecessary. The system has been tried for many years in the largest company in the British Empire, the Australian Mutual Provident Society. No serious difficulties have arisen in connection with the operation of the system. There has been but one revolution in the company, and this one demonstrated the merits of the plan. Incidentally it is worth noting that this company has been one of the best managed in the world. Mr. Dawson says that in nearly all respects, dividends, economy of management, small ratio of lapses, growth, and favorable mortality experience, its career is unprecedented.[1]

Some have said that these large companies cannot be run on the basis of control by policy-holders because the party system cannot be adopted. It is hoped that the last part of this statement is true. The control of these business corporations should be free from politics. It would be suicidal to subject them to a change in management each year. This, as has been pointed out, is not contemplated in the proposed changes. Under the plan which is submitted, it is believed that managements will be just as stable as they have been in the past, indeed more so. At every election it will be the administration against the field, and if the record of the men in power has been satisfactory, it will commend the administration ticket to the policy-holders. The desire to let well enough alone will be sufficiently strong to resist a change, and because there exists an easy method of turning out corrupt managements, these managements will try not to become corrupt. The officers will still have a chance to stay in the business for life, developing a great company, not because they control twenty or thirty thousand proxy votes, but because they are efficient.

[1] "The Business of Life Insurance," p. 128.

CHAPTER XXIII

MISTAKES IN STATE REGULATION OF THE INSURANCE BUSINESS [1]

DURING the last three years we have heard a great deal about the system of American life insurance being on trial, and while, as a whole, it has shown a remarkably clean record, unfortunately some of the charges made have been proved. The public in this situation knew of but one resource, legal regulation, and without stopping to consider how legal regulation has worked in the past, demanded more of it as the remedy for present evils.

The public has not realized that the system of life insurance has not been the only culprit before the bar. Practically every indictment against the insurance companies has been an indictment against state supervision, with which the public has fondly hoped to reform the other criminal. For more than fifty years the states have been trying to regulate the business of life insurance. No constitutional limitations have hindered them in their work. The problem before them has been clear-cut, for the present is not the only time that abuses in management have been exposed. Other exposures have been made, and there has been the same sort of legislation; yet it has failed to prevent a recurrence of the abuses. Before 1905, the State of New York had seen fit to amend her law regulating investments twenty-one times, but it was found necessary to make an entirely new revision in the following year. Since the states have been well aware of the problem

[1] By Lester W. Zartman, Assistant Professor of Political Economy in Yale University. Reprinted from pages 24–43, Volume XVII, *Yale Review*.

before them, and have not been neglectful of their opportunities to try to regulate the business, yet have failed, something must be radically wrong. Either they have pursued wrong methods of supervision, or the system of supervision by the separate states is incapable of accomplishing the desired results, or both reasons explain the half century of failure.

Let us examine the situation and find out wherein the trouble lies. In the first place, have the states attempted to accomplish the desired results by wrong methods of supervision? Without going into any extended history of state regulation, let us summarize, briefly, the main lines along which the states have worked.

1. They have laid down standards of solvency; that is, they have determined what shall be the maximum rate of interest, and the rate of mortality used in computing the liabilities of the life insurance companies.

2. They have regulated investments. Usually the regulations have simply restricted investments to certain classes of securities, though many attempts have been made to prescribe the territorial limits within which the investments must be made. In doing this, the chief object has been to make the companies' investments secure, but there has also been the idea of helping out the commercial interests of the state.[1]

3. They have attempted to secure some measure of publicity. They have provided for annual reports by each company to the state, compulsory investigation by the state into the affairs of the companies, and to carry out the provisions of these laws have created special state machinery, that is, departments of insurance.

4. They have passed measures to secure equitable treatment of the policy-holders, such as non-forfeiture laws, incontestability laws, etc.

[1] For a full description of the limitations placed upon the investment powers of the companies, see the author's "Investments of Life Insurance Companies," Holt & Co., 1906, Chapter VI.

Under these four general headings can be grouped about all the regulations enacted by any state prior to 1906. During that year and the previous one, several legislative committees found the life insurance business apparently so mismanaged that some of the states came to the conclusion that they ought to manage the business of life insurance themselves. They wanted to do this without assuming the responsibility which state life insurance would involve; they would leave the business in the hands of private men who would thus bear the responsibility, but the legislatures would direct the business.

The way in which the states have attempted to manage the business without assuming responsibility has been by enacting laws:

1. Limiting salaries.
2. Limiting amount of expense to secure new business.
3. Limiting surplus.
4. Limiting amount of new business.
5. Prescribing the methods of allotting dividends.
6. Restricting the field of investment.

How much of all this legislation is good; how much of it is bad? How much of it is in the right direction and will accomplish good results; how much of it is in the wrong direction and will do no good and perhaps cause serious injury? These are questions which ought to be settled correctly before the laws are in operation any longer, and before other states follow the example of those which have already enacted such legislation.

Let us examine this legislation in detail. In the first place, should the states lay down standards of solvency, that is, prescribe the rate of interest and the mortality table to be used in computing the liabilities of a life insurance company? There is not much objection to such laws. As a matter of fact, these laws have been practically harmless. The standards adopted by the states have almost always been much more liberal than those which the companies have voluntarily adopted. In laying down these fixed standards of solvency, the states have hindered the development of new plans for cheaper insurance, but, generally speaking, no very serious objections can be raised against them.[1]

Should the states regulate investments? There are grave reasons for believing that they should not. The best that they can do in this respect is to limit the companies to certain classes of securities; to select specific securities would be suicidal. But there is no class of investments of which all in the class are good. A study of life insurance mismanagement will show that mortgage loans have been used just as much for speculative purposes as has any other class of securities. There are good securities in all classes, and good insurance managers ought not to have their privileges in this respect curtailed. To curtail them will mean a loss to policy-holders. The scheming, self-seeking manager will find in any law, which can be enacted regarding investments, so many chances to accomplish his ends, that to limit the field of investments is to injure the good manager without accomplishing any desired results.[2] The history of investments shows that the wise manager of insurance funds will scatter his investments. This cannot be done if the states restrict investments to certain classes. Such laws should therefore be repealed.

While space will not permit of any extended discussion of individual acts, particular attention should be directed

[1] Cf. Emory McClintock, "Insurance, a Text Book," pp. 129, 130. Also Sheppard Homans, Insurance Year Book, 1890, p. 532, and the report of the committee on insurance appointed by the New York Legislature, *Insurance Times*, May, 1882.

[2] The question of restricting investments has been of such importance that many able articles have appeared on the subject. See J. B. Gillison, *Transactions of the Faculty of Actuaries*, Volume II, Part II, p. 104; Mr. Wegenast, *Transactions of the Actuarial Society of America*, Volume VII, p. 361; *the Insurance Spectator*, Volume VI, p. 308; T. B. Sprague, *Assurance Magazine*, Volume XVI, p. 79; also George King, *Journal of the Institute of Actuaries*, 1892, Volume XXIX, p. 496.

to laws compelling investments to be made in certain localities. The states which have had insurance companies of their own have made attempts, from time to time, to compel these companies to invest their assets within the state.[1] On the other hand, the states without such companies, but paying premiums, have thought that they were being drained of their capital, and so have passed laws compelling the companies to invest at least a portion of the reserves within the state where they originated. It seemed a few years ago as if this type of legislation, inspired by such selfish motives, had disappeared. However, within the last year, the demand for such legislation has reappeared, especially in the South, and has resulted in action by one state. In 1907 the Texas legislature passed the Robertson bill, and it became a law. According to the provisions of this act, all companies doing business in Texas must invest 75 per cent. of the reserve upon Texas policies in Texas securities, bonds, stocks, and mortgage loans, and deposit these securities in Texas, subject to local taxation. The motive back of the bill was not to secure safety to the policy-holders; it was passed partly to create a market for Texas securities, but mostly, judging from the debate in the legislature, to secure revenue for certain counties. Since the local rate of taxation is about 2 per cent., the law meant the confiscation of nearly one-half the interest necessary to mature the contracts. Even companies which had a sufficient sum invested in the state to cover their reserves were compelled to withdraw to avoid the excessive taxation. Valuable agency organizations were broken up, and though Texas is already realizing the mistake made, the experiment will cost policy-holders everywhere a goodly sum. This is an extreme example of state regulation of investments, but it is typical of the motives which have actuated much legislation.

[1] Cf. "Investments of Life Insurance Companies," H. Holt & Co., pp. 160–165.

Should the states enact laws to secure the equitable treatment of policy-holders? Like almost all restrictive legislation these laws were passed to remedy certain abuses, but competition among the companies was well on the way to give all the advantages which these laws give, before the first one was enacted. The companies have now gone much further in granting liberal advantages to the policy-holders than the laws require. In fact, if the competition goes much further, the legislators, if they are true to their traditional policy of intervention, will have to enact laws prohibiting the companies from being too liberal to their policy-holders.

Of course, if a state, in attempting to secure equitable treatment of the policy-holders within the state simply secures what the companies have willingly given, no objection can be raised. But some of the states, in trying to secure equitable treatment of their policy-holders, have enacted very bad legislation. A large number of states make it a necessary condition of entrance that out-of-state corporations shall pledge themselves, in the event of any legal difficulties arising, not to take the cases out of the state courts.[1] The purpose of the laws is to prevent companies from making litigation expensive, a situation which they could stand better than most policy-holders; but the result is that the companies are deprived of what really is a constitutional right, the right to a trial in an unprejudiced court.

As another example of similar legislation, Alabama, a few years ago, enacted a law providing that if a life insurance company contested a policy in that State on the ground of misrepresentation in the application, the company should, before the case could be tried, deposit with the court all premiums paid by the assured upon the policy. If the company won the case, that is, proved the mis-

[1] Wisconsin Insurance Laws, section 1947 (5); Indiana Insurance Laws, section 361; Illinois Insurance Laws, section 375; Colorado Insurance Laws, section 29; Kentucky Insurance Laws, section 631.

representation of facts in the application, the court should pay back all the premiums to the defrauding ex-policy-holder.[1] What did this law virtually say to the citizens of Alabama? It told them to go ahead and cheat the insurance companies, to get policies by fraud if they cared to do so. If they were not caught, well and good; if caught, they would get their money back. The law was unjust in principle and demoralizing in its practice; yet it was passed after consideration by an American legislature.

Coming now to the new type of legislation, that enacted since 1905, and which enters into the details of management, what shall be said of it? Is it the wise thing, the proper thing, for the states to limit the salaries which a life insurance company can pay to its officials? Salaries of such men may be too high, but there is serious objection to lowering them by statutory means. How much is a man worth? To most men $25,000 is a large salary; in fact, few men are worth that amount. Yet some men may well be paid twice that sum and still be cheap, because they will effect economies or reap profits which will pay their salaries several times over. There are presidents to-day of insurance companies receiving so-called large salaries, who, from the standpoint of efficiency, are worth twice as much as other presidents who are receiving half as much salary. It takes genius to maintain the agency organization of a life insurance company at the highest point of efficiency; it takes ability to invest and care for several hundred million dollars of assets. State legislatures might well think twice before placing a limit on salaries, lest in so doing they make it impossible for the companies to secure the kind of men they need.

How much ought a company to pay to secure new business? Frankly, it is a difficult question for the most skilful of actuaries to answer.[2] If life insurance is good for the

[1] W. H. Mylrea, "Insurance, a Text Book," p. 871.

[2] Cf., Published letters of the noted English Actuary, George King, to T. B. Macaulay, September, 1906.

individual and, through the individual, for the public, then it is worth a price. Truly enough the price may be too high, but that is a problem for the individual to solve, just as is true of the price of bread and opera tickets. The function of the state in the matter is not to regulate the price, but simply to put the individual in possession of the facts and allow him to judge for himself.

Should the state limit by law the amount of new business which a company can write? The idea back of such a law is either that a company will become so large as to make the men controlling its assets exercise a power dangerous to the welfare of the state, or that if some restraint is not placed on size, the race for bigness will lead the officials into bad practices. From either standpoint the law is a curiosity.[1] If a company is well managed it will not hurt the state by its size; if it is growing rapidly because it supplies insurance cheaply, it ought to be allowed to continue its growth. That is what we want, cheap insurance and lots of it. Therefore, let each company write all the insurance it can. The other viewpoint, to limit expenses by simply limiting size, is absurd. It is an attempt to reverse economic law similar to that made by a Western legislator who offered a bill calling for the repeal of the law of demand and supply.

Finally, should the states regulate the amount of surplus which the life insurance companies may accumulate? Before they do so, they will have to decide how much surplus a company ought to have. It was suggested in the report of the Wisconsin special committee on insurance that 4 per cent. would be about the right amount.[2] The legislature of New York thought that 5 per cent. was the

[1] Mr. D. P. Fackler in an address before the commissioners of insurance in convention at St. Paul, 1892, gave arguments in favor of regulation. See also, Report of New York Legislative Investigating Committee, p. 297.

[2] Report of the Wisconsin Insurance Investigating Committee, 1906, p. 90.

proper amount for large companies, and so enacted.[1] In less than a year events proved that it was a very good thing that the companies had more. If they had not possessed on January 1, 1907, through past accumulations, a greater surplus than 5 per cent. of liabilities, and if the insurance laws of the state had been strictly enforced, we would probably have had, by December 31, 1907, the spectacle of large companies placed in the hands of receivers. The amount of surplus needed depends upon the character of assets, and the states might well leave its amount to be determined by the men who are responsible for the safe conduct of the business.

What then is our conclusion concerning state regulation? It has failed to prevent abuses in management; it has not succeeded in keeping companies from failing. The laws have attempted too much. Many of them have been useless; some of them have been harmful to the business and to the public; and some of them positively dangerous.

Some one asks, have not evils really existed in the business of life insurance for the correction of which the laws were designed? Yes, they have existed from time to time. Were there not abuses which were really serious? Yes. Well, why not remedy them? Every one who has the best interests of the business at heart believes in remedying them. Some insurance men are asking for the repeal of the present restrictive laws, not because these laws are bad in principle, but because the laws place obstacles in the way of their ambitions. These men want the laws repealed in order that the business may be carried on again under the conditions which existed prior to 1905. It is not the purpose of this paper to advocate a repeal of the insurance laws for any such purpose. It is devoutly hoped that many of the conditions existing in the insurance business prior to 1905 have passed away forever.

These restrictive laws are opposed because they are wrong in principle, and are bound to injure the legitimate

[1] Insurance Laws, 1906, section 87.

interests in the insurance business, while all the good which they can accomplish could be accomplished in some other way. This other way has been suggested by others, but since it has not been adopted, it should be urged again. There is good reason for believing that if laws were passed securing real publicity and proper responsibility, practically all the other laws limiting and restricting the insurance business could be repealed.[1]

It is urged against such a simple remedy that we have had publicity in the insurance business for years and years, and that if it were such a panacea, it would have had better results. Some good results have come from publicity, but the trouble is, in spite of assertions to the contrary, that we have not had publicity. To be sure, there have been annual reports of each company published by the state, and investigations of companies by state officials, but until the last year or so very little has been published that the companies have not wanted published. The public has relied upon the state departments of insurance for information regarding the insurance companies transacting business in the state, and these departments have not succeeded in giving the facts. Every state has created a separate department to look after the insurance interests of the commonwealth, and has endowed this department with power to investigate companies and to publish a report of the findings. Either these departments of insurance have not found out the facts in company managements, or, having found the facts, have not revealed them to the public.

Nowhere in our public life can be found better examples of inefficiency than in our state departments of insurance. The reason for this is not difficult to discover. Like all the other state positions, they have been made the spoils

[1] The value of publicity and responsibility in the insurance business was suggested many years ago by Mr. Finch of Indiana in an address before the National Convention of Insurance Commissioners, held at Harrisburg, Pa., September, 1876.

of the politician. In a score of states, the commissioner of insurance, as the head of the department of insurance is usually called, is elected by a direct vote of the people.[1] Under such a condition, the official is bound to be a politician. In several other states he is elected by the legislature, and in the remaining states he is appointed by the governor, in each case with no better results than when elected directly by the people.

To illustrate the political degeneracy of the office, a description of the organization of a department of insurance in one of the states may not be out of place. This department at the time referred to employed fifteen men, besides a number of stenographers. The head of the department was a noted politician in the state, who, after a year's tenure of office, had not yet taken the trouble to read the insurance laws or to post himself with regard to the requirements of the reports which his department was expected to secure from the companies. The attorney for the department, although on a regular salary, found little time to give to his work, since a political campaign was on that year and his chief, the governor, needed help. The chief clerk, on a salary of $3000 per annum, came down to the department each morning to open the mail, a task the two negro janitors might have performed very creditably, and did perform when it was stormy. Similarly, throughout the department, there were men with official titles who knew nothing about the insurance business, rendering no service, but drawing good salaries. In the rear room were three men who were the insurance brains of the whole department. Holding office during successive administrations, no commissioner dared to discharge them, for without their aid not even the routine of the department could be carried through.[2]

[1] In a few states only is the commissioner of insurance as such elected by the people; in a large number of states, however, some state official, who is elected by a direct vote of the people, is *ex-officio* insurance commissioner.

[2] Since one of the charges which Governor Hughes brought against

So it is in most of the states. To be sure, now and then an able man has been given the position of commissioner of insurance, but most of the commissioners have been simply able politicians. Even the able commissioners have not succeeded in accomplishing much, for the tenure of office is short, and time has not been given to learn the details of a very technical business. The able helpers in the rear office have done what they could to protect and foster the insurance interests of the state, but, without authority, they have not exercised much influence. They can only make recommendations to the head of the department, who decides concerning these according to the way in which his political life will be influenced. This, in general, is the kind of state departments which we have had, and now have, to administer the insurance laws.

The states, in giving to the departments of insurance the power to make an investigation of the companies whenever they saw fit, had the idea that the departments would watch the companies carefully, and would make searching investigations of the affairs of the different companies to see that no irregularities took place. How differently has state supervision worked out in practice! In many cases there has been no investigation into a company's affairs until the public demand for such an investigation has grown so insistent that the department could not longer remain inactive.[1] Many of the abuses revealed by the Armstrong committee were common knowledge to insurance men as early as 1903. Syndicate operations, year-end transactions, use of money to help out other enterprises, — all these evils were freely hinted at in insurance circles. Under such circumstances, it was the duty of the insurance departments to make thorough investigations of those companies under suspicion. Instead of doing so, the New

Mr. Kelsey was that he had not yet read the insurance laws, although having been in office nearly a year, it might be well to state that the description here given does not refer to the New York department.

[1] *The Insurance Spectator*, Volume LV, p. 295.

York department held back, and it was not until the public had become thoroughly aroused by the disclosures made in the family quarrel in one company that finally the superintendent of insurance bestirred himself.

Even in the cases where the insurance departments have made investigations, these investigations have not meant much. Sometimes thorough examinations have been made; more often the examinations have been largely a farce. When an examination is made, the laws give the commissioners the privilege of making public only such portions of their findings as each may deem fit. Under such a law, a thorough examination has not much terror to evil-doers. Pressure can be brought to bear upon a complacent commissioner to publish nothing disagreeable. The management promises to reform, the commissioners agree that nothing more could be done if the findings were made public. The result is that disagreeable things are covered over, and no one is the wiser.

Under such circumstances, it is not strange that there has been some mismanagement. Really, the only wonder is that there has not been more, for it must be remembered that notwithstanding the searching investigations which have been made into insurance affairs during the past several years, very little actual stealing has been found. That this has been true speaks well for the high character in general of the men in charge of these great trust interests.

However, the weak managers, the inefficient managers, the wrong-doing managers, must be eliminated from the business. To accomplish this result, there must be publicity. Are there campaign contributions? Find it out. Are some of the officials engaging in syndicate operations at the expense of the policy-holders? Find it out. Are some companies depositing large amounts in trust companies to make those companies profitable? Find it out. Are some of the managers so inefficient that they cannot get business in any other way than by paying twice as much for it as other managers are paying? Find it out. The policy-holders have delegated to the state the duty of finding out these things. The state should find them out, and having found them out should publish all the facts. That would be real publicity.

Opponents of this policy say that since no one reads the insurance reports, there is no use of publishing in them so many facts. It is true that the general public takes but little interest in insurance matters, save in a time of great exposures, but it is a mistake to assume that no one reads the annual reports of the insurance department. The most vigilant lot of men in the country are studying these reports — the agents of rival companies. They are looking for faults of management in other companies, and if there were real publicity of the insurance business, the mismanaged companies would go to the wall quickly or reform their methods of doing business. Just to show what a little publicity will accomplish, let us consider the action of a large company a few years ago.[1] The company was a good one, but it was not accustomed to giving large surrender values to lapsing policy-holders. One year a few of the states demanded that the companies report how large a per cent. of the reserves they gave to lapsed policies. The next year this company practically doubled the amount it had given heretofore. It could not afford to allow rival agents that weapon against it. If a little publicity will secure such a reform, it is easy to see that full publicity will bring great results.

Along with publicity must go responsibility. The day of the trustee who lends his name to dignify the literature of a life insurance company, and expects to give nothing else, cannot pass away too quickly. In theory, the trustees are supposed to watch carefully the conduct of the executive officials, and to pass upon the general business plans to be pursued. No one expects them to manage the com-

[1] Report of the Wisconsin Insurance Investigating Committee, p. 207.

panies, — that is the work of the executive officials; but the insuring public does expect these bodies of trustees to know perfectly well what is going on within the company. That the trustees have not known what was going on has been amply demonstrated. If a trustee has been more than ordinarily conscientious, he has attended the monthly meetings of the board. He has listened to the report of the officials, comparing the month's business with the business of the same month a year before, has approved reports of finance and other committees, perhaps has asked a few questions, and then has gone away none the wiser. What he has learned about the actual condition of the company is whatever the officials have chosen to tell him. The whole system is largely a farce, and one can only wonder that business life will tolerate such conditions.

The practice ought to be changed. Make the trustees something more than dignified figure-heads.[1] Since it is the function of trustees to know what is going on in their company, make them know. This could be accomplished by a very simple law. Make it obligatory for the trustees, or at least a committee of the trustees, to sign the annual report of the company, and then hold these men legally responsible for any misstatement contained in the report. What would be the result? Before the committee of trustees would sign the report they would make a searching investigation of the affairs of the company, or, more probably, would call in professional accountants to make such an investigation as would reveal the true state of affairs. Thus, such a law would accomplish two good results; it would make the trustees familiar with the operations of the company, and it would insure to the public true annual reports.

As an indication of the need of such investigations into a company's affairs by capable men, the experience of a

[1] This question is discussed at length in an article by the author on "The Control of Life Insurance Companies," *Journal of Political Economy*, November, 1907.

large company a few years ago may be cited. Certain changes in the office force made it desirable that an extensive investigation be made into the company's affairs. A well-known firm of accountants was employed, and the officials of the company themselves were surprised at many of the revelations made. There had not been much actual dishonesty, but the officials did not know the business. They had known, in a general way, the total expenditures and total receipts, and that so much was going for agency expenses and so much somewhere else, but of what expenditures were paying and what were not, they were ignorant. Thus a law securing responsibility might not only secure good moral management; it might secure more efficient management.

The simplest and best remedy then for the abuses in insurance management is publicity and responsibility. To whom shall we look to give the public this sort of legislation? The individual states could follow out the suggestions which have been made in this paper, and it is to be hoped that they may adopt them. But if we are ever to have a comprehensive solution of the problem of legal regulation of the insurance business in this country, it will have to come through supervision by the federal government.

The history of the insurance business in this country is pretty well known. The companies started as local concerns, and as such they took out state charters, thus coming under the jurisdiction of the state incorporating them. However, the companies soon found it convenient to expand into other states. Such expansion was necessary to secure a wide distribution of risks and to secure the economies of business on a large scale. That this expansion is desirable for a life insurance company, few would dispute, and in the case of a fire insurance company it is absolutely essential. Thus, some of the companies have come to do business in practically all the states, and all the companies are writing insurance in a number of states. With a system of supervision by the individual states, not only is each company under the jurisdiction of the state which chartered it, but it is also under the jurisdiction of each state in which it writes policies.

Under such a condition, even if we had the very best state supervision possible, there would be trouble. The business of a life insurance company is a unit; it cannot be divided up into forty-six different pieces. Therefore, when any state begins to make regulations concerning the business of one of the companies, it is legislating for the whole country. This would not be so bad if each state would make the same laws, but they do not and they never will. A problem of a course of action put to forty-six good and wise men will be solved in forty-six different ways. Similarly, if the problem of supervising the insurance business is put to forty-six legislatures, no matter how intelligent and broad-minded those legislatures may be, we are going to have forty-six different solutions. Witness the New York, Massachusetts, and Wisconsin laws enacted to remedy the abuses revealed by the Armstrong committee. One would be rash in saying that the legislatures of these states went about their work with an open mind, but in general there was a fairly honest endeavor to get at some solution of the difficulties. All three legislatures struggled with the same problem, yet each reached a radically different solution as to the proper way to supervise the business so as to prevent a recurrence of the evils. So it has been for half a century. Each state has gone ahead and enacted laws regulating the insurance business without giving much consideration to what the sister states were doing. Sometimes the laws passed in various states have been contradictory, but even when they have not been contradictory, they have imposed many hardships upon the companies. Therefore, because it is a good thing for the public that a company should do business in every state, and since the business of a company is a unit, supervision by the federal government would still be preferable to the system of state supervision working at its very best.

However, we must not compare federal supervision with ideal supervision by the individual states, but with state supervision as it actually works out in practice. To have the best state supervision it would be necessary to have legislatures free from prejudice. We do not have such legislatures. They are composed of politicians whose success often depends upon their catering to local interests. They do not go about the task of finding out what is the best thing to do for the insurance business in general, but, actuated by narrow motives, enact laws designed to favor their own particular state. Supposedly, these laws are for the best interests of the people of the state which enacts such laws, but granted that they are, does any state have the right to pass such laws as will interfere with the business of legitimate corporations of other states, and injure the citizens of other states? This question is as old as the country, but the sooner it is answered in the negative concerning insurance affairs the better it will be for the public.

The feeling of animosity shown by many of the states towards the insurance companies of other states has resulted in so much hostile legislation that the big problem before us is not to protect the people from this class of corporations, but to protect these great institutions against the people. Hostile insurance legislation has cost this country far more than has mismanagement of insurance companies.

While much harm is done to the insurance business because of the jealousy among the states, the abatement of that hostility brings out other weaknesses in state supervision. As has already been pointed out, if there is to be any effective publicity in insurance affairs, the supervising officials must make searching investigations into the affairs of the companies. Under the system of state supervision, which state shall make these examinations? Shall it be the duty of every state in which the company does business to make such an investigation? If all the states should do so, the insurance companies would have time for little other than examinations. In the early history of supervision, there was a great deal of examining done by each state of companies, no matter where chartered. It became such an intolerable nuisance, however, that there has grown up a sort of custom among state insurance departments, called state comity. Under this official custom, each department tacitly allows the state in which any company is incorporated to investigate the financial soundness of that company. In substance each official says to the others, you let me manage the companies of my state, and in return I will let you manage your companies. Such a solution of this difficulty was necessary, but what is the result? Simply that the whole country is more or less at the mercy of the insurance official of one state. Frequently it has happened that certain officials have had charge of important companies and have neglected their duties, yet the other commissioners, bound by custom, have been forced to stand by and allow the companies to pursue their wrong course undisturbed.[1] This is bad for the business; it is bad for the country; the remedy is national supervision.

Very few are in favor of national supervision of the insurance business unless it means an end to state interference with interstate business. To have the state departments remain with all their present powers, and to add to these a national department of insurance, would simply be complicating an already very complicated situation. If national supervision, however, would mean an end to state supervision over interstate insurance, there are very few who understand the business who would not welcome the change. The change ought to be made. It is a certainty that state supervision will never be able to cope

[1] For examples of how this works out in practice, see address of Colonel Hahn, Insurance Commissioner of Ohio, *Transactions of the National Convention of Insurance Commissioners*, 1895; also *Journal of Insurance Economics*, 1905, Volume XII, p. 113.

with the situation. It is not a question as to whether one is a believer in states' rights or a disbeliever. It is simply a question as to whether we are going to have efficient governmental supervision over this important business.

Besides the great advantage which national supervision would enjoy over state supervision in securing publicity and in putting an end to selfish, sectional legislation, there would be incidental benefits of great importance.[1]

1. There would be a great direct saving in expense over the present system. It is wasteful to have forty-six departments each duplicating the work of the other. Forty-six voluminous reports are issued each year, all containing practically the same information. Forty-five forty-sixths of this is unnecessary, and would be done away with under national supervision, resulting in the saving of several million dollars annually.

2. National supervision would, it is hoped, result in a more equitable system of taxing the insurance business. Under the system of state taxation, the man who pays his premiums into a life insurance company is frequently taxed twice, and in some cases three times. That such burdens should be placed upon men because, having to provide for their families, they must needs have recourse to life insurance, is a national disgrace, excused only on the ground of ignorance of the real nature of the business. Since much of this taxation is the result of jealous fear of the states that the others are profiting through the insurance business at their expense, national supervision would probably bring at least partial relief from this burden.

Some have objected to national supervision on the ground that the insurance laws enacted by Congress for the District of Columbia are about the worst on record.[2] The

[1] For a discussion of the value of national supervision in Canada, see an article by Mr. Frank Sanderson, *Transactions of the Actuarial Society of Edinburgh*, Volume III, p. 171.

[2] M. H. Robinson, "Government Regulation of Insurance," *Papers and Discussions of the Nineteenth Annual Meeting of the American Economic Association*, p. 149.

laws for the District are bad, but this does not mean much. It takes time, energy, and ability to work out a code of laws regulating so technical a business as that of life insurance, and it is easy to see that while Congress would not be willing to give much thought to a code applying only to the District of Columbia, the situation would be entirely changed if the question involved the insurance business of the whole country. In one case, a few hundred thousand people, with no representative in Congress, are involved; in the other, eighty millions are concerned.[1]

Finally, is national supervision possible? This has been a question of warm discussion during the last ten years. A careful study of the decisions of the United States Supreme Court would seem to indicate that national supervision of the insurance business can come only through an amendment to the Constitution, which makes the situation nearly hopeless. However, notwithstanding the definiteness of the decisions of the Supreme Court, there are two grounds for believing that national supervision may yet be possible. In the first place, all the decisions rendered by the court have arisen from cases dealing with state law. Congress has never passed a law regulating the business, and in our theory of government, a power not exercised by the national government is left to the individual states. If Congress would once exercise control over the insurance business, the Supreme Court very possibly might uphold the action as constitutional. The other ground on which to base hope for federal supervision lies in a possible change of mind on the part of the Supreme Court. Conditions change, the personnel of the court changes. With these changes, the court several times has found occasion exactly to reverse previous decisions.[2] It is not unreasonable to hope that now, since

[1] For further objection to national supervision, see E. P. Marshall, *Transactions of the Actuarial Society of America,* Volume V, Number 19, p. 242.

[2] The Supreme Court has reversed previous decisions regarding the

insurance has become of such national importance, the court may change its decision regarding the power of the states to supervise this business.

Summing up then the main contentions of this paper, the conclusion is that the indictment against state supervision can be sustained. It has failed seriously in the half century that it has been on trial. This failure has been due partly to the fact that the states have directed their activities along wrong lines, and partly to the fact that there are conflicting interests among the states. The remedy which has been suggested is in laws securing publicity and responsibility, these laws to be enforced by a national department of insurance.

legal tender qualities of greenbacks, the constitutionality of income taxes, the citizenship of corporations, and the power of railroads to obstruct navigation on streams.

CHAPTER XXIV

FEDERAL SUPERVISION OF INSURANCE [1]

WITHIN twenty-five years what may be called the "insurance principle" has come to be a notable factor in the traffic, credits, commerce, and the family life of this country. Invited by trunk-line railroads, the telegraph, the telephone, and the welcome of a homogeneous people, the tendency of all our activities has been to expand. Insurance has kept pace with the opportunity. It now has, through its various forms, relations with substantially every man, woman, and child in the Republic, and has large international relations as well. It operates everywhere under governmental supervision. In this country alone it must obey the behests of forty-six different legislatures, each of which claims sovereign authority not only over its activities in that particular state, but, in effect, over all its activities throughout the world. A mere statement of the situation prepares the mind for the confusion and injustice which characterize insurance supervision as it exists to-day.

It is a principle in physics that two bodies cannot occupy the same place at the same time. The Great Teacher said: "No servant can serve two masters. . . . Ye cannot serve God and Mammon." The problem which faces the management of an active insurance company to-day is, how

[1] By Darwin P. Kingsley, President of the New York Life Insurance Company. Reprinted from an address delivered before the students of the University of Missouri. The substance of this address was published as an article in *The North American Review* for April, 1909.

may it profitably, effectively, and peacefully serve forty-six masters. The problem is insolvable. Under the present practice of insurance supervision there is no remedy. But there is elsewhere a remedy, and, to many people, it seems to be the only remedy, viz., federal supervision of interstate insurance.

I by no means think that federal supervision would bring in the millennium, but it would be a long step away from the chaotic and destructive tendencies which have developed under the existing plan. Is federal supervision possible? As against the decisions of the Supreme Court — made not once but several times — is there any probability of such relief? [1]

Relief through an amendment to the Constitution of the United States would be effective, but that is practically unattainable and is probably unnecessary.

Is there not a great deal in the history of the nation, in the development of national sentiment, in the development of national ideals, since the Constitution was adopted, which foreshadows not only the probability but, under an increasing necessity, the certainty that interstate insurance will ultimately come under federal control? I think there is. I ask you now to consider that probability.

President-elect Taft recently called attention to some of the great virtues of the Constitution, namely: it is brief, general in its terms, and obviously constructed so that the powers granted to the general government could be developed and determined as the nation developed. This, as a matter of fact, is what has happened.

It is perfectly clear to one who studies the history of the nation under the Constitution, that but for the wisdom of the great men who interpreted that immortal instrument during the early years of its operation, national development might have taken on a form that would have defeated the purposes of the men who planned it. It is probable

[1] Paul *v.* Virginia, 8 Wallace, 168; Hooper *v.* California, 155 U. S., 646; Cravens *v.* New York Life Ins. Co., 176 U. S., 962.

that we as a people owe almost as much to Marshall, the great Chief Justice who gave the Constitution its national meaning, as to the men who drafted it. The doctrine which Marshall laid down, which was later on reaffirmed, which has now come to be perhaps as fixed in its meaning as the Constutition itself, is substantially this:

"The action of the general government should be applied to all the external concerns of the nation, and to those internal concerns which affect the states generally; while to the states is reserved the control of those matters which are completely within a particular state, which do not affect other states, and with which it is not necessary to interfere for the purpose of executing some of the general powers of the government." [1]

Many of the problems which have arisen since the adoption of the Constitution involve the question of whether it is necessary for the general government to "interfere" for the purpose of executing some of its general powers. Is it necessary now, is it likely to become increasingly necessary, that the government should interfere in insurance for the purpose of executing some of its general powers?

I speak, of course, as a layman. I shall not attempt to make what may be called a legal argument. I speak as one having close relations to an interest which involves people in every state in the Union, and in nearly every country of the civilized world. I speak as a practical man, dealing with one of those situations which make the lawyers now and then understand, and make even the Courts understand, that laws and courts and constitutions exist for the people, that the people do not exist for the benefit of institutions.

In order to consider what the probabilities of federal supervision are, it will be profitable to review briefly some of the things that have happened in the course of our national development.

[1] Gibbons *v.* Ogden, 9 Wheaton, 1.

You understand, of course, that the radical difference between government as it existed under the old Confederation, and government as it has grown up under our Constitution, is this: The Confederation was strictly a union between independent states acting as states; our present government is a union between states in which the central government acts directly upon the individual citizen, and not upon the states composing the government. This is supposed to be our great contribution to the science of government. There is a sharp difference of opinion as to who discovered it. Some credit its discovery to Benjamin Franklin and some to Pelatiah Webster; but Mr. John Fiske has pointed out that the principle was embodied in the ancient federation of Greek cities known as the Achæan League, and is present in the modern federation of the cantons which constitute the republic of Switzerland. He further declares that the principle was never fairly demonstrated and never could be until it was applied to a large and populous country through a considerable period of time. We have supplied these conditions and this is properly speaking our contribution to the science of government. And beyond question in its continued success lies the best hope for the future peace of the world.

The difference between the two kinds of government does not at first blush seem to be great, but, as a matter of fact, the two types are almost as far apart as the poles.

The departure involved in the new type was much clearer to our forefathers than it is to us. Under the Confederation they had won independence. They recognized the pressing need of a different and a stronger plan, but about the old plan clustered traditions and the memory of struggles which went back almost to Jamestown and to Plymouth. In order to create the beginnings of a nation, they had to exercise a forbearance, a charity, and a wisdom which are a constant source of wonder to the student of that period. Once get yourself into the atmosphere of those times, get even an approximate idea of their passion for local self-government — the idea of sovereignty which had seized on the people of each of the original thirteen states — understand the variety and even the hostility of their interests, and then consider the instrument which that devoted body of men wrought out in Philadelphia in 1787, and the marvelous work it has since done in nation building, and you will understand why Thomas Jefferson pronounced it the work of demigods; and you will have a higher appreciation too of the truth of what Gladstone said later, namely, that it is "the most wonderful piece of work ever struck off at a given time by the brain and purpose of man." It was a series of compromises — compromises between the larger and the smaller states, compromises with slavery, compromises all through — but the great principle then adopted, which has more and more asserted itself, which has developed the instinct of nationality, which preserved the nation through a fearful war, which has developed it territorially from the Atlantic to the Pacific and across the Pacific, is, that the general government acts for the general welfare, that it acts directly on the individual and acts in whatever way it is necessary for it to act for the purpose of executing its general powers.

However keen the vision of Washington and Franklin and Madison and Hamilton — the men who dominated the Constitutional Convention — however much they may have seen that the future of free government and the development of human liberty were wrapped up in their plan, the people of that time were impelled by no such motives. They were passionately devoted to their local sovereignty. To them the creation of a new style of government was largely a question of commercial peace between the states and with foreign countries. The situation substantially compelled them to recognize the necessity of a central government strong enough to keep the peace and to regulate commercial intercourse. The Revolution itself had been largely brought about by commercial considerations. The British government sought to keep the colonies in subjection for purposes of favorable trade, and against this the colonies rebelled. After independence had been won a situation bordering on anarchy quickly developed. Foreign countries were unwilling to enter into treaties with the United States under the articles of Confederation. The Confederation had no control over commerce, and commercial war [1] in a variety of forms soon developed. This condition growing out of the feebleness of the federal government resulted in a deep and general

[1] Only British built ships, owned and navigated by British subjects, were allowed to trade between New England and the British West Indies. American ships trading directly with Great Britain were allowed to carry only articles produced in the particular states of which their owners were citizens. Massachusetts, New Hampshire, and Rhode Island prohibited British ships from carrying goods out of their harbors, and imposed a heavy duty on all goods brought in by such ships. New York imposed a double duty on goods imported in British ships. Pennsylvania levied duties for the benefit of local manufacturers. Congress was unable to persuade the states to carry out the recommendations it had agreed to in the treaty of peace with England respecting the treatment of loyalists and the payment of private debts owing to British subjects. In retaliation and to the great humiliation of the new nation, British garrisons were not withdrawn from Ogdensburg, Oswego, Niagara, Detroit, and Mackinaw until eight years after the adoption of the Constitution. The Confederation had no power to lay and collect taxes or duties, and it was unable to pay the ragged Continentals who had won our independence. The nation was too poor to bribe the Barbary pirates and too weak to chastise them, and American ships were plundered in the Mediterranean and American sailors — citizens who had established our independence — were sold as slaves in the markets of Tripoli and Algiers.

Under the union between the states as such, with no power in the central government to act directly on the individual citizen, control over what was common to all the states naturally failed, and it was followed by a commercial war between the states themselves. Connecticut opened her ports to British ships and levied duties on imports from Massachusetts. Pennsylvania discriminated against Delaware and New Jersey. New York required vessels from Connecticut and New Jersey to pay entrance fees and obtain clearances at the custom conviction that commerce ought to be regulated by Congress, and found expression in the commerce clause of the Constitution. As to the breadth of the powers contained in this clause, Chief Justice Marshall said:

"It is not, therefore, a matter of surprise that the grant should be as extensive as the mischief, and should comprehend all foreign commerce and all commerce among the states."

The departures of the new instrument from the old were so radical that many of the states hesitated, and yet, as we can see now and as they came to see, there was nothing

house the same as foreign ships. Crippled in her foreign trade and oppressed with debt, Massachusetts laid a heavy tax on land, and presently what is known as Shay's Rebellion broke out.

The same chaos existed in monetary affairs. There was no national coinage law until 1785, and no money was coined until 1793. The gold and silver coins in use were English, Spanish, French, and German. Notwithstanding the disastrous experience of the country with the irredeemable paper issued by authority of Congress during the Revolution, seven of the states resorted to the same expedient and some of them attempted to enforce its use as legal tender. This resulted in litigation and a general paralysis of local trade. The efforts of Rhode Island to enforce the use of paper money as legal tender gave her the nickname of "Rogues' Island."

That commercial necessities initiated the movement which resulted in calling the convention which framed the Constitution is a fact not generally known. In 1785 Washington became president of a company for extending the navigation of the Potomac and James rivers. This could not be done unless Virginia and Maryland acted together. Washington's plans involved a connection between the head waters of the Potomac and the Ohio, and therefore Pennsylvania was invited to become a party to the enterprise. The papers as finally sent to the legislatures of Maryland and Virginia contained a suggestion made by Washington himself, that these two states should agree upon a uniform system of duties and other commercial regulations and upon a uniform currency. Both states ratified such a compact, and Maryland then proposed that Delaware also be consulted, and that the plan include a canal between the Delaware River and Chesapeake Bay. Maryland finally suggested that all the states be invited to send commissioners to the conference. Nine states complied, and delegates from five states met at Annapolis in September, 1786. New Jersey instructed her delegates "to consider how far a uniform system in else for them to do. It was this or anarchy. But even after the states had all ratified the Constitution, and the new nation had been launched upon its career, the people found it difficult to take their own medicine.

But steadily the national ideal gained ground. Slowly the general government extended its operations from the external concerns of the nation and from those internal concerns which affect the states generally, to those with which it was necessary for it to interfere, and with which it had the right to interfere through its direct operation on the citizen, for the purpose of executing its general

their commercial relations and *other important matters* might be necessary to the common interest and permanent harmony of the several states." The conference noted the phrase "other important matters" and considered it an improvement on the original plan. In this appears a recognition of the necessity of some action dealing with the general commercial chaos which then ruled. The Annapolis conference resulted in no definite action except the adoption of an address written by Alexander Hamilton, urging that commissioners be appointed by all the states to meet in Philadelphia in May, 1787, "to devise such further provisions as shall appear to them necessary to render the Constitution of the federal government adequate to the exigencies of the Union, and to report to Congress such an act as, when agreed to by them, and confirmed by the legislatures of every state, would effectually provide for the same." This address, born of a commercial question, resulted directly in the Constitutional Convention. At first, the Continental Congress refused to notice the Annapolis conference and the address which resulted from it. They said the conference was an irregular body without authority. But the states, wiser than the Congress, led by Virginia, began to appoint delegates, and when New York refused her assent to a plan of Congress for levying and collecting duties on imports, thereby further emphasizing the impotency of Congress itself, a reluctant consent was given, and, as a salve to the pride of its members, Congress itself issued a call for a convention identical with that of the Annapolis conference. This convention in the summer of 1787, working behind closed doors, finally produced an instrument which did not satisfy any one at the time, to which some of the states gave tardy and reluctant assent — and almost no state was more grudging and tardy than New York — but to which all the states finally assented, although in two cases assent was delayed until after government under the Constitution had existed for some time.

powers. Every inch of the ground, however, has been fought over. And that contest, involving always more or less clearly the development of national powers as against the powers of the states, has been a leading issue between political parties — whenever there has been a clear issue — from that day to this.

Naturally the Federalists who had been most active in advocating the adoption of the Constitution favored a liberal construction of it. They wanted it to become effective. Their opponents — then called Republicans — favored a strict interpretation of it. The Federalists, forced by the situation to take the initiative, obliged to do whatever was necessary through taxation and otherwise to carry on the new government, did not long endure. Then came Thomas Jefferson, nominally the founder of the party of strict construction. The burden of the new government, with its then more or less undefined relations to the states, with its powers undeveloped, fell on men who were supposed to be least in sympathy with the national idea. An emergency which put them to the test quickly arose. In the struggle for the possession of the Mississippi, Jefferson proposed and Congress authorized the purchase of the Island of Orleans and what was called West Florida. In the end they bought the whole ancient province of Louisiana, a tract of land richer and larger in area than the original thirteen states. Although Jefferson had advocated the smaller purchase, and there was no difference in principle between what was originally proposed and what was finally done, yet he believed that in signing the treaty of purchase he had "done an act beyond the Constitution." He could find in the Constitution no authority for such a proceeding. His friends believed that in the treaty-making power he had sufficient authority, and Chief Justice Marshall in 1828 confirmed that view in an important decision, when he said:

"The Constitution confers absolutely on the government of the Union the powers of making war and making treaties; consequently that government possesses the power of acquiring territory either by conquest or treaty."

Such are the curious ways of politicians that the Federalists, who before the purchase had urged the most extreme measures to secure navigation of the Mississippi, now vehemently questioned both the constitutionality and the wisdom of an act which not only secured the Mississippi but an empire besides.

The people, however, with an instinct which foreshadowed the decision of Marshall, approved the act; they recognized that it was clearly in the line of national aspirations, that it tended to insure the peace and the safety of the Republic. This was perhaps the first great instance in which, by interpretation and by acquiescence on the part of the people, a way was found.

Following the path upon which Jefferson first entered, we purchased Florida, we discovered, explored, and settled the Oregon country, we annexed Texas on the petition of its people. We acquired California, Nevada, Arizona, New Mexico, and portions of Colorado and Oklahoma. We purchased Alaska. We annexed Hawaii on the petition of its *de facto* government. We took the Philippines, Porto Rico, and Guam. In five of these eight cases, additions to our territorial domain were made and the highest function of sovereignty was exercised, when the federal government was under the control of the party popularly known as the party of strict construction.

Twelve amendments were made to the Constitution during the first fifteen years of its existence. During the next sixty-two years none were made. In this era the Constitution was being interpreted. The executive and the courts were slowly finding out the powers granted either specifically or by implication, and they found all that was necessary to carry on the national government. The growth of federal power during that time was very great, and in that period the citizens of the states transferred to their national citizenship a large part of the love and reverence which they had formerly bestowed upon their state citizenship. The conviction constantly increased that under the Union and the Constitution there was, upon the whole, better freedom and greater happiness than could possibly be secured in any other way. The purchase of Louisiana and the second war with Great Britain led the administration irresistibly along the path of a liberal interpretation of the Constitution. They may not have altogether liked it. There was nothing else for them to do. The embargo which they had denounced in 1793, they employed in 1807. The United States Bank, which they had denounced in 1791 and refused to recharter in 1811, was rechartered by an almost unanimous vote in 1816. They followed so closely the lines laid down by the Federalists that Josiah Quincy declared the Republicans had out-federalized federalism. But the triumphs of both parties were the triumphs of national ideals. This is probably much clearer to us than it was to them. The father of strict construction took the first step in the policy of expansion which has secured us our preëminence on the North American continent, and the last of his great contemporaries, by an equally wise and daring exercise of executive power, put an end to foreign aggressions upon this continent. The Monroe doctrine has no other standing in the Constitution than this: that the Constitution made the United States a sovereign nation with certain ideals which are to be pursued, and with which further foreign aggressions in this hemisphere would interfere. It is curious that this doctrine also has found its strongest supporters amongst the strict constructionists, and in our own day a President who would not annex Hawaii upon the petition of its *de facto* government put more stiffening into the backbone of the Monroe doctrine than it had received since Secretary Seward politely requested Napoleon III to get out of Mexico.

With the expansion of the national domain to the Pacific came the necessity of easier access to that coast and of a naval station in Caribbean waters. The story of negotiations forwarding these purposes is a long one, and includes many failures, but the idea has never been abandoned, and now the United States owns Porto Rico and is making the "dirt fly" in digging a canal connecting the Atlantic and the Pacific, a great waterway which, when completed, will be entirely under the control of the United States.

The supreme event in the development of national ideals came to an issue in 1860. African slavery existed in every state of the Union but one when the Constitution was adopted, and its status under the new government was one of the compromises of the Constitution. The words slave and slavery were carefully avoided in wording that instrument, and it was then the general opinion that the institution would gradually die out. The ordinance of 1787, one of the last enactments of the old Confederation, assented to by all the states, had consecrated the Northwest territory to freedom, but the Louisiana Purchase contained no such provision, and over the settlement and government of that vast region was ultimately waged a conflict which tested the vitality and established the power of the nation. During the years which preceded this conflict, the anti-slavery party pursued its ideal of limiting slavery within a certain area, while the pro-slavery party persistently followed its purpose of protecting slavery in the unorganized territory of the country and in the erection of new slave states whenever the people so desired. Both parties claimed the sanction of the Constitution.

We sometimes lose sight of the great issue of that fearful struggle. We have just celebrated the centenary of the birth of Abraham Lincoln, whose election to the Presidency precipitated the conflict. We have heard much of Lincoln the "Emancipator," and we have been told that the Civil War was fought in order to abolish slavery. Lincoln knew better than this. He realized that the great thing to be done was to preserve the Union and the principles of government and of nationality which it embodied. You remember, in his first inaugural address, he said to those whom he called his "dissatisfied fellow-countrymen":

"You can have no oath registered in Heaven to destroy the government, while I shall have the most solemn one to 'preserve, protect, and defend' it. The mystic chords of memory, stretching from every battlefield and patriot grave to every living heart and hearthstone all over this broad land, will yet swell the chorus of the Union, when again touched, as surely they will be, by the better angels of our nature."

He stated the issue as between the Union and slavery in 1862, when Horace Greeley published in the *Tribune* an open letter urging a more decided policy on the part of the government with respect to slavery. Lincoln replied, in that immortal declaration with which you are all familiar:

"If there be those who would not save the Union unless they could at the same time save slavery, I do not agree with them. If there be those who would not save the Union unless they could at the same time destroy slavery, I do not agree with them. My paramount object is to save the Union, and not either to save or destroy slavery. If I could save the Union, without freeing any slave, I would do it; if I could save it by freeing all the slaves, I would do it; and if I could do it by freeing some, and leaving others alone, I would also do that. What I do about slavery and the colored race, I do because I believe it helps to save this Union. And what I forbear, I forbear because I do not believe it would help to save the Union. I shall do less whenever I shall believe that what I am doing hurts the cause, and I shall do more whenever I believe doing more will help the cause."

Lincoln's supreme purpose and the issue of the war was the preservation of the Union. When he thought that such action would help to save the Union, he issued the Emancipation Proclamation. But it was a war measure distinctly unauthorized by the Constitution up to the time of the adoption of the thirteenth amendment.

Another long struggle which resulted in a great advance in national ideals was in the field of finance. When the Constitution was adopted, the nation as such had no revenue, no credit. But Alexander Hamilton, the first and greatest Secretary of the Treasury, putting into effect the powers granted by the Constitution, soon wrought what seemed a miraculous change. As Webster said: "He smote the rock of the national resources, and abundant streams of revenue gushed forth. He touched the corpse of public credit, and it sprung upon its feet." One of the means employed was a United States Bank, chartered by Congress. The strict constructionists contended that the government had no authority to charter a bank. Its right to do so was upheld by the Supreme Court on the ground that it was a suitable agency in borrowing money which the government had an undoubted right to do. The contest was a long and bitter one and the strict constructionists refused to recharter the bank in 1811, but were glad to do so in 1816 when the currency had been demoralized by the second war with Great Britain. Prosperity brought some abuses, and all the old rancor, and the bank was discontinued in 1836, and a new era of wild-cat money followed in certain sections which lasted until the Civil War. Again the banks suspended specie payments and the federal government issued legal tender notes, established the national banking system, and finally taxed state bank issues 10 per cent. The first and last of these acts were opposed as unconstitutional, but they were upheld by the Supreme Court.[1] Thus what is peculiarly a prerogative of sovereignty was transferred from the states to the

[1] McCulloch *v.* Maryland, 4 Wheaton, 316; Legal Tender Cases, 12 Wallace 457; 110 U. S., 447; National Bank *v.* United States, 101, U. S., 1.

national government through a process of interpretation, in response to national needs and through interference which was necessary in order to carry out the general powers of the government.

Let us consider a little more closely the logic by which this great transformation was accomplished. We may find some comfort therein. Fifty years ago, if any one had said that within ten years we should have only national currency and none issued by state banks, he would have been laughed at. Where would Congress find authority to take this prerogative away from the states? Let us follow the Supreme Court's logic.

The Constitution gives Congress power "to borrow money on the credit of the United States and to coin money, regulate the value thereof, and of foreign coin." The Constitution as a whole makes the United States a sovereign nation. Now notice the links in the chain of reasoning. Congress has power to borrow money; therefore it may charter a bank as an aid in borrowing money. A bank so chartered may be taxed by the states only in such a manner as Congress permits. Congress may borrow money, and the United States is a sovereign nation; therefore it may emit bills of credit and make them legal tender. Congress has power to borrow money; therefore it may enact a national banking law authorizing banks thereunder to issue circulating notes based on the security of United States bonds deposited with the government. Congress may borrow money; having under this power undertaken to supply the country with a stable currency, *it may prevent the circulation as money of any notes not issued under its authority by taxing all other issues out of existence.*

This was going a long way; it was clearly one of the occasions when Congress found it necessary to "interfere," for the purpose of executing its general powers.

A striking example of the exercise of sovereignty which is not contemplated in the Constitution is seen in the control and disposition of what is known as the public domain. To Maryland belongs the credit of taking a step which was of far-reaching importance in arousing a national sentiment. When the Articles of Confederation were proposed, Maryland refused to adopt them unless certain other states would cede their unorganized Western lands to the United States. This was done, and these lands became the first strong bond of union. Settlers on these lands and those afterward acquired took title from the general government, and there are few pages in our history which, upon the whole, record sounder and more constructive statesmanship than those which relate to this subject. Under whatever law the settler took his title, the fact was that the general government was using, and wisely using, the national domain to develop a national ideal. It all followed logically from the act of Maryland, from the Louisiana Purchase, and from the construction put upon the Constitution by Chief Justice Marshall.

But these public lands have also been used to foster education. It is estimated that over one hundred million acres of the public domain have been given to the different states for educational purposes. Where in the Constitution is specific authority given to Congress to give away public lands to men who settle on them and improve them, or to states for educational purposes? The word education does not occur in the Constitution. Congress has power to make all needful rules and regulations respecting the territory or other property belonging to the United States, and from these few words has been deduced the authority to govern territory belonging to the United States as well as absolute control of her lands whether within state or territorial limits. Clearly these provisions for education were made with slight reference to explicit constitutional authority. The action was taken because, under our form of government, homes and education are amongst the most cherished national ideals; because it seemed necessary that the government interfere, in the execution of its general duties and powers.

The states ceded to Congress under the new Constitution the power to regulate commerce with foreign nations and among the several states and with the Indian tribes, but here again they found it difficult to take their own medicine. It was not easy to give up this prerogative of sovereignty. Almost immediately the question arose, What is commerce? It was soon decided that commerce was something more than traffic or trade, — it included transportation, transportation of passengers as well as of goods. When steam came into use as a motive power, that became an issue; but it was decided that commerce included all the means as well as the subjects of transportation. When the electric telegraph came into use, it was decided that this was a medium of commercial intercourse. When the telephone came into use, the same reasoning made its use between states interstate commerce. At first Congress was considered as having jurisdiction only over waters affected by the tide, but this authority was soon extended to all navigable waters upon which interstate commerce is carried on, and to bridges over navigable waters separating two states. At the present time the authority of Congress extends to the places, the means, and the subjects of trade and commerce.[1]

Since the passage of the Interstate Commerce Act of 1887, there has been a remarkable increase in the activity of the federal government with respect to control over interstate commerce. President Eliot of Harvard University not long ago stated that our entire domain between the Atlantic and the Pacific, between Mexico and Canada, was really not as large as New England was sixty years ago, and, as a problem in commerce and transportation, nothing like as large as the original thirteen states. We have

[1] Gibbons *v.* Ogden, 9 Wheaton, 1; Gloucester Ferry Co. *v.* Pennsylvania, 114 U. S., 196; Moran *v.* City of New Orleans, 112 U. S., 69; Passenger Cases, 7 Howard, 283; Walling *v.* Michigan, 116 U. S., 446; Tel. Co. *v.* Texas, U. S., 460; Pa. Tel. Co., 48 N. J., Eq. 91, 20, Atl. 846, 27 Am. St. Rep., 462.

moved on into what is almost a new world. We are facing new problems. We are facing the further development of national ideals. We cling as tenaciously as our forefathers did to what we call the right of local self-government. What we are now and then asked to give up seems to us much more vital than what they were asked to surrender in the general interest. We can see how necessary it was for them to do it. It is not so easy for us to understand the force and direction of the conditions which we face. We have the most extended system of railroad transportation in the world. The use of the telegraph and the telephone has extended throughout the nation. Many important types of business are organized on continental lines. The question, then, is: When we insist on what we call local self-government as against the obvious significance of such facts as these, are we not as shortsighted as our forefathers would have been if they had carried their opposition to the Constitution further than they did? The fact is, we are still entirely devoted to local self-government. But what is local self-government? When a business naturally extends over all the states of the United States, is it local self-government to attempt to regulate it in forty-six different places by forty-six separate sovereign authorities? Under these conditions is not the local idea plainly encroaching on the national prerogative?

On all these large questions the government has not acted until it was obliged to. There has been no aggression as against the states. Looking back at these contests — in which the issue was frequently doubtful — we see that no other solution was possible, that there was nothing else for the government to do, nothing else for the Supreme Court to do. When Livingston and Monroe purchased Louisiana, there was nothing for Jefferson and Congress to do but just what they did. When the question of a national currency became critical, there was nothing for Congress to do but what it did, or something similar, and there was nothing for the Supreme Court to do but to sustain it. When the question of railroads arose, it was already a large question before it became a federal question; it involved interests so extensive that the country generally appreciated its importance and understood that half-way measures would not do.

Unfortunately for us, the Supreme Court declared insurance to be neither commerce nor an instrumentality of commerce in the case of Paul *v.* Virginia (1868), long before many people had any adequate notion of what insurance was to do and to be. It is useless now to conjecture what the makers of the Constitution would have done if insurance had at that time been the large subject it is to-day. It is useless to conjecture, too, what the Supreme Court might have done in the case of Paul *v.* Virginia, if Congress had previously legislated upon the assumption that interstate insurance was interstate commerce.

The chaotic condition which existed in the commerce between the states was, as we have seen, one of the things that drove the states toward a "more perfect union." That condition, in a more or less aggravated form, has existed in insurance for eighty years. In 1829 Pennsylvania levied a tax of 20 per cent. on the premiums of other state companies. This was done under the familiar plea of protecting the business of domestic corporations. There was a similar tax of 10 per cent. in New York from 1828 to 1837. In 1851 New York by means of a deposit law drove all other state companies but two beyond its borders, and when the other states retaliated, the New York State companies withdrew from them. In 1874 California by radical legislation drove twenty-nine companies out of her jurisdiction. Recently nearly all the life companies withdrew from Texas and Wisconsin because of oppressive legislation, and eight withdrew from New York State for the same reason. A Missouri law allows no company to do business within her borders which pays salaries above a certain limit. Many of the states refuse admission to companies of other states unless they in advance agree to surrender the protection of the Federal Courts, and to that extent their rights under the Constitution of the United States. Most of the states have on their statute books, in their insurance laws, that relic of barbarism, the *lex talionis*, the law which exacts an eye for an eye, a tooth for a tooth. The condition is becoming progressively worse. It is akin to those which existed one hundred and twenty years ago with respect to commerce. It is not unlike those which then existed regarding foreign intercourse, public credit, currency, and that comity between states which makes for union and peace. The problems of commerce, of expansion of public credit, of currency, were solved by the action of the general government either through its specific or its implied powers. There is apparently no other method by which the problem of insurance supervision can be solved.

The Supreme Court has said that insurance is not commerce. It has further said that a state may exact from a foreign corporation seeking admission to its borders, compliance with any condition it sees fit to impose.[1] These two pronouncements face insurance on the one side, and the chaos resulting from trying to obey forty-six different masters at the same time confronts it on the other.

Toward these decisions of the Supreme Court we maintain the attitude that Lincoln assumed toward the Dred Scott decision. He said:

"It is not resistance, it is not factious, it is not even disrespectful, to treat it as not having yet quite established a settled doctrine for the country. . . . The Court that made it has often overruled its own decisions, and we shall do what we can to have it overrule this. We offer no resistance to it."

While the Supreme Court has several times flatly said

[1] Nutting *v.* Massachusetts, 183 U. S., 553, 556, 46 L. Ed., 324, 325, 22 Sup. Ct. Rep., 238, 239.

that insurance is not commerce, I think it by no means impossible that later on it may take a different view. I am not sure that it has not already done so. The relations of things have changed. And wise courts interpret constitutions in the light of changed conditions and in the interest of all the people.

Insurance is business. It includes the purchase and sale of contract rights which have become an almost indispensable factor in business, in credit and in traffic. It is a business that from its very nature is most secure when widely distributed, and it naturally and inevitably has become an interstate business. It is a business which from its character requires a reasonable measure of governmental supervision, and at the present time it is more extensively supervised by governments than any other class of business. There is, perhaps, no business in which efficiency and economy are so much promoted by uniformity of legal requirements everywhere; no business that is more easily embarrassed, harassed, and rendered inefficient and unprofitable by conflicting laws and conditions.

But the Supreme Court has said that it is not commerce. The transportation of goods and passengers is commerce, and all the means used as instrumentalities thereof are commerce. The sale of goods by sample by drummers is commerce, but the sale of life insurance policies by agents is not commerce. A telegraphic message relating to a life insurance policy — or any other kind of business — is commerce, but the policy itself, sent by mail or otherwise, is not commerce. If a company talks to an insurant in a neighboring state over the telephone, the talk is commerce, but the subject of the talk is not.

I have now briefly reviewed some of the instances in the history of the country which have resulted in the development of national ideals and the expansion of national power. My purpose has been to show that Congress, under the Constitution and under the wise rulings of the Supreme Court, has always had power sufficient to meet any emergency, and that such emergencies have always been met in the interest of the whole people. I might rest here and have, I think, a very good case. Having pointed out the inevitable chaos and confusion which have followed the attempt entirely to supervise the business of insurance by forty-six different authorities, having shown the hopelessness of any attempt to secure efficient administration through harmony of action amongst the states, it is a fair deduction to say that a business involving such large interests, capable of such great usefulness, a business so necessarily interstate in its nature, is entitled somehow, some way, to just supervision and wise control. And as that cannot be had under the present system, relief from the general government must in time come by force of circumstances and through the logic which has so nobly served the people from the time of John Marshall to the present day.

The force of such conditions has already asserted itself, and unless I misread the mind of the Supreme Court in a leading case, relief from an illogical and reactionary condition is already in sight.

In 1902 the Supreme Court of the United States, in its interpretation of the powers of Congress under the commerce clause of the Constitution, went farther than ever it had gone before. The case before the Court was that of Champion *v.* Ames, and will be familiar to you as the "Lottery Case."[1] By this decision the validity of an act of Congress for the suppression of lottery traffic through international and interstate commerce and the postal service was sustained. As I read the entire case the previous declarations of the Court that insurance is not commerce are therein substantially overruled; and, under the doctrine laid down, it seems reasonably clear that if Congress should now pass an act providing for federal super-

[1] Champion *v.* Ames, 188 U. S., 492.

vision and regulation of interstate insurance, the Supreme Court would be bound to sustain it.

Counsel for the lottery company urged that a contract of lottery was substantially the same as a contract of insurance, and that the principle in the two could not be distinguished. The minority of the Court, for whom Chief Justice Fuller delivered the dissenting opinion, urged the same doctrine, and pointed out that the Court had already decided that insurance contracts are not articles of commerce; that they are not subjects of trade and barter offered in the market as something having an existence and value independent of the parties to them; that they are not commodities to be shipped from one state to another and then put up for sale. The logic of which was that the sale of lottery tickets being indistinguishable in principle from the sale of insurance policies must necessarily fall outside the commerce clause and outside the power of Congress to regulate. In effect, therefore, the relation of insurance to the commerce clause of the Constitution was before the Court and was fully discussed. Not only was it discussed in the briefs of the appellant, but it was apparently a part of the oral argument; and the case of Paul *v.* Virginia was the leading case upon which the minority of the Court based their dissent.

In delivering the majority opinion of the Court in the lottery case, Mr. Justice Harlan, singularly enough, made no reference to the insurance cases. Insurance, as such, was not before the Court, and there was, therefore, no controlling reason why the Court, if it believed that the doctrine laid down in Paul *v.* Virginia was an error, should so state. If, however, a majority of the Court believed that the sale of lottery tickets could be distinguished in principle from the sale of insurance policies, it is fair to assume that they would have said so. This would have been the natural thing to do. The argument of the lottery people was: Lottery is like insurance, therefore it is not commerce. The Court decided, without refuting the argument on that point, that the interstate sale and carriage of lottery tickets is commerce. In reaching this decision the Court sought first for a definition of the word "commerce" as used in the Constitution, and, amongst other things, said:

"Undoubtedly the carrying from one state to another by independent carriers of things or commodities that are ordinarily subjects of traffic and which have in themselves a recognized value in money constitutes interstate commerce. But does not commerce among the several states include something more? Does not the carrying from one state to another by independent carriers of lottery tickets that entitle the holder to the payment of a certain amount of money therein specified also constitute commerce amongst the states?"

After various citations, seeking rather to arrive at a definition of what commerce is, the Court said:

"They (the cases cited) show that commerce among the states embraces navigation, intercourse, communication, traffic, the transit of persons and the transmission of messages by telegraph." (He would now add transmission of messages by telephone.) "They also show that the power to regulate commerce among the several states is vested in Congress as absolutely as it would be in a single government having in its Constitution the same restrictions of the exercise of the power as are found in the Constitution of the United States."

Then without specific reference to that case, the Court met the doctrine laid down in Paul *v.* Virginia in this language:

"It was said in argument that lottery tickets are not of any real or substantial value in themselves, and therefore are not subjects of commerce. If that were conceded to be the only legal test as to what are to be deemed subjects of commerce that may be regulated by Congress, we cannot accept as accurate the broad statement that such tickets are of no value."

This language is very significant. In logical effect it overrules the doctrine laid down in Paul *v.* Virginia. It intimates that an interstate transaction may be commerce even if the article transported has no value in itself. But, finding some actual value in a lottery ticket, the Court brushed all other considerations aside and said: "Lottery tickets are subjects of traffic, and therefore subjects of commerce."

Every element of value which the Court found in lottery tickets exists also in insurance policies. The Court found that lottery tickets had value because of a large capital prize to be paid to the holder of the winning ticket, because of large deposits of money in different banks in the United States insuring the prompt payment of prizes. Lottery tickets were subjects of traffic because they could be sold, and they had a value even in states which made the drawing of lotteries illegal. The parallel between such conditions and those which attach to insurance is almost perfect.

Whether the Court recognized at the time that the doctrine in Champion *v.* Ames overrules the doctrine in Paul *v.* Virginia, must be a matter of opinion until a direct test is made under similar conditions; but it is evident from the text of the two opinions then rendered that there was a vigorous interchange of ideas between the various members of the Court before the opinions were arrived at.

"Could Congress," asked the Chief Justice, "compel a state to admit lottery matter within it contrary to its own laws?" And the answer of the majority opinion clearly would be, "Yes, Congress could." It would simply be unwise legislation, and by way of rebuttal the majority opinion adds:

"The possible abuse of the power is not an argument against its existence. There is probably no governmental power that may not be exerted to the injury of the public. The remedy is that suggested by Chief Justice Marshall when he said: 'The wisdom and the discretion of Congress, their anxiety for the people and the influence which their constituents possess at elections, are in this, as in many other instances, the sole restraints on which they have to rely to secure them from abuse.'"

Apparently anticipating that some one might misconstrue the effect of the lottery decision, the Court said:

"We decide nothing more in the present case than that lottery tickets are subjects of traffic among those who choose to sell or buy them; the carriage of such tickets by independent carriers from one state to another is, therefore, interstate commerce."

Insurance, with a hesitancy which is not readily understood, has never made any serious attempt to secure action by Congress. The insurance cases went before the Court supported by no declaration from Congress that the business is commerce, — a situation which itself invited an adverse conclusion. Whenever the question has been raised since then, immediately Paul *v.* Virginia and the other cases in which opinion has followed the doctrine of that case have been cited, and the matter has been dropped as hopeless. But the lottery case has vastly changed the whole situation. These insurance cases may now be treated as Lincoln treated the Dred Scott decision. They "have not quite established a settled doctrine for the country." The lottery case affords abundant warrant for a request that Congress now act. A law should be drawn on the theory that interstate insurance is commerce, and that the power of Congress to regulate insurance in its interstate relations is absolute. Presented with such an act, the Supreme Court, with the deference which it has always observed toward Congress, would, we believe, be disposed to accept the declaration by Congress that interstate insurance is commerce and is subject to control by Congress. If a case were to arise under such an act, it is difficult to see how the Court could render any different decision from that in the lottery case. In the lottery case the Court was probably seeking to put an end to a great public evil, to abate a great public scandal. It was obvious that the evil would not and could not be ended by the states, and therefore the power to deal with the situation, which must lie somewhere, was recognized as being in Congress under the commerce clause.

Insurance would present a case in which the law and the Court would be invoked, not to abate or destroy an evil, but to conserve and protect a great public utility. It probably would not go before the Court with the pressure of a wide-spread public demand behind it. It would go before the Court stating, first, that it is commerce; second, that it is in distress and confusion and needs the relief which a single authority alone can give; third, that it is irrationally supervised; fourth, that it is harassed by a multitude of exactions and requirements; fifth, that it is unequally and unjustly taxed; sixth, that its operations are, in practice, almost universally interstate and often international; and seventh, that the governmental regulations which it now observes have begun to narrow its field of activities, a condition which, carried to its logical conclusion, threatens ultimately to limit the operations of every insurance company to the state of its domicile.

There must be relief somewhere. The problem will not be solved by the states. It cannot be. The solution lies in the commerce clause of the Constitution, and an act of Congress, drawn on the theory I have suggested, would bring insurance before the Court in a proper way. It would be able to present its just claims, and they could be argued from the standpoint of a powerful precedent. So presented the question would at least be settled and insurance would know finally whether it may go forward or not.

I do not believe, therefore, that an amendment to the Constitution of the United States is necessary. I believe that insurance *is* commerce. I believe the Supreme Court, which has, as I see it, already said so by implication, will ultimately say so by definite decree.

State supervision of insurance is not as logical as the union of the colonies under the Confederation. The colonies had in their Congress at least one point of contact. There is no point of contact in state supervision, no common authority.

There was chaos under the Confederation; there are chaotic conditions now under state supervision. The colonies needed a larger, a stronger, a broader plan. They found that plan in the Constitution. Society itself presents much of the savage individualism that would certainly have destroyed the colonies under the Confederation. The rule of the strong is the law of society. Waste, inefficiency, brutality, selfishness, the lack of any comprehensive plan, make even the best of civilizations more or less inhumane. Society would like to be humane, but it has little time and no sufficient program. Society has advanced only to that condition of efficiency which was exemplified in the Confederation. It needs a Constitution which shall provide a more perfect Union. Insurance — fire insurance as an instrumentality of credit and traffic, and life insurance as a sure and just method of capitalizing human life — presents a plan, and, so far as it goes, an adequate plan. But, like the Constitution, it operates, if it operates effectively, directly on the citizen and not on the several states. In other words, the plan of insurance — especially of life insurance—is the plan of the Constitution.

Through federal supervision we seek the adoption of this social constitution. When that is done, the chaos of the Confederation, of state supervision, will disappear as certainly as it did in 1789. Otherwise the outlook is not hopeful. Reaction has begun. There is no escape ultimately from one of two conditions: either federal supervision, with an increase in the usefulness and the strength of insurance, which always follows a change from confused to sound methods; or, retreat. Retreat means immeasurable loss; it means ultimate retirement for every company to the confines of the state of its domicile.

Will insurance act? Will Congress act? Will Congress and the Supreme Court, through the commerce clause of the Constitution, or through some of the government's implied powers, open the door to that larger field which the business alone is qualified to occupy?

The door is there. It has swung open many times.

It opened and through it passed that stately procession of commonwealths which has added thirty-three stars to the flag.

It opened and through it passed the Monroe doctrine.

It opened and through it came the Emancipation Proclamation.

It opened and through it came a national currency.

It will open again — indeed, it seems almost ajar now — and through it in some form will come federal supervision of interstate insurance

CHAPTER XXV

NECESSITY FOR REFORM OF LIFE INSURANCE TAXATION [1]

LAST year the life insurance companies of this country paid $12,000,000 to the states as the share which the holders of life insurance policies should contribute through the companies to the expenses of government. A number of methods were used by the states in collecting this amount. Two millions were secured by means of fees levied primarily for the purpose of supporting the state insurance departments. The rest was collected through taxes levied on all the assets, or on part of them, and to a much greater extent by means of taxes levied upon gross or net premiums collected by the companies. The problem before us is to determine whether this tax should be levied on life insurance, and if it should, whether the ways in which the tax is imposed are best adapted to secure justice, as far as possible, to every one concerned.

Much of the discussion which has hitherto taken place on the subject of insurance taxation has not accomplished much. On one side have been arraigned those favoring the imposition of heavy taxes on the life insurance business, and on the other those who have taken the standpoint that no taxes on insurance should be imposed whatever. Now it is always of great advantage in clearing up a knotty problem such as this one of insurance taxation to find out as well as we can what are the motives actuating those

[1] By Lester W. Zartman, Assistant Professor of Political Economy in Yale University. Reprint of a speech delivered before the second annual meeting of the Association of Life Insurance Presidents and printed in the proceedings of that meeting.

who are advocating various lines of action. Let us find this out in the present case. In the first place, upon what have the advocates of insurance taxation based their claim that the states ought to levy such a tax? A careful study of the situation will reveal four different reasons. They are, first: the belief that in many cases some tax ought to be levied on the insurance business in order to do justice as between all the citizens of the state. The ideal of legislators is to place taxes so that they will bear equally upon all citizens of the state. To secure this object, they have believed that a tax ought to be levied upon the insurance business in some way, and have adopted the present systems as expedient methods. The second reason why taxes are levied on insurance is that, in the way in which they are imposed, the tax is easy to collect. Suppose that a tax placed upon insurance corporations does fall ultimately upon the policy-holders, as is claimed by insurance experts, the policy-holders do not know it, and if they do, they are unaware of the extent of the burden. In other words, a tax on insurance is an indirect tax and as such possesses all those characteristics which make an indirect tax so pleasing to the legislator whose tenure of office depends upon his pleasing his constituents. The third reason why heavy taxes are imposed upon insurance is popular ignorance as to the true nature of level premium life insurance. Despite all attempts which have been made towards educating the people in life insurance matters, it is perhaps not too much to say that ninety-five out of every one hundred people, yes, even more, do not understand why it is necessary to accumulate a reserve. The public sees millions of assets accumulating in the possession of a corporation. What more fit subject for taxation than this? The legislator who may or may not know the reason why the reserves are accumulating is only too ready in most cases to gratify the popular demand that the business should be taxed. Lastly, the reason why heavy taxes are imposed upon life insurance is that in many states the business is carried on almost entirely by foreign corporations, that is, corporations created by other states. In most of the states, a domestic corporation is none too popular; the foreign corporation is an enemy which should be hurt, and especially when it is one which is supposedly taking millions of dollars out of the state each year. Such a corporation in the popular judgment should be heavily taxed.

It is not maintained that whenever a tax has been imposed on insurance that every legislator who voted for the tax was actuated by all four of these motives. Some have believed in a tax for one reason, some for another. My object has been simply to indicate that no one cause has been back of the action taken.

Three of these reasons for taxing the insurance business will be taken up and discussed. So far as the heavy taxes are due to popular ignorance of the necessity of accumulating large reserves in level premium life insurance, all that can be done here is to urge the spread of general education on the subject. For this purpose nothing will be more valuable than the wholesale failure of fraternal life insurance which is bound to come during the next twenty years.

On the other hand, those who have argued most strongly against life insurance taxation have frequently taken a wrong point of view. They have seen so clearly wherein life insurance differs from any other business, and have felt so keenly the injustice of the present methods of taxation, that they have urged that no taxes whatever should be imposed upon the business, irrespective of the way in which other businesses are taxed, and irrespective of the system of taxation in general. They are wrong. The question of taxing life insurance cannot be isolated from the problem of taxation in general. To have a system of taxation, we must have a plan which takes into consideration all other taxes that are levied. No man, however sound his judgment, or however great his reasoning power, can work out an equitable system of taxing the railroads in a state unless he also knows what taxes are levied on factories, and on real estate. In the same way, a method of taxing life insurance should take into consideration all other taxes that are levied by the governing units having jurisdiction.

Let us examine the situation. We have seen that taxes have been collected in the shape of fees, in the shape of taxes on assets and on premium income, for reasons which have been stated. In the first place, not because of their importance, but mainly to get the subject out of the way, let us consider the fees that must be paid by life insurance companies to maintain the supervisory departments of the various states. From time to time during the past century, the states found it necessary to establish control over various kinds of businesses. First was banking, then followed transportation and insurance. In most cases, it was necessary to create new state officials to exercise these supervisory functions. In order that the burden upon the general state revenues should not be increased, it was usually provided that the new officers should be supported by fees collected from the corporations or individuals engaged in the industries supervised. If this system of fees is applied to banking, transportation, and other specific businesses, then it should be applied to insurance. As a matter of fact, the fee system of supporting supervising departments as it has worked out has not been a success, and cannot be defended. It has resulted in extravagant supervision. Fees have been made so large that with the great increase in business much more has been obtained than is necessary. To use up the surplus, needless offices have been created, with the result that supervision is costing much more than is necessary, and much more than it would have cost without the fee system.

We now come to a consideration of the taxes levied on life insurance for the support of government in general, that is, to taxes based on assets and taxes based on premiums. In this problem, as has been pointed out, there are two distinct questions: first, should taxes be imposed at all upon the insurance business, and secondly, are the present methods the correct methods? Should level premium life insurance be taxed? One cannot answer this question offhand. It all depends upon what the system of taxation is in the state levying the tax. This makes the problem complicated, for the system of taxation varies greatly in different states. As a matter of fact, however, the system of taxation in use in most of the states is the general property tax. Under a general property tax system, taxes are levied on the value of property as a basis, including under the category of property on the one hand such physical things as real estate, railroads, factories, stores, warehouses, and goods, and on the other hand so-called intangible property, namely, rights such as mortgages, bonds, and stocks. Without at this moment going into a discussion as to whether the general property tax system can be defended or not, we must accept it as the existing condition to which the insurance taxation is to be adjusted. Under this general property tax system, when an individual owns real estate he is taxed according to the value of the real estate he possesses. Should not the insurance company which owns real estate also be taxed? No one, so far as known, has had the temerity to deny that it should not be so taxed. Then proceed one step further. When an individual owns mortgages, bonds, and stocks, with a general property tax law in force, he is taxed upon their value. When these are owned by an insurance company, should they not also be taxed as was real estate when so owned? It is here that those who oppose insurance taxation refuse to follow.

The reasons given for not believing in taxing insurance are various. One says that it is a tax upon liabilities. This is not true. What the state is aiming at is to get at the bonds and stocks and the mortgages for purposes of taxation. These assets exist, they belong to somebody, they are subject to taxation. For the time being, the insurance company is the owner, and it is forced to pay the tax.

The chief argument used by those opposed to life insurance taxation is that life insurance is a means of providing for the future. A great deal is said of the widow and orphan and that taxes levied upon insurance are particularly burdensome. As a matter of fact all capital is laid by for the future. A man does not in his own mind differentiate between the capital which he spends for life insurance and that which he invests in corporation and other securities. It is said that the man who pays his money for level premium life insurance does not come to use personally the capital which he saves. This may be true, but with surrender and loan privileges in practically all policies nowadays, he may use for himself the capital which he has saved, and as a matter of fact frequently does so use it. At any rate, the economic unit to be considered is the family and not the individual.

It will not avail anything to say that taxation diminishes the volume of life insurance. Undoubtedly it does, but does not a tax on any industry discourage it? Railroad transportation is important to-day, we could not have the modern organization of society without it, there would be more railroads if they were not taxed, but most people believe that they ought to be taxed. Banking is a beneficial business, the bankers would probably like to have their taxes remitted, to do so would encourage the business, yet we must tax the banking business. We must have government. If we have it we must pay for it. Taxes are not a penalty placed upon a people. The individual is a gainer in so far as he can evade paying any part of the costs of the government, but the people as a whole gain because the taxes are levied and paid.

All these arguments against taxing the insurance business are beside the mark. As a matter of fact, under a general property tax system there is no reason why level premium life insurance should not be taxed in some way. Property rights surely exist, as exemplified by the accumulation of assets by a level premium company. The general property tax includes property rights as taxable possessions. Therefore in levying a tax upon life insurance, the states, so far as they are attempting to bring insurance taxation into conformity with the general property tax systems, are justified in their action.

The simplest method which has been adopted to make the insurance tax correspond to the general property tax has been the taxes imposed directly upon the assets. But a tax upon assets could not be adopted by all the states. Successful companies are located in a few states, the assets have been accumulated in the home office, the states from which much of them have been collected have not been able to get at these assets, and so they have levied a tax upon premiums. Notwithstanding the other arguments which have been made in favor of taxation of premiums, perhaps the great underlying reason for the almost universal adoption of the premium tax and its persistent use has been the feeling that under a general property tax these assets ought to be taxed in some way. Why should they not be taxed under a general property tax system? With every level premium policy there are certain investment features. Level premium insurance involves the necessity of accumulating in the early years of the policy in order that the cost may not increase in the later years. It is claimed that it is the policy-holder who pays the tax. That is true. Why should he not pay it if the state in which he lives continues in force the absurd, mediæval, general property tax. Take a concrete example. Consider two men, A and B. Each has $500 of income yearly with which he wishes to provide for the future. A buys a natural premium life insurance policy for $10,000 at an initial cost of $120. The remainder he uses to purchase bonds. B buys a 20-year endowment policy of $10,000 from an insurance company for $500 annual premium. The company uses $120 of the premium at the start to pay the current death losses, and invests the rest in precisely the same kind of bonds which A purchases. Under a general property tax A is taxed upon his investment in bonds. Under the same system of taxation should not B also be taxed upon the bonds which he has purchased through the medium of the company? If the tax burden is to be borne according to ability to pay and ability to pay measured by what a man is worth, both A and B should be taxed alike.

This is the answer to the question, Should life insurance be taxed? The answer is yes, if we are to continue levying a general property tax, including under it, as taxable objects, mortgages, bonds, stocks, and similar property rights.

But it does not follow from this that the ways in which the states have levied the tax upon the business have been just or practical. Neither the tax on assets nor the tax on premiums can be justified. The state in which a company is located does not have the moral right to levy a general property tax upon all the assets of such companies as happen to have their home offices in that state. No successful insurance company has gathered its assets even for the most part from the savings of citizens within the state where it is located. Its assets are the result of premiums that it has collected from every part of the country. These assets belong in large part to citizens of other states. A life insurance company from the standpoint of taxation is to be compared to a trust company or a savings bank. The assets which it possesses are deposited for the time being in the home office by the policyholders, to be held until the policies mature. Few state legislatures have gone to the extent of taxing a trust company or a savings bank upon its deposits. Why then should they levy a tax upon the deposits in a life insurance company? There would be more justice in a state taxing its trust companies upon their deposits, than taxing an insurance company upon its deposits, since trust companies are more local in their activities. Most of the deposits of a trust company belong to citizens of the state in which it is located. To levy a tax upon its deposits could be justified on the ground of expediency in the collection of the tax. Yet few states have taxed such deposits. How much more then should they not tax the insurance company upon its assets which do not belong to citizens of that state? Whatever rights a state may have in regard to the share of the assets belonging to its own citizens, it does not have the same right over assets belonging to citizens of other states. With but few notable exceptions, the states have realized this and have abandoned the tax on assets.

Neither does it follow from the fact that under a general property tax system insurance ought to be taxed that the states should levy a tax upon premiums. A lax levied on premiums can be defended on one ground only, that of expediency. It is an easy tax to collect and this is a great consideration in the mind of the administrator. But the system of taxing insurance by levying on premiums is an illogical method, the application of which leads to three classes of discriminations:

1. Discrimination between policy-holders of different states.
2. Discrimination between different classes of policy-holders in the same state.
3. Discrimination between policy-holders and non-policy-holders.

Before discussing these discriminations it is well that we should understand in unmistakable language who pays the tax on life insurance. Undoubtedly it is the policy-holder. This fact is so well understood by those who know the nature of life insurance that no attention would need be given it, if there were not so many who do not understand the theory of level premium life insurance. To-day level premium life insurance is sold in two ways:

by means of participating policies, and by means of non-participating policies. In participating insurance, insurance is secured at absolute cost. Whatever increases that cost increases the expense of insurance to the policy-holders. Taxes increase the cost of insurance by even more than the amount of the tax, therefore they increase the expense of insurance to the holders of participating policies. Most policies are of the participating kind, but it can be shown in precisely the same way that the holder of the non-participating policy also pays the tax on insurance. The non-participating policies are sold at a fixed rate. This rate must be high enough to cover all the costs to the company selling such a policy and leave a margin for profit. The margin of profit must remain. In every business where capital is invested there must be some profit, or capital will leave that industry. This is true of non-participating insurance. If the cost of furnishing insurance be increased, the price to the man who wants it must be increased. Decrease the cost and competition between the companies will reduce the price to the policy-holder. A tax is one of the costs. An increase in it means higher prices for insurance. A decrease means lower prices. Thus it is that no matter how life insurance is sold, the tax upon the business is borne by the policy-holders.

Having established the fact that taxes on premiums are ultimately paid by the policy-holders, we are now ready to discuss the discriminations due to the present method of imposing taxes on premiums. The first class of discriminations resulting from taxes levied on premiums is due to the fact that some states levy much heavier premium taxes than other states. Five state legislatures have thought that a tax of 1 per cent. upon gross premiums is the right amount in order to equalize the burden of taxation as between policy-holders and non-policy-holders in their states. Six other states have thought that 2½ per cent. is necessary to make the burden equal as between its citizens holding policies, and those not holding policies. But how does such a tax work out as between policy-holders of different states? A life insurance company does not, it should not, confine its activities to one state. To do so would be bad for the citizens of every state. To do business on such a small scale would increase the expense of insurance, and it would not allow the companies to obtain that wide distribution of risks which is absolutely essential to safety. Therefore we find an insurance company doing business in a large number of states, paying taxes of ½ per cent. in one state for its policy-holders upon their premiums and 2 per cent. in others. In theory life insurance ought to cost more in a state levying a tax of 3 per cent. on premiums than in a state levying only 1 per cent. It does not. Why? Because the companies cannot split up their business into forty-eight units and treat each one independently, giving the policy-holders in each their just deserts. The practical difficulties of such a course of action are insuperable. It would require the uniform action of all companies in placing the burden of taxation upon the policy-holders of a specific state, and such uniform action is impossible. The business is too intensely competitive to allow of uniform action in such a matter vitally affecting the policy-holders. Even if the companies could once agree, they would not be able to prevent this first class of discriminations, as the states levying the high taxes would in all probability pass legislation prohibiting such action. Therefore notwithstanding the higher tax in one state than in another, life insurance costs the same in all. The companies accept the tax as one of the general costs of the business and apportion it upon all policy-holders equally. The result is that premium taxes as they are levied to-day, high in one state, and low in another, force policy-holders in one state to help bear the burdens of government in another state. Such a condition of affairs is repugnant to our sense of justice.

In the second place, a tax on premiums discriminates

and is unfair in that it does not bear equally upon all policy-holders. The theory of the general property tax is that it is levied on individuals according to their ability to pay, ability to pay being measured according to the value of their property interests. A tax of a fixed percentage each year upon the level life insurance premium is a tax levied upon the individual irrespective of his ability to pay. The policy-holder who pays $120 as the second renewal premium on a 20-year term policy, on which a tax of 2 per cent. is levied, is really paying a tax of 10 per cent. upon the value of the equity which he possesses, while the man who is paying in his twentieth renewal premium of $500 on an endowment policy, and is taxed $10, is taxed at the rate of only a fraction of 1 per cent. upon the equity which he possesses. A tax levied in such a way is unjust and unfair.

The third way in which taxes as they are now levied on life insurance are unjust is that they discriminate between policy-holders and non-policy-holders in the state levying the tax. It has been urged in this paper that under a system of taxation based upon the general property tax insurance ought to be taxed. This is true. But whenever a modification is made in the general property tax affecting non-policy-holders, a modification should likewise be made in the tax upon holders of life insurance contracts. This has not been done. In all but four states, if a citizen of a state buys shares of stock in a corporation created by that state, he is exempted from the general property tax upon those shares. If another citizen of the same state, instead of buying the shares directly, buys life insurance, and the company purchases the same shares of stock, no exemption is made in the tax which the company directly, and the policy-holder indirectly, pays to the state. If an exemption should be made in one case, it should be made in the other. It is not, and in this way the policy-holders are discriminated against.

Besides resulting in discriminations as just described,

a tax upon premiums is illogical, that is, if the tax is collected by the state from the companies. If a state decides that premiums must be taxed, it does not follow that it has a right to collect the tax from the insurance companies. The companies have a fixed contract with their policy-holders. The annual premium is determined when the contract is made by the company, and the state insists that this premium must not be increased no matter how urgent are the needs of the company. When a state levies a tax upon premiums, the life insurance company cannot return the reserve upon its policies in that state to the policy-holders, thus terminating its contracts, and in this way avoiding the tax. The state demands that the contracts be carried out to the stipulated time and for the amounts previously agreed upon. At the same time, the state assumes the right to exact payments from the companies which may imperil their ability to carry out their contracts. To say that the states probably will not levy such a burdensome tax is not meeting the objection. The right to levy a tax involves the right to levy a heavier one. The situation is illogical. The state cannot consistently rule that the contract must be a fixed contract, and at the same time make it impossible for the companies to carry out their contracts.

The conclusion then is that even under a general property tax system the tax on life insurance premiums cannot be defended. It is unfair as between citizens of the same state, unfair as between different classes of policy-holders, unfair as between insurers and non-insurers, and essentially illogical.

Two things can be done: first, abolish the general property tax or modify it in such a way as to abolish its offensive features, or secondly, if this cannot be done, to levy a tax on life insurance in such a way as to make it fit in properly with the general property tax as it now exists. The better solution would be the first. The general property tax system must sooner or later be abolished.

Its faults are so evident, its injustices are so burdensome, that a radical change must be made. If the system is to be continued in its main features, at least a careful distinction must be made in the objects which are subject to the tax. Most of the difficulties in our system of taxation are due to the confusion which exists in the minds of men between wealth and the right to the use of wealth. Suppose a man owns a farm worth $10,000. The farm is wealth and as such it is subject to taxation. The deed which he possesses is an evidence of the right of ownership in that wealth. No state taxes deeds to real estate. Let us assume further that there is another man in the community who has no wealth. The assessor on making his annual inspection finds that these two men together possess wealth valued at $10,000. During the year the first man sells his farm to the other for $10,000, taking a mortgage upon the farm for the full amount. This year the assessor finds one man the legal owner of land valued at $10,000 and the other the owner of a mortgage for the same amount. Instead of finding $10,000 worth of taxable value, he finds $20,000. Has the wealth of the two men increased? Is the ability of the two increased doubly? If it has, what an easy thing it would be for a community to grow rich. But no new wealth has been created. No greater ability to pay exists than existed before. Yet practically all our sovereign states act on the assumption that there has been a change, and tax the mortgage as well as the real estate. Two taxes are paid where one was paid before. This is wrong. It is double taxation and as such is unjust.

The same condition exists in the taxation of corporations and corporation securities. If a man lives in one state and owns an unincorporated enterprise in an adjoining state, he is taxed only in the state where the factory or mine or other enterprise is located. Let him incorporate it, and issue the shares of stock to himself in place of the old deed to the wealth, and he will not only pay the same or a larger tax upon the wealth of the corporation in the state where it is located, but he will also now pay a tax upon the same value in the state where he lives, because shares of capital stock are subject to taxation. Has his ability to bear the burden of taxation increased? Is he wealthier than before? Not at all. He is simply the victim of double taxation.

What is the remedy? Let the states give up the plan of taxing wealth and at the same time evidences of ownership in that wealth. It is seriously unjust and has the baneful immoral effect of making men dishonest in their relations with the government. Give up taxing one thing or the other. From the theoretical standpoint it makes little difference which one, wealth or evidences of ownership in wealth. From the practical standpoint, wealth as the concrete, physical thing should be taken as the basis. Since it is physical, and therefore can be seen and found, it would simplify the problem to take wealth, meaning by that term the material objects, as the basis of taxation. In no other way can the injustices of the present methods as easily be abolished.

What would be the effect of this upon insurance taxation? It would mean that an insurance company would be taxed upon its real estate and that alone. The bonds, stocks, mortgages, notes, all these are evidences of ownership and hence would not be taxed. Why should they? The corporation which issues them is already taxed, and they should not be taxed twice. Neither under this system would the policy-holders be taxed in the way they are now. Their equity in the assets is a right to bonds and stocks and mortgages, and these, as we have seen, would not be taxed.

To levy all taxes on wealth exempting property rights would be a real solution of the problem of taxation. But like most good solutions it may be difficult to accomplish. How about compromise measures? Cannot a system be devised for taxing life insurance which can be grafted on to present systems of taxation, and thus not involve such a wide-spread change? Such a method of taxation can be devised. What I have to suggest is that the states give up their taxes on assets and taxes on premiums, and make the policy-holder liable for taxation upon the reserve value of his policy. This method would fit in well with a general property tax. With the modern policy, the reserve upon a policy is always at the disposal of the policy-holder. He can borrow from it and he can withdraw it if he cares to do so. In what essential way does the reserve upon a policy nowadays vary from the deposit placed in a trust company? That the insurance company so far as it is the holder of assets has always been considered simply as the trustee of the policy-holders' funds is amply demonstrated by a study of insurance literature. Most states do not tax trust companies upon their deposits, but they do tax the depositor upon the amount of his deposit. If the states are going to levy a general property tax and under this tax life insurance, the tax which they should impose is a tax upon the individual policy-holder according to the value of his deposit or reserve with the company.

Why should not the tax, if it is to be imposed at all, be imposed in this way? Any unprejudiced man can be shown in a few minutes' time that it is the policy-holder who pays the tax under the present system. This is so easy of demonstration that it would be a waste of time to make the assertion if it were not the fact that many legislators have not realized it as the true situation. The policy-holder pays the tax but he pays it indirectly, and thus does not know how much he is paying. If the truth were known, it would probably show that the policy-holder is in general paying a heavier tax than is the average holder of personal property. Furthermore, the tax is grossly ill-proportioned, amounting to from 10 to 15 per cent. upon the value of the equity which the policy-holder possesses in the early years of the policy. This is wrong. We may not believe that the investor in life insurance should receive any special consideration, but we should insist with all our power that no extra burden shall be placed upon him.

How should such a general property tax as has been suggested be levied upon life insurance? That is a practical question for the practical statesman to solve. Two methods may be suggested. First, make the reserve value subject to local assessment just as is an investment outright in securities, or a deposit in a trust company is made subject to local taxation. The objection to this plan is that it would result in much evasion. Of course it would. But if the states are going to hold on to the general property tax system with all its evasions and its glaring irregularities, it is perhaps but fair that the man who invests in life insurance should have the same privilege of evading the tax upon his insurance reserve. This would be taking a step in the wrong direction for tax reform, but if justice cannot be done in any other way, it is justice that all shall have an equal chance.

The other method would be to retain the insurance tax as a state tax, and have the companies hand in to the state board of tax commissioners a list of all policy-holders in the state, with the values of their reserves. Upon these values the state could impose a fair tax to be collected directly from the individual policy-holders. This would do away with the evasion resulting from local taxation.

What results would be obtained if these suggestions were carried out? It would result in justice as between the policy-holders of various states. It is absolutely wrong that the policy-holders of one state should be taxed to support the government of another state as is done at the present time, and will continue to be done if the method of taxing assets and premiums is continued. The plan would secure justice as between individual policy-holders, something equally to be desired. Lastly, it would result in equalization of the rates of taxation between purchasers of insurance and other taxpayers. The policy-holder pays too much to-day. He does not object because he does not know how much he is paying. Follow the plan here suggested. Substitute a direct tax for an indirect tax and we can safely leave it to the intelligent body of policy-holders to look after their own interests.

Is it possible to secure this reform in life insurance, a reform which would do away with discriminations between policy-holders of different states, between different classes of policy-holders in the same state, and between policy-holders and non-insurers? Some say not. They urge that for a legislator to substitute a direct tax for an indirect one would sound his political death knell. It is to be hoped that it would not; that if such a measure were carefully explained to the public, that public opinion would be intelligent enough to appreciate the situation.

But if this compromise reform, a reform which means simply the substitution of a direct tax for an indirect tax, involves such a radical change in the existing system of taxation that it stands no chance of being adopted, shall we advocate no reform whatever in insurance taxation? No, if we cannot get a reform which will eliminate all three classes of discrimination resulting from the premium tax, let us get a reform which will eliminate one of the discriminations. There is one class of discriminations which has been discussed which the policy-holders have more than the right to ask the states to eliminate. They have the right to demand that it should be eliminated. Reference is made to the discrimination between policy-holders of different states caused by one state levying a tax rate of 2 or 3 per cent. upon premiums while other states impose less than 1 per cent. Discrimination of this sort can be eliminated by all the states levying as nearly as possible a uniform rate of premium taxation upon all the companies.

Uniformity among the states can be secured in two ways, by the states with a low rate increasing their rates to the level of the high-rate states, or by the high-rate states lowering their rates. It is much to be desired that uniformity should be obtained through the decrease in rates by the high states. It would be a move in the right direction. Since some reform is better than none, and since it does seem possible at this time to secure this much, if nothing further can be secured, let us at least secure uniformity of rates of taxation upon life insurance in the various states.

A brief summary of this extended discussion may not be out of place. It has been maintained:

1. That under the existing general property tax system in force in most of the states, some tax ought to be levied on life insurance.

2. That present methods of taxing insurance are unjust.

3. That the best remedy would be for the states to abolish the general property tax, or at least to amend it in such a way as to include only tangible wealth as subject to taxation.

4. That if the general property tax cannot be abolished, substitute for the indirect tax upon the policy-holders a direct tax upon them, making the reserve values of policies subject to taxation, not to the company, but to the policy-holders directly.

5. That if no other reform can be secured, the policy-holders have a right to demand uniform rates of taxation by the various states, uniformity being secured generally by a reduction in the rates of the high-tax states.

CHAPTER XXVI

INDUSTRIAL INSURANCE [1]

INDUSTRIAL insurance is of comparatively modern origin in this country. All forms of life insurance are the result of slow development in theory and practice, but for industrial insurance it may be claimed that it is the outgrowth of ages of experiments to provide, by an effective and absolutely certain method, for the most simple needs of the mass of the population at the hour of death. The mass of the people are confronted by the fact that death means a large expense, usually a burdensome debt, to meet the cost of burial, or a heavy draft on slender savings, the result of years of abstinence and foresight, or the alternative of state or private charity. However remote the chance of death may appear at times, it is an ever-present contingency, for which an effective provision has become a necessity of civilized life.

Industrial insurance is so called because the system is primarily designed to meet the needs of wage-earners employed in manufacturing industries, and the weekly premium payments coincide with the weekly payment of wages and salaries. The premiums are from five cents to seventy cents a week. The system provides for family insurance on a comprehensive plan, and every member of the family at ages one to seventy, if in good health, is insurable. The weekly premiums for a family of five average about thirty-five or forty cents, being respectively

[1] By John F. Dryden, President of the Prudential Insurance Company, Newark. Reprinted from pages 184–199 of the "Yale Insurance Lectures, Life."

ten cents each for the father and mother and five cents each for the children. The amounts of insurance vary with age, but average about one hundred and fifteen dollars. For children under ten the average is thirty dollars, and for persons over age ten one hundred and fifty dollars. The system is sufficiently elastic to meet the needs of the most humble laborer, even though advanced in years, as well as the requirements of the more prosperous mechanic or skilled workman, able to pay premiums for enough insurance to provide for more than the immediate needs of his family after his death. The premiums are collected weekly from the houses of the insured by authorized agents, who also solicit for new insurance. While the collection of weekly premiums necessarily increases the cost of insurance, the difference is relatively small when the convenience of this method is taken into account. Attempts, especially by the British government, to transact a weekly payment system of life insurance without collectors have failed. Attempts to transact a life insurance business on the monthly payment plan have not been successful on any considerable scale. These are the simple elements of a business which has grown to immense proportions during the thirty-four years since The Prudential Insurance Company of America was organized, in 1875, as the first American company to transact this form of life insurance in this country.

Industrial insurance had its origin in England, and the evolution of the business can be traced backwards by an unbroken record through friendly societies and burial clubs to the trade and craft guilds of the fifteenth century. The development was the inevitable result of economic laws making for a higher degree of efficiency and security in social institutions. This is not the place, however, to go into the history of these interesting associations for social betterment under different conditions of life. They served their purpose at the time, but they would ill meet the conditions of the present.

In 1853 a comprehensive investigation was made by a parliamentary committee into the practice of life insurance companies in England, and among other conclusions the committee advanced the view that "the ground hitherto occupied by these useful institutions (life insurance associations) has been comparatively limited, and that their application is capable of a great extension not only in the higher and middle classes of society, but also among the humbler classes, to whom it has recently been very considerably applied."

Acting on this suggestion, The Prudential of London, organized as an ordinary life insurance company in 1848, made inquiries and ascertained that almost without exception the then existing so-called friendly societies and burial clubs were in an unsound financial condition, while many indeed had failed with disastrous results to the people they were supposed to benefit. A modest attempt had been made to transact the business of life insurance for wage-earners on a commercial basis, but the results had not been very encouraging. The Prudential, however, realized the immense opportunity to extend the principles of life insurance to the broad field of workingmen's insurance in general. On the recommendation of the best available actuarial talent, required for the construction of tables and plans, and after purchasing the existing business of a few small companies, The Prudential, in 1854, commenced the business of industrial insurance, destined to make it the foremost life insurance company in the world.

During the fifty years which have passed since the introduction of industrial insurance the business has been extended to almost all civilized countries with more or less success, but the development has been the greatest in English-speaking countries, and there are now more than forty millions of industrial policies in force in the world. Of this number over one-half are in force in the United Kingdom, about four millions in Germany, and not far from one-half a million in Australia.

There are now in force in this country almost fifteen million industrial policies, or, with five persons to a family, it would appear that about three million families in the United States are insured with industrial companies for sums which range from $15 to $1000. When we take into consideration the fact that there are about fifteen million families, we have it that at present about one family out of every five is financially interested in the success and future of this form of life insurance in the United States. When we further consider the fact that the total number of savings banks depositors is only about seven millions, although we have had savings banks since the beginning of the nineteenth century, and industrial insurance for only a little more than one-fourth of that period, you will agree that industrial insurance is a social institution of great magnitude.

The office practice of industrial insurance is in a general way almost identical with the practice of an ordinary company, using that term in a technical way, and nearly all of the industrial companies transact, in fact, an ordinary business as a complement to their particular system of family insurance on the weekly premium payment plan. The essential points of difference arise out of the vast number of necessary office transactions resulting from the weekly collection of premiums from the houses of the insured and the character of the class of risks assumed under industrial policies. It would carry us too far to discuss, even in a general way, the office and field administration of an industrial company, and my remarks are limited to essential points.

First. The calculation of premium charges for both infantile and adult risks is upon an actuarial basis derived from trustworthy mortality tables. The premiums vary with age, but there are practically no restrictions as to occupations or residence, Careful inquiry is made as to the moral character of the risks assumed.

Second. The collection of premiums from the houses

of the insured is made by authorized collectors, or agents, who are under a most effective system of supervision, supplemented by an audit system of weekly accounts and debits and credits, by which defalcation, fraud, and intentional errors are made difficult and, generally speaking, impossible. Every policy-holder has a premium receipt book in which the weekly payments must be entered by the agent, while at the same time a corresponding entry is required to be made in the agent's collection book. The system has worked so well that during the half-century since industrial insurance has been in operation no important alterations have been made in this branch of office practice.

Third. To every person insured a policy is issued which in all essentials conforms to the contract issued to ordinary policy-holders. The language used is so plain and free from confusing technicalities that it is seldom indeed that there are controversies or misunderstandings between the company and the insured. The contract provides for a definite sum payable in the event of death in return for a definite weekly premium, but in addition certain privileges and options are granted to the insured, which provide for a paid-up policy after three years, for additional benefits after five years, for cash dividends after fifteen years, and for cash surrender value after twenty years.

Fourth. Every policy contains a provision that all premiums must be paid in advance on the Monday of the week for which they are due. In the event of a policy being more than four weeks in arrears for non-payment of premiums, the agent is required to report the policy for lapse. Most of the lapses of industrial policies occur during the early weeks of policy duration, when only a few premiums have been paid. Policies can be revived without difficulty provided the arrears do not exceed one year, but it is required that the applicant for revival pass a medical examination, or furnish other evidence of being in good health. There are no fines and every facility is granted to keep the policy in force. If the arrears exceed thirteen weeks the policy may be revived without the payment of arrears, but in place thereof a non-interest-bearing lien will be issued, the amount of which is deducted, in the event of death, from the face value of the policy.

Fifth. In the event of death every effort is made to pay the claim as soon as possible to carry into effect the general intent of industrial insurance, to provide for the burial expenses of the insured. The proof of death, however, requires to be supplemented by documentary evidence — (*a*) claimant's certificate; (*b*) certificate of identity; (*c*) certificate of the superintendent or assistant superintendent; (*d*) certificate of the undertaker; (*e*) certificate of the attending physician.

Sixth. The agency system of industrial companies is in a measure unique and deserving of special mention. A large number of agents are necessarily required to conduct the office and field operations of a company insuring millions of risks, for I may say in passing that 95 per cent. of the entire industrial business is carried on by three companies. The office organization consists of a large number of departments, which cannot very well be dealt with on this occasion. The field operations require a superintendent in charge of a district, who has the assistance of a number of assistant superintendents, under whom is an agency force that varies in number according to the size of the territory. On an average an agent collects from about five hundred to six hundred policy-holders, but his compensation is so adjusted that it is necessary for him in addition to solicit for new business. By this means it is to his pecuniary interest to prevent the lapsing of policies and to increase as far as possible the number of policies in force. The amount of collectible premiums is called the "debit," and the agent is held responsible for the condition of his accounts. His books and papers are periodically inspected by assistant superintendents, who have a thorough knowledge of the business and are personally familiar with all the insured, so that in the event of the resignation or death of the agent there is no interruption or intermission in the collection of the weekly premiums.

We may now consider the place of industrial insurance in practical economics. President Hadley very properly draws a distinction between public and private wealth, and points out that "the growth of material wealth depends upon causes far deeper and more profound than those that the statesman can control." In life insurance we have a species of material wealth representing more than two-and-a-quarter billions of accumulated funds as security for the faithful discharge of promises made and obligations incurred, and in addition a vast amount of economic security resulting from the successful elimination of a risk inherent in the uncertainty of life. May we not properly speak of life insurance, and in particular of industrial insurance, as "public wealth" in the true and complete sense of President Hadley's definition? He insists upon the supreme importance of security and the institution of property, to render possible the progress, social, moral, and ecomonic, of the race, for it is only by accumulated wealth that men are more or less removed from the immediate and destructive pressure of poverty. While, no doubt, much of human poverty is unavoidable and inherent in the very constitution of society, a vast amount of existing misery is preventable by the development of right habits of saving and insurance — by frugality and intelligent industry. Abstinence from the immediate use of money as soon as earned is of the utmost importance in the economic development of the people. No other means have yet been discovered to insure the economic security of the masses as effectually as by insurance. Hadley well says that "Great evils arise from trusting too much to Providence and not making a distinct personal effort to meet the contingencies of life," and no method has yet been devised by which the contingency of death, especially of premature death, can be better provided for than by life insurance. While the sphere of industrial insurance is limited to security against relatively small losses, they are large indeed when considered from the viewpoint of the masses who consume their weekly wages almost as soon as earned.

The place of life insurance in social economics is most important. The accumulation of capital, the struggle of the masses for property and economic independence, the possibility of a more equitable and general distribution of wealth, are all problems which rest fundamentally upon the power and habits of the people to save. But saving habits are acquired only with great difficulty and the ordinary savings bank is far from being the evidence of workingman's thrift which it is often assumed to be. Mr. Carroll D. Wright estimates that not more than one-half of the sum on deposit with savings institutions represents accumulations of wage-earners, the remainder being the investments of the relatively well-to-do. Industrial insurance serves both an economic and a social purpose. It is the most effective, even though perhaps the most elementary, education in thrift which has yet been developed. The weekly premium payments develop systematic habits of saving and lead to the accumulation of millions which, but for this method of insurance, would be expended largely for needless and often for vicious purposes. The usual method of accumulating savings banks deposits is in marked contrast to industrial insurance premium payments, in that as a rule deposits are made at irregular intervals and not in the small sums which represent true foresight, frugality, and abstinence from needless expenditures.

The weekly premium payments soon become a habit of life, even with the young, who in time learn to pay for their own insurance the five or ten cents a week necessary to meet the expense. The education in thrift, however, does not end here. Systematic habits of saving are developed which have their effect in other directions, and the conclusion is quite in accordance with our experience that general saving habits, accumulations in savings banks, or payments for building loans, follow industrial insurance rather than precede it, and are most widely diffused among the people where industrial insurance is most general as a mode or method of family protection. For illustration, in this country, Philadelphia, and Dayton, Ohio, are often referred to as cities in which building and loan associations have made most progress, but they are also cities in which industrial insurance is most general as a method of family insurance. In England, it is claimed on good authority that school savings banks and penny provident funds have been most successful in Manchester, Liverpool, and Birmingham, but these are also the cities in which industrial insurance is almost universal, so much so that at least four-fifths of the entire population hold industrial policies.

Industrial insurance is not only of great value as an aid to the development of general saving habits and the accumulation of property, but it is a contributory agent of great importance in the progress and public appreciation of other forms of insurance — ordinary life, fraternal, accident, fire, etc. Industrial insurance has enormously extended the field of other forms of insurance by familiarizing the mass of the population with the elementary principles and beneficial results of a method of life insurance especially adapted to special needs. It came into existence in the United States at a time when public faith in financial institutions, savings banks, ordinary life insurance companies, and especially so-called workingmen's insurance on the coöperative plan, was profoundly shaken by panics and financial depressions and evidences of mismanagement and fraud. It has kept faith with the people and every promise made has been faithfully performed. Security, stability, permanency has been the watchword, and no social institution of to-day is established on a more scientific and trustworthy theory of mortality and finance than the vast structure of industrial insurance with its forty millions of policy-holders in different parts of the world. It is not going too far to say that this method of life insurance protection forms to-day one of the most effective measures making directly or indirectly for accumulation of property. However small the premium payments and however small in many cases the individual returns, the fact remains that fifty-two times a year payments are made, and these lessons in thrift and accumulation are taught and brought home to an element of the population which is most in need thereof.

We often hear the old complaint that there is no real progress, but only a shifting of wealth, by which the poor are made poorer and the rich grow richer. Relatively this is true, for, by contrasts, in a more advanced society the condition of the very poor becomes more striking and apparently less necessary. Actually, however, our progress during the past half-century has been real and of vast benefit to the mass of our population, who in an ever-increasing proportion are attaining a relatively high degree of economic security and social well-being. The object of all thrift agencies is to aid persons to become savers in the first instance and to accumulate a fund for future contingencies, but, second, "that they may have the consciousness of being removed (by their own efforts) from the burden of relief receiving."

Industrial insurance provides a sum certain, from $15 to $1000, at a time when in many households no ready money is otherwise available for the expenses incident to death and the last illness. The problem reduces itself to the necessity that the burial of the father or the child must be paid for, that it will cost at least from $15 to $100, and that this sum must be provided for either by the convenient method of industrial insurance or by a draft upon a possible sum accumulated during years of careful husbandry of slender resources or by incurring a non-productive debt with the undertaker and the doctor. With the last as the alternative, it is an open question whether an undertaker can be found who will take the risk, and there will often be no escape from the necessity of an appeal to the public poor fund, or private charitable relief. The poor have their standard of life and customs as thoroughly established as the well-to-do or the rich, and, however humble their station, they prefer the burial of their dead at their own expense in a manner which to them represents the common decencies of life. Deep at the root of the problem of life insurance for the poor lies their abhorrence of a pauper burial and their willingness to provide out of present savings for a future contingency, and the ever present possibility of premature or unexpected death. As the result of the introduction of industrial insurance into the United States, which now returns to policy-holders about $25,000,000 per annum in the payment of claims alone, the relative number of pauper burials has been materially reduced during the past twenty years. On the basis of a conservative estimate there would be 25,000 more pauper burials per annum in American cities if this system were not in almost universal operation. From a moral and sentimental point of view, therefore, the value of industrial insurance as making for a higher standard of family life cannot be overestimated. It certainly is a matter of considerable importance in the life and struggle of many who are on the very verge of pauperism and dependency to know that, at the end of their earthly difficulties, they will not be cast away in a potter's field.

But the good effect of industrial insurance as a direct means of reducing pauperism does not end here. In many instances a sufficient sum remains, after the payment of funeral and doctor's bills, to establish the widow in some kind of business, on a small scale, but sufficient to provide the necessary means for herself and children. As a rule there will be other savings available, for, as I have already said, industrial insurance suggests the advantage and importance of other forms of investment and encourages economy in family expenditures. How far the burden of poor relief, indoor and out, is diminished cannot be stated with even approximate accuracy, but we have some very significant data for certain states and cities which indicate that, regardless of a large immigration, there has, during recent years, been a relative and substantial decrease in the number of paupers and the amount paid for poor relief.

The indirect results of industrial insurance are, therefore, of very considerable importance. Just as the vast accumulations in savings banks are to a considerable extent the aggregate of a large number of small deposits, so in industrial insurance the assets of about one hundred and fifty million dollars held as reserve and surplus represent a vast amount of capital as the result of small weekly payments which average about ten cents. These accumulations do not stand for idle capital but for public wealth in the complete sense of the term. It is wealth made available for the conduct of general business, of active enterprise, and other social and economic ends. Of the three billions of assets held by American life insurance companies, 75 per cent. are invested in stocks, bonds, and mortgages, 8 per cent. in real estate, 6 per cent. in loans on policies, and the remainder in other forms of investment and as cash in bank. The absolute necessity for life insurance companies to earn a certain rate of interest on their investments makes it of the highest importance that the assets should be constantly employed in profitable enterprises, thus increasing materially the national prosperity and social security of the people.

I do not go too far, then, when I hold that the indirect results of this form of insurance with its habits of systematic savings are at least equally as important as the direct results represented by the annual payment of over $25,000,000 in claims, etc., to industrial beneficiaries.

The creation of capital by this method of insurance is indeed of far-reaching importance, even to the laborer or wage-earner whose economic security and opportunity for employment is enhanced by the real amount of capital thus made available for increased production. There is no more generally accepted postulate in economics than that "in proportion to the increase in capital the share of the annual product falling to capital is augmented absolutely but diminished relatively, while the share falling to labor is increased both absolutely and relatively." Considered from this point of view alone, industrial insurance makes for a more general and equitable distribution of wealth.

The success of industrial insurance may be summed up in a remark made by Abraham Lincoln that "with public sentiment on its side everything succeeds — with public sentiment against it nothing succeeds." This system of family insurance forms an integral part of the domestic economy of the American people. Organized in the State of New Jersey, the progress in local development has been most complete in that State and in the adjoining states of New York and Pennsylvania. In New Jersey there are now about 1,500,000 industrial policies in force, representing about 65 per cent. insured population. In certain sections of Newark, of New York City, of Philadelphia, and other large cities, the system is so general that from 75 per cent. to 95 per cent. of all insurable persons hold industrial policies.

We have made a number of investigations to ascertain the actual extent of industrial insurance in various cities and there is one significant fact which we have learned, especially in and around Newark, that the proportion of population insured on the industrial plan is somewhat higher among those who own their own homes than among those who do not. Whether as cause or effect, the fact remains that the progress and development of the business has been most satisfactory among the thrifty and stable element of our industrial population. We can go further and say that policy-holders are in other respects a superior class. For illustration, we find by our mortality statistics that the death rate of insured children is less than the normal mortality in the general population as determined by the census. Our percentage of deaths from intemperance and alcoholism is less than the expected by the general standard of mortality, and finally, we find that our ratio of deaths from homicide and suicide is below the average for the country at large. I mention these facts, which are supported by irrefutable evidence, to show that there is a close relation between industrial insurance and the progress and well-being of the industrial population, and that the policy-holders represent a more thrifty, more temperate, and more law-abiding element than the uninsured.

It remains for me to speak of the evolution of industrial insurance and the adaptation of the business to new conditions. When established in 1875, the financial and industrial conditions were such as to call for an elementary form of life insurance with absolute security as the first consideration. By slow degrees public confidence in insurance and financial institutions was restored, and as early as 1881 it become necessary to issue a special policy for the round sum of $500 to meet a distinct and increasing demand from the superior element of our industrial population. By 1886 the insurance education of the masses had gone far enough to make it seem advisable, and in fact necessary, to establish an ordinary department. That was less than twenty years ago, but during the intervening period the three industrial companies which transact 95 per cent. of the business in this country have built up a vast ordinary business, with about 720,000 policies and $800,000,000 of insurance in force. At least one-half of this sum, and perhaps three-fifths, represents ordinary insurance on the lives of wage-earners, or persons in positions or situations practically outside of the field of the solicitor for exclusively ordinary companies. The number of persons insured with industrial companies for both industrial and ordinary is indeed quite large and constantly increasing. The industrial policies are held for the payment of expenses incident to death, the ordinary for family protection, child education, and other purposes of social and economic importance. Coincident with the progress and evolution of industrial insurance there has been a material improvement in the industrial policy contract, which to-day contains all the essential and important provisions and privileges of the regular ordinary policy. Thus we see how close the relation is between the two forms of insurance and how important industrial insurance is as an education in general insurance theory and practice, making gradually but with certainty for the social and economic security of the people.

If there is any one thing that "social classes owe to each other," it is that all shall aim and work to diminish the needless suffering and unnecessary burdens of those for whose well-being and future protection we are individually or socially responsible. The mass of our population is engaged in a heroic struggle to escape from poverty to relative economic and social freedom, and whatever contributes toward this much-to-be-desired end is deserving of sympathetic consideration. I believe that in industrial insurance we have a most valuable aid in this determination for social betterment on a large scale, and the evidence is conclusive that a vast amount of direct and indirect good is accomplished by this elementary but effective form of thrift. During the almost thirty years since industrial insurance has been in active operation in this country, gradual but constant progress has been made toward a higher degree of social efficiency, so that we may hopefully look forward and anticipate a time when this form of insurance will be indeed a social institution of universal utility, in every respect a far-reaching power for good, directly to the people and indirectly to the nation.

I believe that the evidence warrants the conclusion that industrial insurance makes first for private wealth and second for public wealth, as well as directly and indirectly for the all-important aim and end of a higher degree of security for the industrial population of this land.

INDEX

P

R